MASQUES OF GOD

MASQUES OF GOD

FORM AND THEME IN THE POETRY OF HENRY VAUGHAN

by

JAMES D. SIMMONDS

UNIVERSITY OF PITTSBURGH PRESS

PR
3744
.S5

Library of Congress Catalog Card Number 78-170144
ISBN 0-8229-3236-9
Copyright © 1972, University of Pittsburgh Press
All rights reserved
Henry M. Snyder & Co., Inc., London
Manufactured in the United States of America

In Memoriam
E. L. MARILLA
scholar, teacher, friend

CONTENTS

	Preface	*ix*
I	Introduction	*3*
II	Ben Jonson and the Craft of Poetry	*22*
III	The Well-Ordered Poem	*42*
IV	Love Poetry	*65*
V	Satire	*85*
	A. Anti-Puritanism	*85*
	B. Classical Themes	*116*
VI	The Form of Nature	*138*
VII	Archetype and Wit: The Bed-Grave Image	*165*
	Appendices	
	I. Vaughan's Illness	*197*
	II. Amoret, Etesia, and Catherine Wise	*204*
	III. Immorality and Profane Literature	*208*
	Notes	*219*
	Bibliography	*241*
	Index	*249*

PREFACE

HAVING RECITED my first lessons at the knee of Brooks and Warren, *Understanding Poetry*, I am aware of my affinities with what T. S. Eliot once memorably disparaged as "the lemon-squeezer school of criticism." Wishing to avoid the method's unfortunate tendency to usurp the reader's right to his own perceptions, I have generally refrained from saying as much as might be said about any poem. On the other hand, rather than comment briefly on a large number of examples, I have left out many poems which might have illustrated my general arguments. The reader may particularly notice the omission of such famous poems as "The Morning-watch," "Regeneration," "The Night," and "The World," which have been extensively discussed in Vaughan criticism. I have left them out because I wanted to introduce less familiar poems into the critical conversation.

The organization of most chapters, and of the book as a whole, is deliberately diachronic. The last chapter is not a conclusion. Chapters which seem to break off without being concluded do indeed break off without being concluded. There is some repetition, as the same poems and the same topics reappear in different contexts and are discussed from different points of view. I have tried in these ways to approximate a "mosaic" or "field" mode of presentation, rather than a linear sequence of time or argument, because it seemed better to exemplify Vaughan's way of reading the world and my way of reading him.

I am grateful to the University of Pittsburgh and the Charles E. Merrill Foundation for two research grants, in 1963 and 1967, which enabled me to begin this book, and to the University of Pittsburgh for a sabbatical leave which enabled me to finish it. Any vestigial similarity to my doctoral dissertation on Vaughan is more or less coincidental; but I am deeply indebted to my teachers at Louisiana State University—particularly John Olive, Lawrence Sasek, and the late E. L. Marilla—whose encouraging responses to that version stimulated me to persist with Vaughan. To my students at the University of Pittsburgh, who have patiently listened and responded to some of these ideas, adumbrated with varying degrees of crudity in my seventeenth-century seminar and at meetings of the Graduate Humanities Club, I extend my thanks and admiration. I am especially grateful for the sympathetic and intelligent interest of Bob Davis, Dorothy Saladiak, Mary Ager, John McNavage, Bill Karn, Pat Pinka, Jim Marino, Judy Rosenthal, Ted Brodie, and Greg Goekjian. For their helpful comments on my early work in the field, I am grateful also to Louis Martz, Marjorie Nicolson, Waldo McNeir, Arnold Stein, and the late Helen White. Several chapters have benefited indirectly from discussions of Vaughan with my colleagues Charles Crow and Austin Flanders. And Louis Martz's comments on the manuscript clarified several minor problems and suggested major improvements in organization.

My work on this book has been aided incalculably by the unfailing helpfulness and efficiency of Roberta Heine, secretary nonpareil. And I am also indebted in a number of personal ways to Charles Peake, Frank Wadsworth, and the late George Crouch, and to my colleagues Bob Marshall, Tom Philbrick, Ed Marrs, and Bob Whitman.

The reader cannot fail to notice how fundamentally my thinking has been shaped by E. L. Marilla's work on Vaughan. The dedication of this book says all that I need say about the gentleman to whom, since becoming his student fourteen years ago, I have owed most.

I am grateful to the Clarendon Press for kind permission to quote extensively from *The Works of Henry Vaughan*, ed. L. C. Martin, 2nd ed. (Oxford, 1957). Portions of the text, now thoroughly revised, appeared first in a number of scholarly publications: *Modern Language Quarterly, Philological Quarterly, Modern Language Notes, English Studies, Die Neueren Sprachen, Anglia, Studies in English Renaissance Literature,* ed. Waldo F. McNeir (Baton Rouge, La., 1962), *Neophilologus, Modern Philology,* and *Essays in Honor of Esmond Linworth Marilla,* ed. Thomas Austin Kirby and William John Olive (Baton Rouge, La., 1970). Full details are given in footnotes.

MASQUES OF GOD

*In these Masques and shadows I may see
Thy sacred way.*
                                HENRY VAUGHAN

Chapter

I

INTRODUCTION

CRITICAL JUDGMENTS on Vaughan usually seem to imply the superiority of the Christian elements in seventeenth-century culture to the secular, classical, humanistic elements. But this bias is reserved especially for Vaughan, not extended to all the poets of the period. Vaughan was a more versatile poet than is generally understood, for the great variety of his work in subject, mood, and style is poorly reflected in anthologies and critical discussions. The reader who has heard it rumored that Vaughan was the peer of Carew, Herrick, Suckling, Lovelace, and sometimes even of Jonson, Donne, and Dryden, in the urbane secular modes of the period—amatory, satiric, reflective—will find little support for this anywhere but in the texts. When one compares the secular Vaughan with his contemporaries, one soon confronts a dilemma: we must either erase much of the seventeenth-century canon or include Vaughan's secular poetry in it.

To take such a position may be to number oneself with those whom patience finally must crown. The persistence of the secular Vaughan's exile may be illustrated by a recent anthology, which includes selections from Jonson, Herrick, Carew, Waller, Suckling, and Lovelace, and even from Richard Corbett, Aurelian Townshend, Thomas Randolph, William Habington, John Cleveland, and Thomas Stanley, but not one secular poem by Vaughan.[1] When anthologists go beyond the sacred verse, they rarely go beyond "To Amoret gone from him," which is neither the most interesting nor the most representative of Vaughan's early poems, but owes its unearned distinction to its dependence on Donne. When criticism acknowledges the secular Vaughan's existence, attitudes usually hover between objurgation, condescension, embarrassed tolerance, and pained regret, although more sympathetic comments appear briefly and sporadically.[2] But the strongest voice in this wilderness is that of E. L. Marilla, whose edition of the secular poems, with its extensive commentary, is the first major recognition of their value and an invaluable aid to anyone interested in this neglected portion of Vaughan's work.[3]

A basic fact about Vaughan's secular and sacred poems is that they are all poems, and students of literature should find this interesting. Remembering Frank Kermode's caveat about "the critical error of refusing to treat Vaughan's poetry as poetry so long as it may be treated as prayer,"[4] I have declined to follow the usual custom of treating the secular and sacred verse as separate categories, for the crude distinctions which are commonly made between them have simply not survived my reading of the texts. The discussion of most topics freely crosses and recrosses the barrier commonly supposed to divide the secular from the religious poems. If Vaughan surmounted it only with divine aid, in the form of a conversion which totally transformed him and his poetry, this should be a formidable obstacle. But I have found that the concept itself, rather than anything in the poetry, obstructs our view of close poetic relationships between the early and later work.[5] Whatever the status of Vaughan's "conversion" in his biography (another, quite different, and probably insoluble problem), as a generic and evaluative term in criticism it has distracted our attention and muddled our judgment. We will learn more about Vaughan's poetry and poetic development if we disregard the barrier than if we assume it to be impassable.

I am not concerned either to affirm or deny that Vaughan experienced a conversion, regeneration, or spiritual awakening. With the kind of evidence we have, the proposition seems to me simply inarguable. Certainly the sacred poems contain many expressions related to such an experience, and one can easily make the case that regeneration is a major theme of the poetry. But, in the absence of direct personal testimony to corroborate them (and there is no such testimony), these expressions justify no conclusion about Vaughan's religious life except that he had one. It is certain, too, that his poetry underwent a major development or reorientation in the late 1640s, and these changes are marked enough to warrant our conceiving of his poetic development in two (overlapping) phases. It is one of the functions of criticism to describe the developments within a writer's work, and it is precisely this function which has been hindered by the use to which Vaughan's hypothetical conversion has been put. Thus I object to the "conversion" concept on two levels: as a biographical concept, it is unfounded; and as a critical concept, an exegetical tool, it is misleading. A magnet introduced into a pile of metal shavings will attract only the steel. Vaughan's "conversion" has been used to build a total interpretation of his work on some elements in the sacred verse, distorting those elements themselves in the process. This has produced severe distortions of the sacred verse, the secular verse, the relationships between them, Vaughan's poetic development, and the distinctive nature of his poetry.

Following Marilla, I believe that it is more helpful to see Vaughan's poetic, intellectual, and religious development as essentially organic, continuous, and natural rather than radically disjunctive and marked by the preternatural transformation which is meant by "conversion."[6] Critics who visualize the poet's development in terms of a biographical crisis approach the mature verse with a mind dominated by the metaphor of rebirth. Thus they are disposed to believe that everything significant in the sacred verse is new, or that only the new things are significant—to see the poetry as responsive only to the experience of conversion itself and to the literary and intellectual experiences which accompanied or followed it. And thus they are disposed to value content, apprehended as biographical experience, for its own sake. There is no other way to explain the fact that sacred poems which are equally remarkable for good Christian intentions and tawdry writing have won critical admiration at the expense of poems which express the values of classical humanism in language worthy of a Jonson or a Dryden, or the fact that critics attribute to Herbert's influence the appearance in *Silex Scintillans* of "everyday" images, arresting openings, and octosyllabic couplets,[7] which, as anybody familiar with the secular verse knows, had always been characteristic of Vaughan's poetic style and simply continued to be so.

The view that Vaughan's poetic development was radically disjunctive is enforced either by disregard of the earlier verse altogether or by juxtaposition of some feeble example and an impressive passage from the sacred verse. Thus Joan Bennett judges the secular verse as a whole by one of the weakest of the Amoret poems, Helen Gardner speaks of "the conversion which turned the tepid wooer of Amoret into a poet who brings us 'authentic tidings of invisible things'," and F. E. Hutchinson begins his chapter on Vaughan's conversion by quoting the famous opening of "The World" and then proceeds: "Here is authentic poetry of such arresting quality as had not been apparent in the *Poems* of 1646 or would be found in the *Olor Iscanus* of 1651. . . . The author of *Silex Scintillans* was a changed man."[8] We are invited to infer that the conversion made all the difference between routine versifying and inspired greatness, but one's suspicion that the matter is not so simple is encouraged by the observation that, using the same logic but different examples, it is possible to argue that Vaughan's conversion made him soar like Icarus. True, the earlier poetry contains a good deal of routine versifying; but it is also true that it more consistently achieves a satisfying aesthetic level and that nothing in it can rival the dismal nullities of sacred poems which are really bad.[9] Hutchinson excuses the neglect of the secular verse by observing that, at its best, it is surpassed by the best of the sacred verse: "There is . . . general agreement that no poems in *Olor Iscanus* reach the standard of the best poems in *Silex Scintillans*." And Arno Esch puts the matter similarly: "Trotz E. L. Marillas verdienstvollem Versuch, Vaughans weltliche Lyrik stärker zur Geltung zu bringen, ist die künstlerische Überlegenheit seiner religiösen Dichtung unbestreitbar."[10] Vaughan's more mature work is indeed his more mature work, but this is a phenomenon for which we seldom require supernatural explanations. And for a poem to be judged inferior to Vaughan's best is hardly a crippling indictment. If we should ever take seriously the proposition that only poems which are as good as Vaughan's best are worth reading, we would have to give up not only his secular verse, and most of his sacred verse, but half the poetry in the language.

The nineteenth century made Vaughan in its own pious-romantic-sentimental image, which still floats before our eyes whenever we look for the poet who was "ingeniose, but prowd and humorous,"[11] who could scorn and scoff, gibe, laugh and rail, denounce Puritans and libidinous poets, as well as dream of paradise and light. The rainbow-browed recluse whispering of star-filled visions, fancied by Blunden, merited Eliot's duly meted scorn, but Eliot himself took this for portrait instead of parody.[12] Hutchinson deprecated the intrusion of earthly matters into the remote ecstasies that he thought Vaughan recorded.[13] "The rest were long to tell," but critics still speak of Vaughan's "rejection of the contemporary world and withdrawal into an inner realm of peace and light and unity" and of "the bright stillness of his visionary, ideal world."[14] When "nostalgia" and "yearning," with their suggestions of sentimental weakness and escapism, are joined with "ideal," "visionary," "otherworldly," and "mystical," the critical vocabulary yields a composite portrait of Vaughan as a kind of simpleminded saint. We are advised not to expect logical subtlety, coherent argument, consistent or unified structure, ingenious or provocative development of images, intricate patterns of implication, irony, wit, paradox, baroque tension, or complex analogies. But we are assured of moods of religious and mystical intensity, passionate devotion to God and Nature, authentic and sincere feeling and experience, flashes of insight into an ideal world, and the vivid evocativeness of isolated images, stanzas, and lines.

Thus the overwhelming impression one gets from the criticism is that Vaughan was critically naïve, an artless poet whose artlessness was a necessary condition of his distinctive achievement rather than an impediment to it. In his youth, self-consciously emulating Donne's fashionable conceits, he produced prosaic nullities without personal conviction, genuine commitment, or a controlling purpose. His poetic salvation was his religious conversion, an upsurge of the unconscious and a total surrender of the self to profound intuitions. Thereafter he failed when he strained for an effect, sought to edify his readers, tried to imitate the logical techniques of Herbert and Donne, or strove to exploit such conventional forms as the emblem and the meditative exercise—in short, when he ceased to respond compulsively to his private ecstasies and agonies, took thought for what he was doing, and shaped his poetry according to his awareness of an audience and of the traditional forms of artistic expression. His conscious exercise of artistic choice imposed alien restrictions on the free flow of his native genius, with the result that many of his poems are prosaic, flat, uninspired, conventional, and routine, or (when his true voice breaks through in spite of himself) uneven, disjointed, and fragmentary. Thus Elizabeth Holmes finds that "Vaughan's real subject is often indefinable and so eludes his efforts to present it. Many of his poems . . . begin with vivid inspiration, which later dies and leaves the rest of the poem dull and forlorn, because the gleam has returned to its source in the subconscious, and Vaughan's conscious mind, which is not strong or subtle, cannot follow it."[15] Similarly, E. C. Pettet endorses the popular charge of "constructional weakness" and attributes Vaughan's successes to a process of "subconscious association" between images.[16] Margherita Leardi speaks of Vaughan's oscillations "tra l'abbandono all'intuizione e l'atto della volontà," and finds that "il vero Vaughan vada cercato tra le righe delle sue poesie" because of "un dualismo alla base stessa dell'espressione vaughaniana: dualismo tra i temi della sua poesia e il linguaggio di cui si serve per dar loro corpo, tra la qualità della sua immaginazione e quella della tradizione letteraria a cui attinge."[17] And R. A. Durr will not have Vaughan called a meditative poet because the term "denotes a mental exercise . . . a formal regulation and arrangement of devotion," and "it is not in this spirit that Vaughan's poems live," but "with a poignancy not compatible with a calculated use of the mystical language."[18]

By thus insisting on feeling or experience as a sufficient motive for Vaughan's poems, critics unconsciously align him with those poets from whom T. S. Eliot radically distinguished the Metaphysicals: those poets of the nineteenth century who, according to Eliot, "thought and felt by fits, unbalanced," whereas in Donne "there is a direct sensuous apprehension of thought, or a recreation of thought into feeling."[19] We are given to understand that Vaughan's occasional taking of thought is responsible only for his inferior poetry, whereas his best poems proceed by intuitive associations and the like. And so he is presented as primarily a poet of isolated and uncomplicated moods and (a natural corollary) of brilliant fragments rather than of whole poems. The insistence that Vaughan's secular verse has nothing to do with his sacred verse is related to this assumption that his feelings have nothing to do with his thoughts. Similarly, it is assumed that his worldliness has nothing to do with his "otherworldliness"—that when he put on the one he put off the other; that his love of God has nothing to do with his hatred of the Parliamentarians; that his devotional moods have nothing to do with his satirical moods; that his "love of Nature" has nothing to do with his ironic attitude toward time. Thus Vaughan is implicitly presented as a classic victim of dissociated sensibility or romantic agony. Leardi, in the passage quoted in the previous paragraph, is most explicit in ascribing to Vaughan a dichotomy and a conflict between understanding and will, between thought and word, between the private, subjective idea and its public, objective representation. She thinks that his essential quality "non si determina con lo studio del linguaggio della poesia," and that the elements of conventional religion in his poetry function as "cifra usata a dare un crisma di razionalita e di ortodossia al magico mondo della sua fantasia."[20] Similar disjunctive assumptions, less explicitly voiced, are involved in Pettet's discovery of the secret of Vaughan's power in "a private 'world' of imagination" which is somehow distinct from "every poet's dower of imagination" and even "in some sense distinct from the poems that embody it. It is the poetry behind the particular poems."[21] Durr apparently conceives of Vaughan's meaning as something prior to his language, in excess of it, and independently knowable, for he implicitly treats Vaughan's poetic imagery (which, for the most part, is common, traditional poetic imagery) as a system of occult signs. Thus he acknowledges that Vaughan uses "the conventional vocabulary and symbolism" but warns us against assuming that he refers to " 'nothing but' the ordinary Christian life."[22] Similarly, Pettet claims that "the stars and streams of *Silex Scintillans* are the stars and streams of *Poems* and *Olor Iscanus*; but they are something else too."[23] And Itrat-Husain uses any image of light in the sacred poems (but not in the secular poems) as evidence of Vaughan's achievement of Illumination, the third stage of the *via mystica*.[24]

The source of these views is the belief that Vaughan's sacred poetry was inspired by a single radical experience—conversion or spiritual awakening—and that this experience was essentially characterized by a withdrawal of his mind from ordinary human experience into a reflexive preoccupation with its solitary self. The world of his experience, and hence of his poetry, is seen as a Christian analogue of the psychological world of fantasies and dreams and of the world of natural miracle found in myth and romance. The reader is encouraged to regard Vaughan's poetry as a means of vicarious escape from ordinary experience into an autotelic, magical, ideal, "other" world and to believe that it served a similar function for its author. Critics may disagree about whether "otherworldly" or "mystical" is the best word to describe Vaughan's private experience, but there is basic agreement about its privateness and about its remoteness. The implication of either term is that his religious experiences were *sui generis*, unavailable through practice of the formal disciplines of institutionalized religion, recognizably distinct from the common piety signified by Vaughan's own practice of those forms, and therefore both incommunicable and inexplicable in terms of the symbolic language of Christian mythology which characterized Vaughan's culture and his conscious mind. Thus there is a plausible parallel between the kind of religious consciousness and the kind of poetic consciousness usually ascribed to Vaughan.

Vaughan's reputation as a mystic consists mainly in a long tradition of vague and casual allusion to him as such. Pettet acknowledges "some elements" of mysticism in Vaughan, but declines Itrat-Husain's argument for use of the term, following Helen White by speaking more vaguely of Vaughan's "strange otherworldliness," a quality which he associates with "glimpses . . . of the quiet, tranquillity, and ineffable radiance of heaven," but does not otherwise define.[25] Durr aptly objects to "otherworldly" as "unnecessarily vague and general." Believing Itrat-Husain to have placed the issue of mysticism in Vaughan beyond dispute (though he objects to Itrat-Husain's conclusion, reached by the same methods, that Donne and Herbert were also mystics), Durr takes it for granted that "to read the poet on his own terms" is to read him in the context of Christian mysticism—a context which he describes as "the *right* one."[26] On the other hand, Kermode insists that, qua poet, Vaughan makes a poet's use of the mystics' language—a position on the relation of literature to life for which he has been chidden more than once.[27]

If "mysticism" is to survive Occam's razor, it ought to refer to a special class of religious experiences. Itrat-Husain defined it in terms of the five phases of the *via mystica*, but his argument that Vaughan was a mystic is inconclusive, even on his own terms— that is, even if one grants the crude correspondence between literature and life which his method assumes.[28] As Durr says, "It is necessary first of all to make clear what one means by mysticism." The two pages of quotations which he gives to illustrate his usage seem to me to cover enough ground to include virtually any emotion related to religious matters.[29] To the extent that they illustrate "widespread agreement on the fundamental definition of the term," their common denominator seems to me to be the *experiencing*, or the *feeling*, of the relationships between the individual and God which theology describes and ritual celebrates, as distinct from conceptualization or routine observance. Here I am in general agreement with Ross Garner, who defines "mysticism" in Vaughan in terms of Cardinal Newman's distinction between notional and real assent, the latter being assent "to images derived from experience, to data provided by the senses and imagination."[30] This makes "mysticism" equivalent to what Vaughan and others of his time were wont to call "living faith," differentiating it from what in modern parlance might be called alienation. In this sense, of course Vaughan was a mystic, and of course he wrote mystical poetry. But this means more than that "mystical experience" is a tautology. It means that "mystical poetry" is a tautology as well, for, by its use of images derived from experience, data provided by the senses and imagination, poetry is essentially affective. And it means that the affective qualities of Vaughan's sacred verse do not have that exceptional, distinctive, private character which the use of "mystical" implies and which Durr insists on, enforcing his claim with a *reductio ad absurdum* of the affective quality of the devotional experiences common to many Christians ("titular Lip-labouring Christianity," "syllogistic priming of the pump of piety").[31] As Garner says, "mysticism and poetry have in common an imaginative apprehension of experience"[32]—which means, I would say, that precisely what is distinctive about Vaughan's religious poetry is that it is poetry. His poetic gift, not anything esoteric in his religious experiences, is what distinguishes him from countless mute, inglorious Miltons who have also worshipped with "living faith."

Vaughan himself had nothing but contempt for those Puritan exponents of "inner light" who claimed the sort of private dispensation of divine knowledge commonly attributed to him. In a time when such issues were sharpened by controversy and civil war, he never swerved from his dedication to the ecclesiastical and political systems which opposed the accumulated wisdom of man, as exemplified by institutions and customs, to the claims of individual liberty and individual conscience. Discipline was one of his favorite themes, the claim to authority based on personal revelation his prime bête noire. He simply denied the possibility that the insights offered by individual experience or individual conscience might be superior to those offered by history and sanctioned by public institutions. He continually derided "these new lights," "a presumptuous assuming to our selves of the stile of *Saints*," and "the stale shift of liberty of Conscience."[33] The period of his supposed withdrawal from the mundane world into a private realm of ideal vision was actually a period of intense activity and effort directed toward solution of what he considered the most important practical problem of his society: the problem of preserving "distressed Religion" during the suppression of the English Church, of keeping alive the true faith in a time of heresy and schism. Far from being a withdrawn contemplative, solely preoccupied with his personal relationship to God and the problem of his own salvation, he was a religious militant, an indefatigable preacher. When the Royalist and Anglican cause was finally defeated in the Civil War, the King executed and the Church suppressed, he appointed himself a lay preacher of the "underground" church, his pulpit the press and his congregation anybody who would read. The sacred verse and prose treatises which poured from his pen between 1648 and 1655 all had the same pastoral purpose: to *"turn many to righteousness,"* to provide "nourishment or help to *devotion*" (Martin, p. 391).

His desire to preserve the traditional forms of worship is revealed by his opposition to extemporaneous prayer. His response to the Puritans' intolerance of set prayers, and specifically to their abolition of the Prayer Book, was to compose the series of set prayers and formal meditations which make up the first part of *The Mount of Olives: Or, Solitary Devotions* (1652). He introduces the book by deriding those who imagine they can come to God by some other route:

> I know the world abounds with these Manuals, and triumphs over them. It is not then their scarsity that call'd this forth, nor yet a desire to crosse the age, nor any in it. I envie not their frequent *Extasies*, and raptures to the third heaven. . . . Nor should they, who assume to themselves the glorious

stile of Saints, be uncharitably moved, if we that are yet in the body, and carry our treasure in earthen vessels, have need of these helps. (Martin, p. 140)

The confinement of Vaughan's poetic inspiration to a single kind of experience is insidiously Procrustean. The critic's characterization of the experience becomes an exclusive touchstone of literary value, and passages in the works which seem to express the "essential" experience most fully or directly are identified as true poetry while others are repelled as impure metal. In practice, this approach manifests itself in an excessive emphasis on a single thematic and imagistic strain in Vaughan's verse. The most cherished passages are those which seem to express large, general, simple feelings (nostalgia, yearning, admiration, wonder, awe, joy) in relation to exotic symbols of transcendent spiritual states (Eden, the Golden Age, Nature redeemed, Heaven). The "essential" Vaughan is a dreamer of ethereal dreams, a seer of cosmic and apocalyptic visions. He yearns for the perfect order of the stars, the angelic innocence of childhood, the simple faith of Abraham, the naïve obedience of stones and trees and birds and flowers. He is ecstatic, joyful. He saw eternity the other night.

Pettet identifies the essential Vaughan with "a private 'world' of imagination," which is "in some sense distinct from the poems that embody it ... the poetry behind the particular poems ... perfectly reflected through a number of poems that are really one poem ... often to be glimpsed only in the gleams and flashes of fragmentary but intensely suggestive lines and phrases." Similarly, he distinguishes "three notes that are pervasive throughout *Silex Scintillans* and memorably concentrated in its masterpieces."[34] But Pettet's description of this private "world" of Vaughan's imagination and experience is really no more than a severely curtailed index of his images and themes. The restrictive implications of Durr's presumption that the context of Christian mysticism is "the *right* one" for Vaughan should be obvious. Durr finds that there are basically only three figures in Vaughan's carpet, "and each of them serves to embody a single theme: regeneration"; but, for one of these "major metaphors," he cites only two examples from all of Vaughan's work.[35] Surveying the early verse, Leardi finds "il vero Vaughan" in "lo sbrigarsi della fantasia in visioni cosmiche, in rarefatte atmosfere fuori dal tempo e dallo spazio," in "immagine di vastità favolosa e infinita," and her survey of *Silex Scintillans* concentrates on these qualities: "Vaughan rinuncia sí al mondo esterno, al mondo dell'apparenza, ma per meglio impadronirsi del mondo della realtà eterna al di là dei veli mortali; e proprio da questo nasce libero il vero Vaughan, il lirico soggettivo, tutto a sé nel suo mondo magico e visionario."[36]

The conception of true poetry involved in this use of Vaughan's "conversion" as a critical touchstone might be described as a sentimentalized version of the Romantic concept of poetic sublimity. It is primarily responsible for the popular view of his work: a handful of successful lyrics, a scattering of brilliant fragments, and a bulky mass of obtuse verse. Readers who go to Vaughan for visionary raptures and exotic transports will often be disappointed. They will often miss the central subject of a poem, placing primary emphasis on a passage or image which is only subsidiary to the whole and insulating it from the modifying pressures of its context. Those poems and passages which do not fit these restrictive criteria will be slipped into the Vaughan file under "Inspiration, failure of." These readers will not expect, and thus will not find, integral relationships between the "otherworldly" and "mundane" elements within a poem, and thus will miss the poem's wholeness. And they will conclude that the poet's imagination was powerful but erratic, that he wanted art, could not sustain a unified poetic structure, and lacked the judgment to stop when his inspiration dried up—in short, that Vaughan had genius, but no talent. The genesis of this view of Vaughan in the selective emphases which I have been discussing is dramatically illustrated by the critical history of "The World." The "cosmic vision" of the first seven lines has been cited interminably as a peak of both his religious experience and his poetry, while at the same time the portrayal of worldly vanity in the other fifty-three lines (which Vaughan emphasized by the poem's title) has been deplored as so much drab versifying, so much evidence of the involuntary and transitory nature of both his poetic and his mystical inspiration. Some anthologists have even gone so far as to print only the first seven lines, a procedure which, as Pettet remarks, "produces a quite attractive, if somewhat obscure poem."[37] The inadequacy of the assumptions and expectations which produced this mutilation of Vaughan's work is suggested by the recent studies which have amply demonstrated the poem's complex unity.[38]

The Romantic bias which persists in Vaughan criticism is part of our heritage from his nineteenth-century readers, who responded to his treatment of Nature in terms of Wordsworth's poetry.[39] This heterogeneous yoking was encouraged by the coincidence, in "The Retreate" and Wordsworth's *Intimations of Immortality*, of the Platonic concept of the soul's preexistence and an idealized image of childhood. Vaughan was regarded as a precursor of Wordsworth, even as a direct influence upon him. This habit of thought eventually produced the myth that Wordsworth had owned a copy of *Silex Scintillans*, and he was even reputed, sometimes, to have annotated it with care. In 1870, R. C. Trench went so far as to report the "discovery" of this fugitive volume, but the myth was eventually demolished by Helen McMaster, although not before several critics had shored it up with parallels, and not before William Empson, Edmund Blunden, and T. S. Eliot had authorized the nineteenth-century reading of Vaughan, differing only in their attitudes toward it.[40] Vague suggestions of an affinity between Vaughan and Wordsworth, claims that Vaughan vaguely foreshadowed or anticipated the Romantic treatment of nature, are standard in the books on Metaphysical poetry which appeared in the 1930s[41]—some of which have been reprinted without revision in recent years. The association of Vaughan with Wordsworth remains a staple of Vaughan folklore, appearing regularly (with or without the claim of direct influence) in such popular sources as histories, anthologies, surveys, and guides. Since the 1930s, specialized critics have usually been more careful. But Hutchinson consistently associates Vaughan with Wordsworth as "an observant lover of nature," dwelling on the landscape of the Usk valley because Vaughan "would not have questioned Wordsworth's view of the influence of natural beauty upon the growing child."[42] And Pettet, while insisting that Vaughan "was essentially of his age, not a Romantic born out of his time," that "certain writers have made far too much of him as a poet of Nature," nevertheless describes him as the "tutelary spirit" of the Usk valley, finding in his poetry "the clear impression of a distinctive landscape," which is "unmistakably the Usk valley below the Brecon Beacons and Alt yr Esgair."[43] And Miriam K. Starkman is equally ambiguous: "We are still a long way from the secular transcendentalism of Romanticism, from Nature as landscape and teacher, but we can see the distant prospect of Romanticism in the future."[44]

The only unequivocal details of local topography that I can find in Vaughan are the titles of two poems, "Upon the Priorie Grove" and "To the River *Isca*" (Martin, pp. 15, 39). But the poems describe a traditional *locus amoenus*, not an observed scene. One of the most extended examples of what looks like natural description in Vaughan's poetry is the first stanza of "The Water-fall" (Martin, p. 537), a poem which contains the suspiciously Wordsworthian lines, "Dear stream! dear bank, where often I / have sate, and pleas'd my pensive eye." Wordsworth composed some lines "a few miles above Tintern Abbey, on revisiting the banks of the Wye during a tour, July 13, 1798," sat "Here, under this dark sycamore," and pleased his pensive eye by viewing "These plots of cottage-ground, these orchard-tufts, / Which at this season, with their unripe fruits, / Are clad in one green hue," and by remembering, among many other personal experiences and feelings stimulated by the occasion, how the sounding cataract had once haunted him like a passion.[45] For all anybody knows, Henry Vaughan may have often sat by a waterfall and pleased his pensive eye in just such a way. But what does that have to do with his poem? The stream which is dear to the speaker in "The Water-fall" is an artificially constructed emblem representing temporal life, death, resurrection, and immortality. The details of the description, the sequence in which they appear, and the pattern which that sequence creates, are chosen for their symbolic value, not—as Wordsworth's are—as "beauteous forms," chosen for their aesthetic and emotional value in the life of the poet. That is to say, they are determined by the preconceived complex of ideas which they are to represent, not by Vaughan's personal experience of a place. And the language of the passage, the central tendency of which is to personify the stream, and thus to render its course analogous to human life, consistently emphasizes the ideational, general level of meaning, not the locally descriptive or uniquely personal.

This stream has precisely as much in common with a real stream, which Vaughan may have actually observed and responded to with personal emotion, as the emblematic heart on the title page of *Silex Scintillans* has in common with the physical organ which beat in his breast. The form of the poem may be referred to the Ignatian meditation on death; the simulation of the speaker's presence in an imagined situation is related to the Ignatian practice of "seeing the place," and to the tendency, characteristic of Metaphysical poetry, to dramatize an evolution of experience. The treatment of the imagery may be referred to the compositional and analytic phases of meditation, to allegory, to the illustrations in emblem books, to religious iconography in general, and to the conception of nature (derived from Biblical and Neoplatonic tradition) as a system of hieroglyphs, a metaphorical expression of the mind of God. The provenance of the imagery is not the Usk river flowing near Vaughan's home, but archetypal images of the river of time and the waters of life, baptismal water, Biblical fountains of life, the dark waters of the first chapter of Genesis, on which the spirit of God moved and created light, and the Red Sea and the river Jordan as elements in the Christian symbolism of life as a pilgrimage to the Promised Land. The meaning of the poem is related to Vaughan personally only insofar as he shares the general Christian experience of sin, expiation, forgiveness, mercy, grace, regeneration, and redemption.

All in all, the last place in the world to look for precedents for Wordsworth's treatment of nature is the poetry of Henry Vaughan. When earlier critics differentiated Vaughan's treatment of nature from a Wordsworthian "personal response," they located its source in the writings of the mythical Hermes Trismegistus and of such Hermetic philosophers as Cornelius Agrippa, Jacob Boehm, and the poet's twin, Thomas Vaughan. The critical literature on the question of Vaughan's indebtedness to Hermeticism, and on the related question of his closeness to his brother, is perhaps more extensive than on any other aspect of his work.[46] One effect of explicating Vaughan's poetry in terms of Hermeticism is that it appears esoteric, intellectually sophisticated, and "difficult." In the 1920s, when A. C. Judson opened the debate on Hermeticism in Vaughan, T. S. Eliot had made a great impression with his dictum, uttered in an essay on Metaphysical poetry, that modern poetry must be difficult.[47] Difficulty was thought a hallmark of the Metaphysical style, and especially of its prime exemplar, John Donne. Judson, and others who followed him, may have been unconsciously motivated, perhaps, by a desire to make Vaughan respectable in the accepted terms, to rescue him from the status of a third-rate Romantic. However that may be, it seems to me that those areas of thought in which Vaughan's poetry has most in common with Hermeticism are precisely the areas in which Hermeticism has most in common with the mainstream of Christian and Neoplatonic tradition. As Garner insists, it is superfluous at best, and at worst it deforms our sense of the poetry, to adduce an esoteric text in explanation of a commonplace.[48] The Hermetic writers placed great emphasis on God's immanence and on the related view of nature as divine metaphor. Vaughan's readings in Hermeticism may, indeed, have intensified his awareness of nature in these terms, but it is both unnecessary and potentially misleading to suppose so, because such a view was fundamental in a culture permeated by the Bible, Christian theology, and popularized Neoplatonism. Occasionally, it is true—very occasionally—Vaughan draws on a Hermetic source for specific terminology or a specific image. But, as Frank J. Warnke notes, "Vaughan's Hermeticism almost always appears within a framework of orthodox Christian reference."[49] And, as Garner's analyses of some of Vaughan's most "Hermetic" poems demonstrate (to my satisfaction, at least), the framework almost always explains the Hermeticism, not vice versa. Vaughan was indeed a learned man, and he was familiar with some esoteric lore; but his poetry is no more esoteric, learned, or "difficult" than it is Romantic and third-rate.

A critical approach which enables us to respond to only a fraction of a poet's work must at least abide our question. I would like to discourage descriptions of Vaughan's typical quality in terms associated with emotional rapture, ecstasy, or excitement of one kind or another, whether it be called a passionate response to nature, a mystical vision of another world, or a nostalgic yearning for childhood innocence or the New Jerusalem. The contemporary world is very much in his poems, inextricably involved with the bright, ideal vision. His "otherworldliness" is involved with his fanatical Royalism and his consciousness of self, the metaphysical idealism with the political and the personal, for the heavenly paradise has individual and social analogues, and all are lost and to be found. Problem corresponds to problem and solution to solution on different levels, and the levels variously interact and coalesce with one another. The reader who expects starry visions, but can see the words on the page, may well be at a stand to choose whether "The Brittish Church," for example, or "The Constellation," or "The Proffer" is *either* religious idealism *or* sociopolitical propaganda. When Vaughan transcends hatred, or bitterness, or despair, it is a struggle, and he expresses the hatred, the bitterness, the despair, and the struggle—not just a transcendence. He does not find peace by withdrawing into himself, for there he finds rebellions and disorders as much as in England. He does not reject the contemporary world, or the world in general, or withdraw from it. He absorbs it until his perspective becomes broad and tragic rather than local and elegiac.

Not stillness, but energetic, dynamic, conflicting action is the characteristic mode of Vaughan's poetry. He does not withdraw into peace and light and unity, but fights for them against tumult, darkness, and disorder—in himself, in the world around him, in the way things are. What he gives us is not a bright, static vision; it is a fierce tension, a dynamic struggle, a delicate balance—always lost, always renewed.

Vaughan was good at hatred, and he can make it sting in acidulous, crackling couplets or bruise in hard, powerful rhythms. His poems reveal, among other things, a humor, a sense of fun, a delight in the incongruous and absurd, a relish for the concrete touch of things, a gusto—whether for wenching, or wining, or detesting Puritans. Vaughan was a worldly man—hence the brilliant, sensuous surfaces of his poems. Hence, too, their vitality—their dynamic, delicate energy. His experience of the world—of its folly, tumult, vanity, darkness, disorder, sin—enlivened his sardonic spirit, gave him his Democritean laugh, his bitterness, his savage tone, his self-pity. It gave him his haunted, heavy sense of mortal coils; his deep, troubled, tragic vision not only of his own time but of human nature and history; and it gave him his glittering images of the heavenly city, the supernal analogue of the lost world. As these currents cross and combine, they yield the somber glamor of his greatest lyrics—"The Night," for instance, or "The World," or "They are all gone into the world of light!" His range was great, the bright vision only one point—and this is not to deny the essential simplicity which all recognize. But Vaughan gives us simplicity, not simplification, and we cannot apprehend it without apprehending the complex diversity out of which it is wrought.

Chapter

II

BEN JONSON AND THE CRAFT OF POETRY

THOUGH CRITICS SPEAK constantly of his early interest in Donne, Vaughan himself never spoke of it at all. In the first poem in his first book, he elevates Jonson to the place of honor in the underworld to which Dante had assigned Homer:

> First, in the shade of his owne bayes,
> Great *BEN* they'le see, whose sacred Layes,
> The learned Ghosts admire, and throng,
> To catch the subject of his Song.   (Martin, p. 3)

Praising "Mr. *Fletchers* Playes" (Martin, p. 54), he again puts Jonson first, with capitals *and* italics, not only before Fletcher but before all poets past and to come:

> This, or that *age* may write, but never see
> A *Wit* that dares run *Paralell* with thee.
> True, *BEN* must live! but bate *him*, and thou hast
> Undone all *future wits*, and match'd the *past*.

We are rightly inclined to doubt the sincerity of literary compliment in the Renaissance. As an indicator of personal conviction and taste, Vaughan's gratuitous exaltation of Jonson and complete disregard of Donne is, by itself, no more significant than his occasional attempts to imitate Donne in diction, theme, and argumentative technique. But it should at least make us hesitate to conclude that criteria drawn from Donne's poetry constitute the most appropriate framework within which to evaluate Vaughan's early efforts. Judgment by these criteria invariably produces the conclusion that Vaughan failed to achieve anything remarkable in the Donne manner, and from this has followed the standard view of the early Vaughan as a dilettante—a superficial, unsuccessful imitator of Donne—whose work lacks any clear focus or sense of purpose and direction.[1] This stems from the idolatry of Donne which impelled critics of thirty or forty years ago to concentrate on signs of his influence on later poets of the century, minimizing or disregarding other possibilities, and to elevate his work as an ultimate standard for seventeenth-century poetry and even for English poetry in general. When Vaughan spoke of an ultimate standard in poetry, he spoke of Ben Jonson. Could it be that he usually "failed" to write like Donne because he usually tried to write poetry of quite a different sort?[2] What were his poetic aims and standards of poetic excellence? What was his conception of poetry's nature and function and of his role as a poet? What did *Vaughan* think he was trying to do?

Practicing the art of literary compliment with the conventional ardor of his age, Vaughan adumbrated the aesthetic principles and criteria which the writers he praised are alleged to fulfill so lavishly. His remarks are squarely in line with the traditional, classical principles propagated by Jonson in defiance of the new fashion for "strong-lined" verse of which Donne's is the most conspicuous example. In the controversy over strong lines, Vaughan stood solidly in the opposite camp, with Jonson, Lord North, Drummond, D'Avenant, and Hobbes. He endorsed, in language that is remarkably similar to D'Avenant's preface and Hobbes's reply, the revived emphasis on "naturalness" represented by *Gondibert*, and explicitly condemned ornate, obscure, and bizarre writing. He saw poetry as a public institution, not as an instrument of private satisfaction, and believed the poet's first duty to be the clear communication of "good sense." He regarded extemporaneous or "inspired" writing with distrust and aversion, and insisted on the need, in poetry as in religion, for discipline and formal order. In short, practically everything that he said about poetry was a restatement of something in Jonson's *Timber*. Comparison with *Timber* is a convenient way of explicating Vaughan's views and—since this is an anthology of traditional ideas rather than an original work—of showing by the way that, in poetry as in politics and religion, Vaughan was one who loved to keep the road.

Perhaps the most distinctive feature of Jonson's criticism was his refusal to grant autonomy or even primacy to the role of inspiration or intuition in the creative act and his emphasis on the relative importance of conscious, deliberate choice. He wrote his own poems "first in prose, for so his master Cambden, had learned him," thought good poets were "made, as well as borne," and wished Shakespeare had blotted a thousand lines: "His wit was in his owne power; would the rule of it had beene so too."[3] In rhetorical terms, *inventio*, or the finding of poetic matter, must be complemented and controlled by *dispositio*, or the organization of matter. Fancy or wit, the synthetic, image-making power of the mind, or the capacity to perceive similarities between disparate phenomena or experiences, must be regulated by judgment, the analytical capacity to classify phenomena or experiences by perceiving differences. Vigor, variety, or richness of matter were not enough; Jonson demanded that matter be *orderly*, and therefore stood always at sword's point with "the obstinate contemners of all helpes, and Arts: such as presuming on their owne *Naturals*. . . . utter all they can thinke, with a kind of violence, and *indisposition*; unexamin'd, without relation, either to person, place, or any fitnesse else" (Tayler, p. 104). Invention was easier, more spontaneous, more "natural" than disposition, because fancy was more closely allied than judgment with the senses and the appetites. For that reason, a poet was easily enticed to surrender himself entirely to the pleasing activity of his natural wit; but the factor which made the free exercise of a fecund imagination pleasant also made it an unreliable arbiter of artistic order, which could best be assured by the rule of judgment—that is, by self-criticism, intellectual detachment, and rational control of the lower faculties.

Complimenting "Mr. M. L. *upon his reduction of the* Psalms *into Method*" (Martin, p. 628), Vaughan expresses a typically Jonsonian view of the roles of fancy and judgment and of the need for a balance between matter and form:

> You have oblig'd the *Patriarch*. And tis known
> He is your Debtor now, though for his own.
> What he wrote, is a *Medley*. We can see
> Confusion trespass on his Piety.
> Misfortunes did not only Strike at him;
> They charged further, and oppress'd his pen.
> For he wrote as his *Crosses* came, and went
> By no safe Rule, but by his *Punishment*.
> His *quill* mov'd by the *Rod*; his witts and he
> Did know no *Method*, but their *Misery*.
>   You brought his Psalms now into Tune. Nay, all
> His measures thus are more than musical.
> Your *Method* and his *Aires* are justly sweet,
> And (what's *Church-musick* right) like *Anthems* meet.
> You did so much in this, that I believe
> He gave the *Matter*, you the *form* did give.

Vaughan does not value the expression, per se, of intense emotion, but its expression in orderly, measured, "methodical" language. The first ten lines quoted above isolate the writer's submergence in his own subjective response to experience and his unrestrained expression of strong feelings as the principal enemies of artistic success. Far from evincing any belief in the autonomous efficacy of strong emotion to express itself naturally or intuitively in artistic form, Vaughan clearly suggests that the risk of confusion increases with the strength of the feeling and advocates intellectual detachment and the deliberate exercise of artistic choice as the only "safe Rule." Vaughan's complaint against the Psalmist is that he was one of those who presume, in Jonson's phrase, "on their owne *Naturals*," for "without Art, Nature can ne're bee perfect" (Tayler, p. 136). Vaughan is speaking of the perfecting of Nature by Art.

In the seventeenth century, the writers of strong lines were often chided for deliberate obscurity, as in Jonson's celebrated confidence to William Drummond that Donne "for not being understood would perish." But deliberate obscurity did not lack apologists for whom not being understood was praise. The Orphic and Pythagorean conception of the poet as *vates*, a guardian of religious mysteries, was reinforced by Plato's theory of poetic rapture or *furor poeticus*, and, on this basis, medieval and Renaissance Neoplatonism fostered the view that the poet's priestly office required him to build defenses against sacrilege into his style. Deliberate obscurity is the most time-honored of literary values, for literary criticism might be said to have begun as the search for hidden meanings in Homer's epics and the surface trivialities of classical myths, and it was deliberate obscurity, or what Spenser was later to call "dark conceit,"[4] that was rationalized in the earliest theories of allegory. The metaphysical conceit was one product of the search for "inwardness"—the expression of more than meets the eye—in what Bacon called "Poesie Allusive, or Parabolical," which he found to be "of ambiguous use, and applied to contrary ends. For it serves for *Obscuration*; and it serveth also for *Illustration*. . . . for that tendeth to demonstrate, and illustrate that which is taught or delivered, and this other to retire and obscure it" (Tayler, pp. 148–49).[5] The *Mythomystes* of Henry Reynolds was a vigorous defense of the "mysticall manner of writing" sponsored by Neoplatonic theory. Reynolds found the ancients superior to the moderns not only in prophetic knowledge, "those extaticke elevations; or that truly-*divinus furor* of theirs," but in their "closenesse, and care to conceale," their use of "Enigma's and mysticall riddles. . . . that high and Mysticall matters should by riddles and enigmaticall knotts be kept inviolate from the prophane Multitude" (Tayler, pp. 234, 238, 242).

There is much in Vaughan that is Neoplatonic, including some interest in "those extaticke elevations; or that truly-*divinus furor*," but he preferred a poetic style that, in Bacon's words, "tendeth to demonstrate, and illustrate that which is taught or delivered." "The chiefe vertue of a style is perspicuitie," said Jonson, "and nothing so vitious in it, as to need an Interpreter. . . . Order helpes much to Perspicuity, as Confusion hurts. *Rectitudo lucem adfert; obliquitas et circumductio offuscat*" (Tayler, pp. 120–22). The central points of Jonson's recommendations on style are rendered metaphorically in Vaughan's praise of Cartwright (Martin, p. 56):

> Thy matchless *Genius*, in all thou didst write,
> Like the *Sun*, wrought with such *stayd heat*, and *light*,
> That not a *line* (to the most *Critick* he)
> Offends with *flashes*, or *obscuritie*.
> . . . .
> Thus, thou thy *thoughts* hast *drest* in such a *strain*
> As doth not only *speak*, but *rule* and *raign*.
> Nor are those *bodyes* they assum'd, *dark Clouds*,
> Or a *thick bark*, but *clear, transparent shrouds*,
> Which who so *lookes* on, the *Rayes* so strongly beat
> They'l *brushe* and *warm* him with a *quickning heat*,
> So *Souls* shine at the *Eyes*, and *Pearls* display
> Through the *loose-Chrystal-streams* a *glaunce of day*.

That these passages express a common animus for strong lines is too obvious for comment. Vaughan's opposition to "riddles and enigmaticall knotts" is underscored by the way "Nor are those *bodyes* they assum'd, *dark Clouds*, / Or a *thick bark*, but *clear, transparent shrouds*" reverses Reynolds' praise of Moses for keeping the true meaning of the Law "hidden and concealed under the barke, and rude cover of the words" (Tayler, p. 243). Vaughan does not merely parrot Jonson's attitude; he expresses, in similar language, the traditional assumption about the relation of words to matter on which the attitude was based: "In all speech, words and sense, are as the body, and the soule. The sense is as the life and soule of Language, without which all words are dead" (Tayler, p. 119). The Platonic metaphor insists on the primacy of "sense," and Jonson says just what he means by it: "Wee doe not require in [the poet] meere *Elocution*: or an excellent faculty in verse; but the exact knowledge of all vertues; and their Contraries; with ability to render the one lov'd, the other hated, by his proper embattaling them" (Tayler, p. 110). Thus Vaughan praises Cartwright above all for his exact knowledge of human nature and his power to move men's minds:

> When thou the *wild* of *humours* trackst, thy *pen*
> So Imitates that *Motley stock* in men
> As if thou hadst in all their *bosomes* been
> And seen those *Leopards* that lurk within.
> The am'rous *Youth* steals from thy *Courtly page*
> His *vow'd Addresse*, the *Souldier* his *brave rage*.

Later in his life, he complains to "*the Editor of the matchless* Orinda" about the desuetude of "noble numbers with good sense" and the prevalence in poetry of trivial, childish, and absurd matter:

> Long since great witts have left the Stage
> Unto the *Drollers* of the age,
> And noble numbers with good sense
> Are like good works, grown an offence.
> While much of verse (worse than old story,)
> Speaks but *Jack-Pudding*, or *John-Dory*.
> Such trash-admirers made us poor,
> And *Pyes* turn'd *Poets* out of door.   (Martin, p. 641)

In this demand for solid intellectual substance in poetry there is nothing that divides Jonson and Vaughan from Reynolds, who excoriated "the mont'ibanke Rimers of the time" as vigorously as Jonson deplored the popularity of "*Heath's Epigrams*, and the

Skullers Poems." But there is a fundamental conflict in their ideas on style, and this proceeds from their concern with different kinds of knowledge and a corresponding difference in their beliefs about the function and purpose of poetry. The "sense" which Jonson wishes poetry to express is based on "the observation, knowledge, and use of things. . . . wrought out of experience, the knowledge of humane life, and actions" (Tayler, p. 119). It is primarily knowledge of man's moral nature and behavior and is limited to the realm of nature or second causes. But when Reynolds speaks of knowledge he emphasizes knowledge of first causes or essences, the Platonic *divinus furor* or intellectual rapture which culminates in contemplation of the Idea of the Good. This knowledge is sacred, secret, and autotelic. Reynolds speaks of its possessor's "neglect of the body, and businesse of the world. . . . blindnesse to all things of triviall and inferiour condition" (Tayler, p. 234), just as Vaughan's modern critics speak of his renunciation of the world and withdrawal into private visions. Poetry turns in upon itself, the private endowment of a coterie of ascetic *cognoscenti* who preserve the integrity of their mystical wisdom "inviolate from the prophane Multitude" by means of a style which deliberately does not communicate beyond the pale.[6]

Jonson and Vaughan, however, believe that the end of poetry lies not in the reflexive satisfaction of the writer or a coterie but in its effect on a wider public. They follow the maxim that the end of poetry is delightful teaching. Its purpose is the persuasive communication of knowledge that is useful in the broadest sense, the eloquent expression of intellectually and morally sound ideas. Vaughan's comparison of poetry to "good works" (as distinct from "faith") suggests that, for him, the moral responsibility of the poet is something quite different from the enjoyment of private visions. "The principall end of Poesy," said Jonson flatly, "[is] to informe men, in the best reason of living." This fundamental belief determines the views on style which Vaughan and Jonson share. The eloquent expression of "good sense" will move the reader to admiration, and thence to emulation, of the best reason of living. The poet "doth raigne in mens affections . . . invade, and breake in upon them; and makes their minds like the thing he writes," said Jonson; and Vaughan extolled Cartwright's eloquence in similar terms: "thou thy *thoughts* hast *drest* in such a *strain* / As doth not only *speak*, but *rule* and *raign*"; the lines "*brushe* and *warm*" the reader "with a *quickning heat*." In a poem to Katherine Philips (Martin, p. 62), Vaughan expresses this idea of the contagious effect of poetry through images of magnetism, celestial motion, and musical vibration:

> So *Lodestones* guide the duller *Steele*,
> And high perfections are the *Wheele*
> Which moves the lesse, for gifts divine
> Are strung upon a *Vital line*
> Which touch'd by you, Excites in all
> Affections *Epidemicall*.

Perspicuity is the chief virtue of a style because a style that is clear, orderly, and direct is the most eloquent: it best enables the poet's matter to "invade, and break in upon" the reader's mind. This is what Vaughan and Jonson mean by the equation sense : language :: soul : body and by their speaking of style in terms of light. The body should *express* the soul; the sense should shine through the language as "*Souls* shine at the *Eyes*." Perspicuous language is the best conductor of light.

Their more conservative contemporaries deplored the writers of "strong-lined" verse as exhibitionists and regarded their extravagant inventions as not only obscure but fantastic, bizarre, and "unnatural" as well—that is, as violations of *mimesis,* which Jonson transcribed as the writing of "things like the Truth" (Tayler, p. 131). William Drummond appeals to the *consensus gentium* to justify his opinion that the verse of those who "endeavoured to abstract" poetry "to *Metaphysical* Idea's, and *Scholastical* Quiddities. . . . is no more *Poesy* than a Monster is a Man" (Tayler, pp. 215–16). Jonson, insisting no less on the proper imitation of Nature, similarly defines the truth of Nature in terms of the *consensus gentium*: "The true Artificer will not run away from nature, as hee were afraid of her; or depart from life, and the likeness of Truth. . . . *Custome* is the most certaine Mistresse of Language. . . . that I call Custome of speech, which is the consent of the Learned" (Tayler, pp. 104, 120–21). In his preface to *Gondibert*, D'Avenant decried "what are commonly called *Conceits*, things that sound like the knacks or toyes of ordinary *Epigrammatists*" and described himself as "one that travelled not to bring home the names, but the proportion and nature of things," thus "bringing Truth (too often absent) home to mens bosomes" (Tayler, pp. 273–74). His efforts were commended in very similar language by Hobbes and Vaughan:

> There are some that are not pleased with fiction, unlesse it be bold not onely to exceed the *work*, but also the *possibility* of nature: they would have impenetrable Armours, Inchanted Castles, invulnerable bodies, Iron men, flying Horses, and a thousand other such things which are easily feign'd by them that dare. Against such I defend you . . . by dissenting onely from those that think the Beauty of a Poem consisteth in the exhorbitancy of the fiction. For as truth is the bound of Historicall, so the Resemblance of truth is the utmost limit of Poeticall Liberty. (Tayler, pp. 285–86)

>   where before *Heroick Poems* were
> Made up of *Spirits, Prodigies*, and *fear*,
> And shew'd (through all the *Melancholy flight*,)
> Like some dark Region overcast with night,
> As if the Poet had been quite dismay'd,
> While only *Giants* and *Inchantments* sway'd,
> Thou like the *Sun*, whose Eye brooks no disguise
> Hast Chas'd them hence, and with Discoveries
> So rare and learned fill'd the place, that wee
> Those fam'd *Grandeza's* find out-done by thee,
> And under-foot see all those *Vizards* hurl'd,
> Which bred the wonder of the former world.
>   (Martin, p. 64)

The rule of judgment over fancy in the poetic imitation of Nature was psychologically analogous to the rule of reason over the passions, the psychological model of moral order imprinted on men's imaginations by Plato's myth of the charioteer in the *Phaedo*. As examples of *discordia concors*, both were models or microcosmic reflections of the order of Nature, whose various plenitude was regulated by the wisdom of God. Thus "follow Nature" was both an artistic and a moral injunction. Poetic fancy unrestrained by judgment was concupiscence of wit, and the poem it produced was, in Drummond's words, "as if Nature should bring forth some new *Animal*, neither Man, Horse, Lyon, Dog, but which had some Members of all" (Tayler, p. 216). It was unnatural, or disordered, in the same way as a person whose reason was ruled by passion. Such a poem not only failed to imitate Nature; it subverted the moral end of poetry, which was to set the reader's affections in right tune. And this end required not only that the poem's content should inform people in the best reason of living, but that its form should reflect the order of Nature, the archetype of the moral order of the individual soul. The proper imitation of Nature, according to Jonson, required imitation of the form as well as of the things of Nature:

> The order of Gods creatures in themselves, is not only admirable, and glorious, but eloquent; Then he who could apprehend the consequence of things in their truth, and utter his apprehensions as truly, were the best Writer, or Speaker. . . . Neither can his mind be thought in tune, whose words doe jarre; nor his reason in frame, whose sentence is preposterous. (Tayler, p. 126)

The moral implications of formal order in poetry color the indignation which Jonson, Drummond, and North express on the subject of poems in which fanciful language overbalances sense. A good poem will ultimately reflect the order of Nature; but it will most directly reflect the moral order of the author's soul. This is the significance of Jonson's celebrated remark, echoed by

Vaughan (and by Milton), on "the impossibility of any mans being the good *Poët*, without first being a good *Man*" (Tayler, p. 79).[7] The discipline required to write well is psychologically identifiable with the discipline required to achieve moral perfection: a moral poem and a moral soul alike reflect the perfecting of nature by art.

The central topic of Vaughan's preface, written in 1654, to the enlarged reissue of *Silex Scintillans* published in 1655, is the question of the fittest subject matter for poetry, which is virtually synonymous with "the best reason of living." The issue is predicated on the traditional assumption that the end of poetry lies in its moral effect on the reader, and therefore the discussion also involves the allied topic of the poet's moral and social responsibility, the proper use of poetic talent:

> It was wisely considered, and piously said by one, *That he would read no idle books; both in regard of love to his own soul, and pity unto his that made them, for* (said he) *if I be corrupted by them, their Composer is immediatly a cause of my ill: and at the day of reckoning (though now dead) must give an account for it, because I am corrupted by his bad example . . . I will write none, lest I hurt them that come after me.* (Martin, p. 390)

The old issue is now placed in the explicitly Christian context of personal salvation; eternal as well as temporal consequences are now attributed to temporal acts. Wrongdoing which in pagan or secular terms had been thought of as a violation of reason or Nature, a crime against the humanity of writer and reader, is now seen as a theological crime, a violation of the law of God which Nature and man's reason embody. Nature and man are vessels of divine grace, and therefore acts which affect humanity are sacred. The shift strengthens the moral imperatives involved, and has other important consequences for Vaughan's thinking about poetry; but it does not change the basic pattern of relationships between writer, poem, and reader.

"It was well noted by the late L. St. *Alban*, that the study of words is the first distemper of Learning," said Jonson, "Vaine matter the second" (Tayler, p. 125). Vaughan's preface begins with the first distemper, decrying "those ingenious persons, which in the late notion are termed *Wits*" for their "deliberate search, or excogitation of *idle words*, and a most vain, insatiable desire to be reputed *Poets*." Sacred poets are among those guilty of this imbalance between words and matter; a pious subject is no guarantee of a well-ordered poem:

> After [George Herbert] followed diverse,—*Sed non passibus aequis*; they had more of *fashion*, then *force*: And the *reason* of their so vast *distance* from him, besides differing *spirits* and *qualifications* (for his *measure* was eminent) I suspect to be, because they aimed more at *verse*, then *perfection*; as may be easily gathered by their frequent *impressions*, and numerous *pages*: Hence sprang those wide, those weak, and lean *conceptions*, which in the most inclinable *Reader* will scarce give any nourishment or help to *devotion*; for not flowing from a true, practick piety, it was impossible they should effect those things abroad, which they never had acquaintance with at home; being onely the productions of a common spirit, and the obvious ebullitions of that light humor, which takes the pen in hand, out of no other consideration, then to be seen in print.

Vaughan does not attribute Herbert's eminence as a sacred poet simply to the quality of his religious feeling. It is also a matter of "differing *spirits* and *qualifications*"—knowledge and training, and that "goodnes of naturall wit" which Jonson thought the basic qualification of a good poet (Tayler, p. 133). The basic criterion which Vaughan is applying to Herbert and other sacred poets is the one he had applied to Cartwright and Katherine Philips—the criterion of *"force"* or eloquence, the power to move men's minds, specified here as the provision of "nourishment or help to *devotion*." His unfavorable attitude toward "strong-

lined" sacred verse ("those ingenious persons . . . termed *Wits*.
. . . those wide, those weak, and lean *conceptions*") suggests that
he still favors a style which "tendeth to demonstrate, and illustrate that which is taught or delivered." The "matter" of the
poem will not be primarily doctrinal, theological, abstract, or
theoretical. Since the poem can only "effect those things abroad"
which it has "had acquaintance with at home," and since its public function is to *"turn many to righteousness,"* to provide
"nourishment or help to *devotion*," it will be an imitation of the
poet's own "true, practick piety." That is, it will eloquently portray the poet's own unitive religious experience—not his affections only, and not his beliefs only, but his affections as shaped
by knowledge and faith.

Vaughan's thinking here participates in a central movement of
the Reformation and the Counter-Reformation—a movement,
variously illustrated by Erasmus's *Praise of Folly*, the Ignatian
Exercises, the *Imitatio Christi*, and the renewed emphasis on
preaching, from "works of Law to works of Faith"[8] and from
conceptualized belief to felt belief, the actualization of faith in
the mind and heart of the whole person. According to Vaughan's
preface, the central aim of sacred poetry is the propagation of this
kind of faith. The relation of poet and reader is therefore directly
analogous to the relation of priest and congregation. The kind of
poetry which Vaughan envisages here is the diametric opposite
of anything that can be meant by "otherworldly." The nature of
the private matter of the poem is absolutely determined by the
poem's public function, and the two are indissolubly linked. The
poet is to be an exemplar of perfect faith because the poem is to
be a persuasive paradigm of "true, practick piety," an eloquent
model of living faith to be internalized and thus imitated by the
"inclinable *Reader*."[9] The end of poetry is delightful teaching.
The perversion of this end by a disproportionate emphasis on
"delight" and a neglect of "good matter" is the reason for
Vaughan's complaint against sacred poets who "aimed more at
verse, then *perfection*."

Vaughan's dissatisfaction with those who aim more at verse

than perfection does not imply that a sacred poet may neglect his craft, any more than the dissatisfaction of Jonson and others with the disproportionate study of words implies a contempt for art. He is simply, at this point, emphasizing the importance of good matter and hence of the moral qualifications of the sacred poet. He presents the "true, practick piety" of the poet as a necessary precondition for the achievement of his purpose, but not as a sufficient qualification. There is nothing in the preface to suggest that a sacred poet need only be sincere, need only respond intuitively to the motions of the Spirit, however authentic and profound. In his poem on the Psalms, Vaughan did not exempt Scripture itself from judgment by the criteria of perspicuity and order. On the contrary, he criticized the Psalmist for writing in direct response to the pressure of experience, without the degree of detachment necessary for the perfecting of nature by art. Besides, the moral perfection that Vaughan speaks of is in no sense an autonomous faculty, whether naturally or divinely endowed. For the most part it is a product of deliberate and disciplined exercise and laborious control of contrary forces, though completed by the gift of grace:

> It is true indeed, that to give up our thoughts to pious *Themes* and *Contemplations* . . . is a great *step* towards *perfection*; because it will *refine,* and *dispose* to devotion and sanctity. And further, it will *procure* for us . . . some small *prelibation* of those heavenly *refreshments*, which descend but seldom, and then very sparingly, upon *men* of an ordinary or indifferent *holyness*; but he that desires to excel in this kinde of *Hagiography*, or holy writing, must strive (by all means) for *perfection* and true *holyness*, that a *door may be opened to him in heaven*, Rev. 4. 1. and then he will be able to write (with *Hierotheus* and holy *Herbert*) A *true Hymn.*

There is nothing particularly artless or spontaneous about striving by all means for perfection. And, since Vaughan thinks of sacred poetry as cognate with prayer, it is worth remembering at this point that he regarded extemporary prayer with distrust, if not contempt, and preferred the formal order of devotion sanctioned by Anglican ritual. For him, sacred poetry was a form of devotion; is it implausible to suggest that he regarded devotion as a form of sacred art? The poem "Dressing" is suggestive:

> Give me, my God! thy grace,
> The beams, and brightnes of thy face,
> That never like a beast
> I take thy sacred feast,
> Or the dread mysteries of thy blest bloud
> Use, with like Custome, as my Kitchin food.
> Some sit to thee, and eat
> Thy body as their Common meat,
> O let not me do so!
> Poor dust should ly still low,
> Then kneel my soul, and body; kneel, and bow;
> If *Saints*, and *Angels* fal down, much more thou.
> (Martin, p. 456)

It is likely, I think, that Vaughan regarded the neglect of order and form in sacred poetry as analogous to carelessness in devotion. He might well condemn as worldly vanity an excogitation of idle words prompted by an insatiable desire to be reputed poets. But a sacred poem is a vessel of God's Spirit, and the things of the world are sanctified by their use. In such poetry, he is likely to have considered the carefulness of art in perfecting the product of a fallen nature a proper expression of humility as well as part of the proper imitation of a well-ordered soul. The dedicatory verses prefixed to *Silex Scintillans* (Martin, pp. 394-95) present the poems to God as a sacred gift, a sacrifice. In them, Vaughan is speaking *to* God, and he is also, as poet-priest, speaking *for* God. "Were it not a dishonour to a mighty Prince," asked Jonson, "to have the Majesty of his embassage spoyled by a carelesse Ambassadour?" (Tayler, p. 126).

Vaughan's continuing conception of poetry as a vehicle of moral persuasion brings him once again to the question of obscurity. Expressing the hope that *Silex Scintillans* will be "as useful now in the *publick*, as it hath been to me in *private*," he ambiguously acknowledges the possibility of ambiguity in his verse:

> In the *perusal* of it, you will (peradventure) observe some *passages*, whose *history* or *reason* may seem something *remote*; but were they brought *nearer*, and plainly exposed to your view, (though that (perhaps) might quiet your *curiosity*) yet would it not conduce much to your greater *advantage*. And therefore I must desire you to accept of them in that *latitude*, which is already alowed them.

He may be referring to the various elegies which do not clearly identify their subjects; he may be referring to poems which employ imagery and terminology based on the esoteric doctrines of Hermetic philosophy; or he may be referring to the numerous poems which, without explicitly identifying Puritanism or republican government, lament the bondage of the Church, the oppression of God's truth, the temporal supremacy of evil men, the apparent subversion of Providential order, and the general corruption and disorder of society. Or he may mean all of these dubious and oblique elements. But it is important to notice his insistence that they are inessential, that they will not impair the usefulness of the poems. In the case of the poems that have, broadly speaking, political implications, he may mean that he relies on the reader to discover the oblique meaning, to make the right connection between the poem and contemporary circumstances. In the case of the metaphors based on Hermetic ideas and using Hermetic terminology he may mean that the tenor will be clear from the context without the reader's having a technical knowledge of the vehicle's provenance. In the case of the elegies, he may mean that the biographical genesis of the poems is irrelevant to their meaning.

Besides this new willingness to countenance what Jonson

called "doubtfull writing," the main difference between the preface and Vaughan's earlier thinking about poetry is his exclusive choice of Christian faith as "the best reason of living," his exclusive preference for "*divine Themes* and *Celestial praise*" as the best subject matter for poetry. He declares that he has been "converted" to this view by the example of George Herbert, and calls upon all other "gifted persons" to follow the same example. This new indifference to moral matter of an inferior order (of course it had been a commonplace of Christian culture for centuries that all other moral matter was inferior to Christian faith) was largely stimulated by Vaughan's awareness that the Christian faith in England was in mortal danger. This was how he interpreted the cataclysmic political events of the 1640s and 1650s. For him, the issue at stake in the Civil War was no less than whether the English people should or should not continue to be a just and holy nation, whether they should remain part of Christ's flock or relapse into barbaric idolatry, whether they should be God's children or Satan's, whether they should keep alive the light of faith or be overrun by the powers of darkness. For him the Civil War was a holy war, an antitype of the War in Heaven. Its outcome was a severe trial of his faith in the temporal manifestation of divine Providence.[10]

Vaughan had adumbrated these terms and given some hints of his sense of danger in earlier poems (for example, in "The King Disguis'd"),[11] but his awareness of a temporal crisis of faith and Providential order increased sharply in response to the events of 1648–1649, and it is only in *Silex Scintillans* and the prose treatises published between 1650 and 1655 (when the two parts of *Silex* appeared) that his apocalyptic interpretation of the war and its outcome is fully expressed. In 1648 the Royalist army was finally defeated; in 1649 the victorious enemies of God executed the King, in Vaughan's view the temporal head of the true Church as well as of the state, and God's temporal vicegerent in both capacities; and in the same year the Anglican ritual (i.e., God's true worship) was proscribed in Wales.[12] The sharp intensification in the militancy of Vaughan's faith in these years was essentially a movement toward greater involvement in the problems of the temporal world, rather than the withdrawal into private visions which figures so prominently in most accounts of his "conversion." The change which took place between 1651 and 1654 in his thinking about the fittest subject matter for poetry resulted, not from a commitment to private contemplation, but from an intensified commitment to the Church Militant, in response to the progressively solid establishment of republican government and Puritan forms of worship.[13] Anxiety about the welfare of the Church and the temporal manifestation of Providence is far more prominent in the prose works and the second part of *Silex Scintillans* than in the 1650 volume. And it is only in the 1654 preface that Vaughan appeals to all of his fellow writers to abandon other themes and join in the effort to "*turn many to righteousness*" or formally dedicates his own talent to the services of the embattled Church.

He is trying, as one of presumably more than "an ordinary or indifferent *holyness*," to do something toward filling the gap left by the proscription of Anglican preachers. He sees himself as a vessel of God's spirit, an agent for communicating to others, in a time of the direst need, "those heavenly *refreshments*, which descend." The role of poet-priest involves participation in the *activa vita*; it involves a threefold, reciprocal interaction between the external world and the self. The mind moves from the perception of external conditions back into the self, there to discover, in experiential terms, the evidences of faith, and then returns to communicate its vision to other minds in an attempt to impose the form of that vision on an external world which seems in imminent danger of collapse. This interaction between public and private visions, between knowledge of the world and knowledge of God, is part of the basic pattern and structure of Vaughan's sacred poems. Similarly, his early love poems and satires take their characteristic form, meaning, and mode of development from the mutual pressure of experience and an ideal order.[14] This points to a fundamental continuity in the development of Vaughan's imagination. And the development of his ideas on the craft of poetry was likewise continuous. The new emphasis on sacred themes and the new admiration for Herbert which he expressed in the 1654 preface were not merely compatible with his admiration of Jonson and the poetic theories articulated earlier; they were organic developments of those attitudes in response to new exigencies in the world around him.

Chapter
III
THE WELL-ORDERED POEM

RAPID MUTATIONS of imagery and meaning, expressed in terms of motion and light and achieved through the sharp juxtaposition and blending of opposites, give Vaughan's poetry a quality at once vibrant and elusive. And his use of a poetic language that is particularly rich in associations and suggestions tends to arouse emotions which the reader cannot quite identify. This subliminal eloquence, coupled with the hectic but somehow evanescent activity of the language, makes it particularly difficult to *see* a Vaughan poem, to identify what is going on and how one thing leads to and relates to another. Donne's style is more densely allusive, and weaves a dialectical thread into tighter and more elaborate networks. But Donne is always at the reader's elbow, signaling with a nudge that now he is changing the minor premise, now he is treating accidents as essences, now he is taking this thread and crossing it over that and joining it to another. Vaughan does not so insistently proclaim his method. He sets an unfolding pattern in motion, shines a light on it, and retires to let reader and poem take their chances together. If readers are dazzled, as they well may be, they may always remember the poem in terms of brilliant confusion.

Vaughan's poems are often confused, and often far from brilliant. Nobody can produce uglier rhymes, flatter, stiffer, more ungainly and limping rhythms, or more monotonous meandering through drab wastes of prosaic banality and puerile platitude.

Surely one of the most inane lines in all poetry is Vaughan's "O holy, happy, healthy heaven" (Martin, p. 513). One is inclined to understand why he was so aware of the difficulty involved in writing well:

> O! 'tis an easie thing
> To write and sing;
> But to write true, unfeigned verse
> Is very hard! (Martin, p. 526)

A generous selection of Vaughan's poems, chosen for their provision of an aesthetic experience that a reasonably sophisticated reader might wish to repeat, would exclude perhaps one third of the total. But the remainder would be an impressive body of verse, and we usually characterize poets in terms of their achievements rather than their failures. Vaughan does indeed deserve his reputation for unevenness, but the critical commonplace that he lacked ability to sustain a unified poetic structure, that his verse is fragmentary and unbalanced, is intended to identify not only his obvious failures but a flawed quality in his most admired poems, to define the limits of his talent rather than mere lapses in power. His admirers applaud brilliant images and profound sentiments and uneasily deprecate wavering structures and blurred forms.

The poetic theories adumbrated by Vaughan have been examined in chapter 2. His dual insistence on eloquent vividness and formal clarity points to a poetic style in which a vigorous mobility of language, images, symbols, and sensuous impressions would be stabilized by interaction with an encompassing form marked by regularity and order. Such an achievement of unity in diversity may be regarded as a fusion of thought and feeling, or of abstract and concrete, or as an imitation of Nature. The form or model of Nature which Vaughan inherited was a *discordia concors* containing infinite variety within a unified pattern, an order which maintained its integrity through an infinite process of adjustment and balance between conflicting internal forces which threatened its wholeness. The central activity of Nature was a tension between the reciprocal challenges of anarchy and oneness. And such an activity is reflected, early and late, in Vaughan's poetic style.

William Drummond reports that Ben Jonson "had ane intention to perfect ane Epick Poeme . . . it is all in Couplets, for he detesteth all other Rimes, said he had written a Discourse of Poesie both against Campion and Daniel especially this last, wher he proves couplets to be the bravest sort of verses, especially when they are broken, like Hexameters and that crosse Rimes and Stanzaes . . . were all forced." And, on the same subject: "Some loved running verses, *plus mihi comma placet.*"[1] Vaughan was somewhat more tolerant of running verses—that is, couplets with very loose enjambment—and of such cross rhymes as the quatrain, but he seems also to have thought couplets the bravest sort of verses, for he used them in all his verse more extensively than any other pattern. He relied less heavily on couplets in his later career than he had earlier, making considerable use of quatrains, which earlier he had practiced seldom but skillfully, and of simple combinations of quatrains and couplets. These are the basic measures of his poetry, for nearly all of his poems employ them, either separately or in combination, with the occasional variation of triplets. Of his most famous poems, only "The Morningwatch" reveals a genuinely complex pattern of rhyme. Vaughan's most basic, constant patterns are those which are best known for their regularity, symmetry, clarity, and order.

The symmetry, balance, and precise definition of some of Vaughan's couplets would please the most ardent lover of the comma:

> So wee are meerly thrown upon the stage
> The mirth of fooles, and Legend of the age.
>
> 'Las! they're but quibbles, things we Poets feign,
> The short-liv'd Squibs and Crackers of the brain.
>
> (Martin, p. 45)

In each example, the breaking of one line slows the rhythm and gives the line internal balance and compact force, in contrast to the thrusting vigor of the unbroken line. In the second example, there is a hint of duplication of the balanced pattern if the second line is read with a brief pause after "Squibs." The use of synonomy enhances the deliberate force of the balanced rhythms. The aural vigor of the mainly monosyllabic language is particularly notable in the second example, with its repetition of hard consonants and of the short *i*-sound. The total impression is of controlled and ordered energy. Nor are these isolated examples:

> Harke! how his rude pipe frets the quiet aire,
> Whilst ev'ry Hill proclaims *Lycoris* faire.
> (Martin, p. 10)

> So fals ambitious man, and such are still
> All floating States built on the peoples will. (p. 21)

> And holy *Orpheus*, Natures *busie* Child
> By headlong *Hebrus* his deep *Hymns* Compil'd. (p. 39)

> But wilt have money *Og*? must I dispurse?
> Will nothing serve thee but a *Poets* curse? (p. 43)

Vaughan's use of couplets in the sacred poems is often marked by a similar smoothness, balance, and control. The breaking of the line often marks a play of antitheses within the couplet:

> Heale then these waters, Lord; or bring thy flock,
> Since these are troubled, to the springing rock. (p. 405)

> Here of this mighty spring, I found some drills,
> With Ecchoes beaten from th' eternal hills. (p. 418)

> Souls sojourn here, but may not rest;
> Who will ascend, must be undrest. (p. 482)

> Seeing thy seed abides in me,
> Dwell thou in it, and I in thee. (p. 488)

> The Rock of ages! in whose shade
> They live unseen, when here they fade. (p. 540)

One of Vaughan's most famous poems, "The Retreate" (Martin, p. 419), exhibits this unity under tension, this balanced control of energy, throughout its length. The activity of the language is contained and ordered within the end-stopped couplets:

> Happy those early dayes! when I
> Shin'd in my Angell-infancy.
> Before I understood this place
> Appointed for my second race,
> Or taught my soul to fancy ought
> But a white, Celestiall thought,
> When yet I had not walkt above
> A mile, or two, from my first love,
> And looking back (at that short space,)
> Could see a glimpse of his bright-face;
> When on some *gilded Cloud*, or *flowre*
> My gazing soul would dwell an houre,
> And in those weaker glories spy
> Some shadows of eternity;
> Before I taught my tongue to wound
> My Conscience with a sinful sound,
> Or had the black art to dispence
> A sev'rall sinne to ev'ry sence,
> But felt through all this fleshly dresse
> Bright *shootes* of everlastingnesse.

This first paragraph expresses the tension in the speaker's mind between memory of a lost spiritual unity and awareness of present disorder. Except in lines 11–14, the state of unity symbolized as "Angell-infancy" is never expressed in isolation.[2] Each couplet forces us to contemplate both states simultaneously and thus to be aware primarily of the tension between them rather than merely of the ideal. As Milton describes Eden first through the eyes of Satan, forcing us to see this symbol of innocence and order from the perspective of a fallen creature, and thus to be simultaneously aware of the symbol, its antithesis, and the delicate poise which separates them, so Vaughan defines a state of ideal innocence and order in terms of its opposite, and thus focusses attention on the "black art" which has willfully effected the transformation. The opening and closing couplets emphasize the ideal more than the others do, but even here the backward glance of "Happy those early dayes," "when I / Shin'd," and "felt" hint strongly of an antithetical sequel, the oppressive quality of which is suggested by "all this fleshly dresse." In the intervening couplets, the bright radiance of innocence is more strongly shadowed, and one might even suggest that there is a progressive darkening of the prospect until the final couplet is reached. The speaker's mind becomes progressively more absorbed in awareness of his present state, rather than in memory of the lost ideal, which remains dominant only through line 14. The language insistently forces us to look, not merely at innocence, but back at a state of innocence from a state of sin, and then to retrace the forward movement by which the one became the other. Thus we are constantly aware of the contrary pressure, within the speaker's mind, exerted by motion forward and backward through time. The forward motion is from innocence to sin, and retraces the temporal sequence of the speaker's life; the backward movement through the memory reverses that sequence, and the realization of it would involve a reverse transfiguration of the soul. Thus the backward motion corresponds to what we call progress, though in Vaughan's spherical universe it is conceived as the completion of a circle.[3]

The form of the paragraph imitates this circular progress and thus contributes to the expression of the soul's proper life. The speaker begins with a vivid apprehension of former innocence in terms of light: "Shin'd in my Angell-infancy." But then his mind moves, as his soul has moved, away from this state, downward (or forward) into sin. We still have references to "a white, Celestiall thought," "a glimpse of his bright-face"; but gradually, as he walks more than "A mile, or two," the light fades, and we have "weaker glories," "shadows of eternity," and finally "black art." As the pressure of this movement increases, so too does the contrary pressure, until, from "had the black art to dispence / A sev'rall sinne to ev'ry sence," the speaker's mind leaps back to "felt through all this fleshly dresse / Bright *shootes* of everlastingnesse." It is more than an effective contrast. The final couplet completes a circle by reverting to the vivid apprehension of innocence in terms of light expressed by the first.

Other details contribute to this formal symmetry. As we have seen, the first and final couplets reflect one another. The eight couplets enclosed by these are joined in pairs by the clausal structure and are introduced as follows: *before . . . or; when . . . and; when . . . and; before . . . or.* The paragraph is twenty lines in length, and the second *when . . . and* pair of couplets begins with line 11. Thus two ten-line passages face each other like mirror images or the halves of a divided sphere. From primitive cosmology and the tale that Aristophanes tells in the *Symposium* we remember the divided sphere as a mythic figure of the conflicting forces of unity and diversity. The diversity here consists in the gradual wasting away of light in the second half of the passage, the increasing emphasis on present sin rather than past innocence, and in the constant juxtaposition of the two in a single unit of verse. But all of this is contained within a symmetrical pattern which mirrors the great circle of time from Creation to Apocalypse and the little circle made by the fallen soul that perfects itself through struggle. As it develops and unfolds, the form of the paragraph reflects the process of creating order out of disorder, which is the burden of the theme and of the speaker's spirit. The second paragraph explicitly identifies the paradox of progress by backward motion and explicitly presents this progress under the figure of pilgrimage. The balanced order of the couplets still speaks of the unity of the desired ideal, but the vivid expression of the goal of the quest only intensifies the sense of the speaker's alienation. And the image of the soul as a staggering drunkard hints of a dark undertone of hopelessness.

Vaughan normally overrides the smooth, even rhythm of the couplet. By a free use of enjambment and great variation in the placement of midline pauses, he creates a line that is both free and strong, a flexible and versatile line capable of the most extended or compressed rhythmical effects. The tendency of his modifications of the basic rhythm is toward a marked increase in the internal activity of the verse; the normative line becomes an organic form molded by the dynamic pressures of imagery and thought. When the pressure is less great, we have the "sinewy" verse preferred by Ben Jonson, a restrained interweaving of intrinsic and extrinsic form. However much Vaughan increases the internal pressure of the language, the containing form of the line does not give way. In the verse satires discussed in chapter 5, for example, he creates extended and extremely varied rhythmic patterns by pushing his syntax across line endings for many lines, often freely mingling closed couplets with run-on lines, and finally bringing the swirling pattern to rest in a closed couplet that sharply marks the completion of thought.

This kind of versifiication is characteristic of Vaughan's early work. In the sacred poems, about half of those written in couplets evince a kind of flaccid sprawl. This is particularly true of the couplet poems in the second part of *Silex Scintillans*. But comparison with the secular poems mentioned above, or with the sacred poems that use couplets successfully—for example, of "Repentance" or "Misery" with "The Lampe" or "Christs Nativity"; of "Jesus weeping" (II), "The Ass," or "Jacobs Pillow, and Pillar" with "And do they so?" "The Constellation," or "The Starre"; of "The day of Judgement" or "To the Holy Bible" with "The Water-fall" or "The Book"—reveals that the cause of Vaughan's failure does not lie in any lack of mastery over the subtle potentialities of the form. It lies rather in tenuous imagery and diffuse thought. In the absence of close-knit, vigorous, and various thought unified by the consistent development of a central metaphor or interrelated group of metaphors, the regular couplets of these poems merely constitute a vacant form. They do not indicate that Vaughan could not construct or could not sustain a structure for more than a few lines. They indicate that on these occasions he wrote irresponsibly, with no more than a vague conception of his subject. In Jonson's words, he neglected to "first thinke, and excogitate his matter; then choose his words, and examine the weight of either. Then take care in placing, and ranking both matter, and words, that the composition be comely."[4]

An outstanding example of Vaughan's achievement of an organic form through his versatile and flexible handling of the couplet is offered by "*Monsieur Gombauld*" (Martin, p. 48). In its expression of light and airy motion, the movement of the verse catches perfectly the dreamlike atmosphere of romance:

> Thy Journall of deep Mysteries, and sad
> Nocturnall Pilgrimage, with thy dreams clad
> In fancies darker than thy *Cave*, Thy *Glasse*
> Of sleepie draughts, and as thy soule did passe
> In her calm voyage what discourse she heard
> Of Spirits, what dark Groves and ill-shap'd guard
> *Ismena* lead thee through, with thy proud flight
> O'r *Periardes*, and deep, musing night
> Neere fair *Eurotas* banks, what solemn *green*
> The neighbour shades weare, and what forms are seen
> In their large Bowers, with that sad path and seat
> Which none but light-heel'd *Nymphs* and *Fairies* beat . . .

One of Vaughan's most remarkable achievements in this kind of organic versification is "Love-sick" (Martin, p. 493). Only in the two opening, end-stopped couplets, which propose the subject of the poem, is the rhythm of the decasyllabic line allowed its natural expansion:

> Iesus, my life! how shall I truly love thee?
> O that thy Spirit would so strongly move me,
> That thou wert pleas'd to shed thy grace so farr
> As to make man all pure love, flesh a star!

The lines define the love between God and the soul in terms of two reciprocal actions: an infusion of grace which enables the soul to destroy the internal barriers of sin and thus to love God, and the response by which it realizes that potential. The rest of the poem does not define or describe these actions further; it renders them in a sensuous image, a speaking picture of the soul strongly moved by the Spirit. The second sentence is linked to the first by repetition of the star image. By means of abruptly abbreviated phrasing, heavy internal repetitions, and repetitions of rhyme words, Vaughan creates a compact, constricted, but very powerful rhythm which dramatically portrays the thematic struggle of the soul with fleshly obstacles:

> A star that would ne'r set, but ever rise,
> So rise and run, as to out-run these skies,
> These narrow skies (narrow to me) that barre,
> So barre me in, that I am still at warre,
> At constant warre with them.

Then follow two cognate sentences which appeal to the Spirit to release the soul from the bondage, the stagnant immobility, of which it has just complained. The image speaks of dissolving, of massive inertia transformed into liquid motion:

> O come and rend
> Or bow the heavens! Lord bow them and descend,
> And at thy presence make these mountains flow,
> These mountains of cold Ice in me!

Here the repetitions are less oppressive, and the rhythm expands as the language anticipates release and freedom. In the two sentences which conclude the poem, the speaker imagines the mighty battle joined in the soul, and the verse renews its former abrupt intensity. In the final sentence particularly, the mind of the speaker winds a sinuous thread of sequential actions following the descent of divine heat—"Heat motion gives." The thread links together, as the bases of love, man's sin and Christ's Atonement. The final linkage is the joining of God and man in mutual love. The ecstatic conclusion renders, in dramatically realized terms, or what Sidney called "lively truth," the meaning of the opening phrase, "Iesus, my life!" As phrase follows from phrase, motion from motion, the verse gathers a massive, controlled momentum, and all that power issues in the final expression of union:

>   Thou art
> Refining fire, O then refine my heart,
> My foul, foul heart! Thou art immortall heat,
> Heat motion gives; Then warm it, till it beat,
> So beat for thee, till thou in mercy hear,
> So hear that thou must open: open to
> A sinfull wretch, A wretch that caus'd thy woe,
> Thy woe, who caus'd his weal; so far his weal
> That thou forgott'st thine own, for thou didst seal
> Mine with thy blood, thy blood which makes thee mine,
> Mine ever, ever; And me ever thine.

The quatrain is a more spacious form than the couplet, and offers readier opportunities for varied music. Vaughan usually respects the integrity of the unit, and limits his inventiveness to modulations of its internal structure. Like the couplet, the quatrain is naturally disposed for the coordinate expression of qualities, impressions, or ideas, whether antithetical or cognate, and for the balanced statement of logical relationships, such as premise and consequence or thesis and antithesis. Vaughan often enhances these resources for symmetry, balance, and clarity by causing his syntax to divide the quatrain neatly in the middle, where the rhyme divides it. And, as in "A Song to *Amoret*" (Martin, p. 8), he usually adds to this by alternating lines of different length:

> If I were dead, and in my place,
>   Some fresher youth design'd,
> To warme thee with new fires, and grace
>   Those Armes I left behind;

> Were he as faithfull as the Sunne,
>   That's wedded to the Sphere;
> His bloud as chaste, and temp'rate runne,
>   As Aprils mildest teare;
>
> Or were he rich, and with his heapes,
>   And spacious share of Earth,
> Could make divine affection cheape,
>   And court his golden birth:
>
> For all these Arts I'de not believe,
>   (No though he should be thine)
> The mighty Amorist could give
>   So rich a heart as mine.

The internal symmetry of these stanzas may be briefly indicated by the second, where the first two lines speak of faith and compare it to the relation of the sun to its sphere, and the next two speak of the blood, comparing it for chastity and temperance with April's rain. It is important to notice also the clear logical relationship between one stanza and the next, the steady, continuous evolution of the whole sentence. The first stanza hypothesizes a posthumous rival, the second hypothetically grants him fidelity and temperate passions, and the third, riches (all attractive qualities); but the fourth denies him the most important quality of all, attributing it instead—actually, not hypothetically—to the still-living lover, and assisting the logical coherence of this transfer by speaking of the heart in terms of true riches. And the final rejection of the hypothetical rival is marked by the phrase "mighty Amorist," which attributes to him the unpleasant qualities of egotism and pride, thus making explicit the third stanza's hint that these qualities accompany wealth. The stanza following those quoted above distinguishes the fortune and beauty of greater men from his own "true resolved minde," and the final stanza explicitly asserts the constancy and the divine origin and nature of his feelings. The fiction developed in the preceding stanzas prepares for the positive affirmation of the climax by defining the qualities of the speaker's love through exclusion.

One of Vaughan's greatest poems, "They are all gone into the world of light!" (Martin, p. 483), exhibits just this symmetry and balanced progression in the handling of quatrains. The poem is unified by the imagistic contrast of darkness and light, which expresses the contrast in the speaker's mind between temporal and eternal life. And these terms subsume other contrasts—between knowledge and ignorance, vision and blindness, freedom and bondage. The treatment of the subject may be referred to the practice of formal meditation on death, the fulcrum which balances these opposites. The speaker's point of view is just this point where two ways meet, and their poised opposition on the stage of his mind is precisely expressed by his balanced disposition of the quatrains:

> They are all gone into the world of light!
>   And I alone sit lingring here;
> Their very memory is fair and bright,
>   And my sad thoughts doth clear.
>
> It glows and glitters in my cloudy brest
>   Like stars upon some gloomy grove,
> Or those faint beams in which this hill is drest,
>   After the Sun's remove.
>
> I see them walking in an Air of glory,
>   Whose light doth trample on my days:
> My days, which are at best but dull and hoary,
>   Meer glimering and decays.

As the speaker remembers those who have gone, he composes an image of light in the midst of darkness, corresponding to their memory in the midst of his saddened mind, the hope of immortality in the midst of world weariness. Sometimes the syntax balances these antitheses within the line, sometimes in successive lines; always the strong pause at the end of the second line clarifies their mutual pressure. In the first stanza "all gone into the world of light" opposes "I alone sit lingring" in the next line;

and the pattern is repeated in the next two lines, as their "fair and bright" memory opposes "my sad thoughts."[5] Then the pattern is compressed within the line, as "glows and glitters" and "star" oppose "cloudy brest" and "gloomy grove," then expands again with the opposition of "faint beams" and "this hill . . . / After the Sun's remove." In the third stanza, the second half of the second line, "trample on my days," marks the point of balance between the "light" and "Air of glory" in which the dead walk and the "dull and hoary" days, "Meer glimering and decays" of the speaker's life. And all the time our minds move smoothly from stanza to stanza, pausing as a sentence ends at the end of each.

Implicit in this contrast between two kinds of life which the speaker "sees" is a contrast between two kinds of knowledge, one that sees the surfaces of things and one that sees beyond them. This begins to develop as a paradoxical relationship of blindness and sight, and is expressed by an inversion of the normal value of images:

> O holy hope! and high humility,
>   High as the Heavens above!
> These are your walks, and you have shew'd them me
>   To kindle my cold love,
>
> Dear, beauteous death! the Jewel of the Just,
>   Shining nowhere, but in the dark;
> What mysteries do lie beyond thy dust;
>   Could man outlook that mark!

Laid low in death ("humility"), the dead are raised "High as the Heavens above." The heat of cold death kindles the cold heart of the speaker with warm love for "beauteous death." Its deformity is beauty, its dust is a jewel, its darkness shines in the darkness of life. These are the mysterious "walks" of death whereon is based the holy hope of immortality. The implication that they cannot be seen by ordinary light, that ordinary vision cannot "outlook that mark," but that to see through this darkness one needs insight that to the world is blindness, is the basis of thought in the following three stanzas:

> He that hath found some fledg'd birds nest, may know
>   At first sight, if the bird be flown;
> But what fair Well, or Grove he sings in now,
>   That is to him unknown.
>
> And yet, as Angels in some brighter dreams
>   Call to the soul, when man doth sleep:
> So, some strange thoughts transcend our wonted theams,
>   And into glory peep.
>
> If a star were confin'd into a Tomb
>   Her captive flames must needs burn there;
> But when the hand that lockt her up, gives room,
>   She'l shine through all the sphaere.

The echo of "I see them walking in an Air of glory" in "And into glory peep" may alert us to the fact that the middle stanza quoted here defines what the speaker has done since the beginning of the poem. He has seen what death seems (darkness, dust: lines 18, 19) and he has seen the truth of death, which is the antithesis of what it seems. And he has seen his life as it is. Death marks the boundary line between the world in which truth is what seems (that is, in which there is no truth), and a world of mysteries which subvert common sense. The observations of the bird watcher (not the speaker, but a hypothetical "he") belong to the first kind of knowledge: knowledge of the temporal world derived from sensory observation and the exercise of natural judgment. It is limited to the temporal world, cannot outlook that mark, cannot penetrate mysteries, can see things only as they seem, not as they are—dust as dust, but not dust as jewels. The "strange thoughts" are, in theological terms, spiritual knowledge, or knowledge of Scripture illuminated by the Spirit. The difference from natural knowledge is expressed by a play on blindness and sight. The observation of birds' nests is a function of sight, and Vaughan uses the word; but the transcendence of wonted themes is compared to sleep: the action of the soul in apprehending immortality is like the action of the soul in attaining it.

The speaker has never doubted the promise of immortality; he begins by expressing his faith in the destiny of the dead: "They are all gone into the world of light!" The development of his meditation does not involve the questioning or the recovery of faith.[6] It involves the clarification, confirmation, and strengthening of faith, and a focusing of feelings in an attitude of personal hope and love. Thus the final paragraph quoted above, which sums up the speaker's faith with a decisive image of the mysterious transformation wrought by death, is followed by a personal address to God. The dominant terms in which he now sees life and death are bondage and liberty, and ignorance and knowledge, as well as darkness and light:

> O Father of eternal life, and all
>   Created glories under thee!
> Resume thy spirit from this world of thrall
>   Into true liberty.
>
> Either disperse these mists, which blot and fill
>   My perspective (still) as they pass,
> Or else remove me hence unto that hill,
>   Where I shall need no glass.

The stanzas still maintain their balance. In the penultimate stanza, the vocative address and the prayer itself are evenly distributed, and the even balance of the alternative forms of liberty prayed for in the last stanza is signalled by *either . . . or* in the first and third lines.[7]

Sometimes, as in "Thou that knowst for whom I mourn," "White Sunday," "The Timber," and "The Seed growing secretly" (Martin, pp. 416, 485, 497, 510), Vaughan's quatrains enclose subject matter and imagery that are too diffuse to satisfy any but the most ardent devotee of edification at any price. But it seems that he relied more often on couplets when his mental energies slackened, for most of his poems in quatrains are notably successful. The reader may consider for himself how much the formal balance and symmetry of Vaughan's versification contribute to such poems as "Death. *A Dialogue*," "Religion," "The Incarnation, and Passion," "H. Scriptures" (formally a Shakespearian sonnet), "Corruption," "Idle Verse," "The Burial Of an Infant," "The Tempest," "Begging," "The Daughter of *Herodias*," "The Knot," "Tears," "Quickness," and "The Queer."

In "The Palm-tree" (Martin, p. 490), Vaughan achieves in his handling of quatrains both this formal symmetry and the kind of organic versification observed in early poems and in "Love-sick." The relation of the two kinds reflects the pattern achieved with couplets in many secular poems: a supple, varied rhythm, expressing activity or the evolution of thought and achieved by weaving the syntax across line endings and stanza divisions, is brought to rest in a regular pattern that expresses fulfillment and stability:

> Deare friend sit down, and bear awhile this shade
> As I have yours long since; This Plant, you see
> So prest and bow'd, before sin did degrade
> Both you and it, had equall liberty
>
> With other trees: but now shut from the breath
> And air of *Eden*, like a male-content
> It thrives no where. This makes these weights (like death
> And sin) hang at him; for the more he's bent
>
> The more he grows. Celestial natures still
> Aspire for home; This *Solomon* of old
> By flowers and carvings and mysterious skill
> Of Wings, and Cherubims, and Palms foretold.
>
> This is the life which hid above with Christ
> In God, doth always (hidden) multiply,

And spring, and grow, a tree ne'r to be pric'd,
A Tree, whose fruit is immortality.

Here Spirits that have run their race and fought
And won the fight, and have not fear'd the frowns
Nor loved the smiles of greatness, but have wrought
Their masters will, meet to receive their Crowns.

The sinuous winding of the syntax and rhythm through the first three stanzas expresses the sinistral growth of the tree, which by indirections finds directions out. It is an emblem of the *felix culpa*, of the spiritual life of man growing toward God and immortality through sin and death. No stanza is whole and single, no point of rest in the language marks the completion of a formal pattern. The lines are always off balance, always restlessly moving onward. The form of the verse expresses the divided, blurred, mixed condition of the soul as it seeks to compose itself among the conflicting pressures of temporal existence. But, by its suggestion of natural, organic growth, the verse also expresses motion through time as a successful quest, a steady growth of the soul into the life hid above with Christ. The emergence of the soul into its perfect form, of this tree into that hidden tree whose fruit is immortality, is marked by a shift to independent stanzas, each a single, self-contained sentence whose supple, interwoven rhythm and organic unity symbolize the perfect balance of *discors* and *concors*, the vibrant unity of the perfected soul and immortal life. More immediately, it reflects the image of the interwoven circlet, in Christian iconography always the symbol of eternity, immortality, and perfection:

> Here is the patience of the Saints: this Tree
> Is water'd by their tears, as flowers are fed
> With dew by night; but One you cannot see
> Sits here and numbers all the tears they shed.
>
> Here is their faith too, which if you will keep
> When we two part, I will a journey make

> To pluck a Garland hence, while you do sleep
> And weave it for your head against you wake.

In other poems, Vaughan achieves a similar suggestion of motion toward an end with stanzas consisting of a quatrain followed by a couplet. For example, in "Cock-crowing" (Martin, p. 488), only the fourth and sixth lines of each stanza are end-stopped. The syntax weaves the lines of the quatrain together into an organic unity of thought and rhythm, and the balanced couplet sums up or draws an inference from the preceding lines:

> If such a tincture, such a touch,
> So firm a longing can impowre
> Shall thy own image think it much
> To watch for thy appearing hour?
>   If a meer blast so fill the sail,
>   Shall not the breath of God prevail?
>
> O thou immortall light and heat!
> Whose hand so shines through all this frame,
> That by the beauty of the seat,
> We plainly see, who made the same.
>   Seeing thy seed abides in me,
>   Dwell thou in it, and I in thee.

Some of the stanzas of "Ascension-Hymn" (Martin, p. 482) reveal a similar structure; others weave quatrain and couplet together into a single unit. Here the normal rhythm is given by the octosyllabic couplet; since the lines of the quatrain are half this length, they have the effect of a couplet with internal as well as end rhyme. The result, particularly because each stanza is end-stopped, is an impression of rapid movement culminating in rest:

>   Dust and clay
>   Mans antient wear!
>   Here you must stay,
>   But I elsewhere;

> Souls sojourn here, but may not rest;
> Who will ascend, must be undrest.
>
> > And yet some
> > That know to die
> > Before death come,
> > Walk to the skie
> > Even in this life; but all such can
> > Leave behinde them the old Man.

The relevance of this mobile pattern to the meaning of the poem should be sufficiently indicated by these quotations. The poem is unified by the patterning of descending and ascending motions, corresponding to mutations of darkness and light, and through these images expresses the interactions between sin, the Atonement, and redemption. The transfiguring pressure of opposites, bringing wholeness out of chaos and transforming inert flesh into dynamic spirit, is starkly and beautifully expressed in the final stanza, based on a famous passage in Ezekiel:

> Hee alone
> And none else can
> Bring bone to bone
> And rebuild man,
> And by his all subduing might
> Make clay ascend more quick then light.[8]

Poems such as "Regeneration," "The Brittish Church," "Mount of Olives," "Joy of my life! while left me here," "The Storm," "Easter-day," "Man," "I walkt the other day," "The Proffer," and "The Night" owe much of their ordered wholeness to the flexible interdependence of lines of varying length and to the organic linking of regular patterns of rhyme. The syntax and rhythm are often loose and free, but the stanza is stabilized by a clearly perceptible pattern of sound and the firm pause which marks completion of the pattern. And the transition from one rhyme pattern to another is often strongly marked by an end-stopped line—for example, in "The Night" (Martin, p. 522):

> Through that pure *Virgin-shrine*,
> That sacred vail drawn o'r thy glorious noon
> That men might look and live as Glo-worms shine,
>   And face the Moon:
> Wise *Nicodemus* saw such light
> As made him know his God by night.

Here the pattern of line length and rhyme is: 6*a*, 10*b*, 10*a*, 4*b*, 8*c*, 8*c*. The couplet, the only perfectly harmonic pattern, is the basic measure of order, for although there is also a pair of ten-syllable lines, one is rhymed with a six and one with a four. The central image and theme of "The Night" is paradigmatic of Vaughan's poetry as a whole: the mind, inundated by chaos, strains for signs and means of order, meaning, and unity within and without. Such a theme is aptly articulated by a verse form whose basic stresses are between disintegration and wholeness, freedom and control.

Vaughan's achievement of flexibility and variety within a unified form may be illustrated also by "Christs Nativity" and "Easter-day" (Martin, pp. 442, 456). In the latter, the imperious commands in the fifth line of each stanza are intensified by the abrupt shift from alternating ten- and eight-syllable lines to one of four syllables and from alternating to paired rhymes. The shift gives the verse a dynamic impetus that mirrors the vigorous mobility which the poem speaks of, thus enriching the figurative linking of resurrection, spiritual awakening, and awakening from sleep:

> Thou, whose sad heart, and weeping head lyes low,
>   Whose Cloudy brest cold damps invade,
> Who never feel'st the Sun, nor smooth'st thy brow,
>   But sitt'st oppressed in the shade,
>   Awake, awake,
>   And in his Resurrection partake,
>   Who on this day (that thou might'st rise as he,)
>   Rose up, and cancell'd two deaths due to thee.

"Christs Nativity" uses the same pattern in a similar setting. The poem is unified by the interrelating of various images of movement with each other and with images of light and song. The internal liveliness of the stanza is greatly aided by the way enjambment links the short central couplet to the others:

> Awake, glad heart! get up, and Sing,
> It is the Birth-day of thy King,
>   Awake! awake!
>   The Sun doth shake
> Light from his locks, and all the way
> Breathing Perfumes, doth spice the day.
>
> Awak, awak! heark, how th' *wood* rings,
> *Winds* whisper, and the busie *springs*
>   A Consort make;
>   Awake, awake!
> Man is their high-priest, and should rise
> To offer up the sacrifice.

The stanzas of "The Brittish Church," "Joy of my life! while left me here," and "The Morning-watch" (Martin, pp. 410, 422, 424) extend and develop the potentialities of this pattern. They may be viewed as an inversion, with some variations, of the stanzaic pattern in "Ascension-Hymn." The basic form consists of a pair of decasyllabics or octosyllabics followed by a series of four-syllable lines. A more restrained version of the form appears in "Vanity of Spirit" (Martin, p. 418), which is naturally divided by the syntax into four paragraphs, each composed of a decasyllabic couplet followed by three octosyllabic couplets. Vaughan's earliest experiment with more extreme variations is found in "*To* Amoret, *of the difference* . . ." (Martin, p. 12):

> Marke, when the Evenings cooler wings
>   Fanne the afflicted ayre, how the faint Sunne,
>   Leaving undone,
>   What he begunne,

> Those spurious flames suckt up from slime, and earth
> > To their first, low birth,
> > Resignes, and brings.

Most critics do not care for this poem, although the slow, halting rhythm and the abrupt shifts in line length might be defended as enrichments of the subject. In "To the River *Isca*" (Martin, p. 39), Vaughan employed the device to achieve an effect of dynamic rapidity more characteristic of his verse:

> *Noones* as mild as *Hesper's* rayes,
> Or the first *blushes* of fair dayes.
> What *gifts* more *Heav'n* or *Earth* can adde
> With all those *blessings* be thou *Clad*!
> > *Honour, Beautie,*
> > *Faith* and *Dutie,*
> > *Delight* and *Truth,*
> > With *Love,* and *Youth*
> Crown all about thee!

Chapter
IV
LOVE POETRY

MOST OF VAUGHAN'S LOVE POEMS are grouped in two distinct sequences, addressed to "Amoret" and "Etesia" respectively.[1] Each brief story of courtship begins in the traditional way with love at first sight, but each develops toward a different resolution. The sequences reflect in their thematic emphases two distinct modes of the Renaissance love lyric. Like Spenser's *Shepheardes Calender* and the sequences of Petrarch and Sidney, the Etesia poems record the torments of an idealizing passion denied possession of its object. Though they begin in this vein, the Amoret poems, like Spenser's *Amoretti and Epithalamion*, record the satisfying growth of a sustaining, mutual love which is completed and symbolized by marriage. The Etesia poems descend from the medieval fusion of Platonic idealism with erotic passion in adulterous courtly romance; the Amoret poems are products of the Protestant, middle-class effort, beginning in the sixteenth century, to escape the social, moral, and psychological dilemmas of the medieval tradition by romanticizing a mutual affection of "true plaine hearts" which culminates in married union. In *The Allegory of Love*, C. S. Lewis made the classic case for Spenser, especially in the central books of *The Faerie Queene*, as the author of "the final defeat of courtly love by the romantic conception of marriage," as "the greatest among the founders of that romantic conception of marriage which is the basis of all our love literature fom Shakespeare to Meredith."[2]

But Grierson's earlier presentation of Donne as a rebel against Petrarchan conventions and a pioneer in the expression of natural passion had already accustomed critics to seeing a predominant influence from Donne in seventeenth-century treatments of love as an innocent, happy union.[3] It happens that a few of the less successful poems to Amoret on this theme follow Donne in imagery, phrasing, and technique, and this has prompted some critics to dismiss the whole sequence as a series of weak, insignificant experiments in the Donne manner.[4] Worse still, the more derivative of the Amoret poems have been taken as representative of Vaughan's achievement as a love poet, the poems to Etesia being seldom noticed and almost never anthologized. I agree with S. L. Bethell that the Etesia poems are more often successful than those to Amoret, although, in his words, the latter have "a gracious tenderness about them and a combination of pretty delicacy and sober strength which gives some indication of greatness to come."[5] Worst of all, the Amoret poems have often been spoken of as though they were the summit of Vaughan's accomplishment as a secular poet. For example, Helen Gardner speaks of "the conversion which turned the tepid wooer of Amoret into a poet who brings us 'authentic tidings of invisible things'."[6] Thus Vaughan's secular poetry as a whole, and not just the love poetry, comes to be popularly regarded as trivial and uninteresting.

The ideal form of love, according to Vaughan, is a reciprocal love between two persons whose souls are in harmony with divine law; their passionate union is therefore innocent, natural, and happy. It is symbolized by the coupling of roses and is closely associated with nature's self-perpetuating fertility and the plenitude of nature's beauty. Treating love as an aspect of nature's innocence and creativity, presenting love, virtue, and natural fertility as components of an ideal order which is, in a sense, permanent, Vaughan is far from Donne. He is close to the pastoral tradition, to the Shakespeare of the sonnets on "increase," and to the Spenser of the *Epithalamion*, the Garden of Adonis episode in book III of *The Faerie Queene*, and the Mount Acidale episode in book VI. The poem "To I. Morgan ... *upon his sudden Journey and succeeding Marriage"* (Martin, p. 637) is typical of Vaughan's ideal of love:

> So two sweet *Rose-buds* from their *Virgin-beds*
> First peep and blush, then kiss and couple heads;
> Till yearly blessings so increase their store
> Those two can number two and twenty more,
> And the fair *Bank* (by heav'ns free bounty Crown'd)
> With choice of *Sweets* and *Beauties* doth abound;
> Till time, which *Familys* like *Flowers* far spreads;
> Gives them for *Garlands* to the best of heads.

Earlier in the poem love is seen as an elixir, a philosopher's stone which contains the essence of nature's creativity and can transfigure dull matter into a thing of precious beauty. The lover, impregnated with divine "*Love* and *Wisdom*," is likened to the sun, whose analogous "*Light* and *Heat*" work on "senseless *Stones*" to convey "Fire into *Rubies*, into *Chrystalls* day." Human procreation is analogous to this alchemical transmutation of base matter; the lover recreates and perpetuates the "bright Blessings" which have been generated in him by a higher power:

> you, like one ordain'd to shine, take in
> Both *Light* and *Heat*: can *Love* and *Wisdom* spin
> Into one thred, and with that firmly tye
> The same bright Blessings on posterity;
> Which so intail'd, like *Jewels* of the Crown,
> Shall with your *Name* descend still to your own.

The sense of a continual interchange between the natural and spiritual orders is intensified if we may read the "best of heads," to which Time eventually gives the offspring as garlands, as referring to the Son of God, head of the mystical body of the Church.[7] By this reading, the conceit is close to some more explicit lines in the penultimate stanza of Spenser's *Epithalamion*, when he prays to the "high heavens"

> That we may raise a large posterity,
> Which from the earth, which they may long possesse,
> With lasting happinesse,
> Up to your haughty pallaces may mount,
> And for the guerdon of theyr glorious merit
> May heavenly tabernacles there inherit,
> Of blessed Saints for to increase the count.[8]

Similarly, in the poem "To the best, and most accomplish'd Couple ─────── " (Martin, p. 57), the end of love is seen as the prolongation of nature's beauty through "that mysterie / Your selves in your Posteritie"; and the physical union of the lovers is presented in its ideal form through the metaphorical union of a rose with the sun:

> Fresh as the *houres* may all your pleasures be,
>   And healthfull as *Eternitie*!
> Sweet as the flowres *first breath*, and Close
> As th'*unseen spreadings* of the Rose,
> When he unfolds his Curtain'd head,
> And makes his bosome the *Suns* bed.

In "To the River *Isca*" (Martin, p. 39), through the hypothetical form of an invocation and prayer, Vaughan presents us with a composite symbol of nature as an ideal order. As symbol, the valley of the river Usk is "*The Land redeem'd from all disorders*"; completely alien to it are

> those *lowd, anxious Cares*
> For *dead* and *dying things* (the Common *Wares*
> And *showes* of time.

Redeemed from all disorders, it is redeemed from time, change, and death, and from lust as well. Its qualities are "*Freedome, safety, Joy and blisse / United* in one loving *kisse.*" The river itself is the central symbol of love's fertilizing, transfiguring power, generating all forms of natural beauty and dispelling everything harsh, ugly, or violent. From this valley the *"wilie, winding Snake"* is banished, as are *"sullen heats"* and offensive flames; the symbol of human love is the innocent, natural union of roses. All the rich, spicy odors of nature are concentrated here, deceit and lust are unknown, and innocent love is celebrated joyfully with *"Garlands, and Songs, and Roundelayes."* This is Vaughan's version of the ancient figure of the enclosed garden of love. Rooted perhaps equally in classical pastoral and the *Song of Solomon*, its best-known Renaissance forms are the Garden of Adonis in *The Faerie Queene* and the Garden of Eden in book IV of *Paradise Lost*:

> May thy gentle *Swains* (like *flowres*)
> Sweetly spend their *Youthfull houres*,
> And thy *beauteous Nymphs* (like *Doves*)
> Be *kind* and *faithfull* to their *Loves*;
> . . . .
> In all thy *Journey* to the *Main*
> No *nitrous Clay*, nor *Brimstone-vein*
> Mix with thy *streams*, but may they passe
> Fresh as the *aire*, and cleer as *Glasse*,
> And where the *wandring Chrystal* treads
> *Roses* shall *kisse*, and *Couple* heads.
> The *factour-wind* from far shall bring
> The *Odours* of the *Scatter'd* Spring,
> And *loaden* with the rich *Arreare*,
> *Spend* it in *Spicie whispers* there.[9]

Spenser's Amoret was raised up "In all the lore of love, and goodly womanhead" in the "thickest covert" of a wood where "all plentie, and all pleasure flowes."[10] Vaughan's Amoret is discovered by him wandering in the "coole, leavie House" of the Priory Grove, whose "sacred shades" are now consecrated as the garden symbol of their union:

> Henceforth no melancholy flight,
> No sad wing, or hoarse bird of Night,
> Disturbe this Aire, no fatall throate
> Of Raven, or Owle, awake the Note
> Of our laid Eccho, no voice dwell
> Within these leaves, but *Philomel*.
> The poisonous Ivie here no more
> His false twists on the Oke shall score,
> Only the Woodbine here may twine,
> As th' Embleme of her Love, and mine.
>
> (Martin, p. 15)

The poet's imagined transfiguration of the grove into a symbol of an ideal natural order expresses the power of love to transfigure a fallen world. As in the Usk poem, the description of the ideal qualities of the garden by exclusion of their contraries makes us fully aware of all the destructive forces of nature which threaten its beauty and peace. Thus we perceive the stability and contentment of the love which the garden symbolizes, not as a given, but as something won out of opposition to the forces of the fallen world which impinge upon and threaten to impair its harmony. The force which the language exerts to exclude these contrary qualities expresses the psychological force which is needed to transcend them and assert the supremacy of love. The image of the grove eventually clothed "in an aged Gray" is an image of the lovers' future selves. Like the grove, they must yield to "the consuming yeares," and the irrefragability of their union is secured, not in time, but only through their immortality. In imagination, the grove, transplanted, becomes "A fresh Grove in th' Elysian Land," the scene of a renewal of the lovers' "first Innocence, and Love." The earthly paradise of the grove, subject to time, is only a fragile antitype of the heavenly paradise, where "in thy shades, as now, so then, / Wee'le kisse, and smile, and walke agen."[11] By contrast, in "To my Ingenuous Friend, *R. W.*" (Martin, p. 3), Vaughan imagines an Elysium without love and without women, an Elysium where "learned Ghosts" admire one another's poetry and the souls of "murther'd" lovers seek dolefully to appease the torments of "th' inconstant, cruell sex."

In *The Faerie Queene*, the antithesis of the Garden of Adonis is the Bower of Bliss. The beautiful plenitude of the natural, innocent garden is replaced by an artificial ersatz, and the free exchange of passion between lovers is distorted into a lust to possess or to use the other. An aspect of the distortion is that, in a sense, the body of the beloved comes to be seen as itself a garden to be plundered of its beauty. The essential egotism and impersonality of the attitude is clearly evident in Donne's Elegy XIX:

> O my America! my new-found-land,
> My kingdome, safeliest when with one man man'd,
> My Myne of precious stones, My Emperie,
> How blest am I in this discovering thee![12]

Vaughan creates such an antithesis of the garden of love in the poem *"In Amicum foeneratorem"* (Martin, p. 43), as the speaker mocks the usurer by offering in repayment of his debts an imaginary kingdom of erotic fantasies. Typically, predatory metaphors invite the usurer to imagine limitless feminine beauties, depersonalized by metaphors of coral, gold, and timber, as mere agents of his pleasure:

> Wee'l suck the *Corall* of their lips, and feed
> Upon their spicie breath, a meale at need,
> Rove in their *Amber-tresses*, and unfold
> That glist'ring grove, the Curled wood of gold,
> Then peep for babies, a new Puppet-play,
> And riddle what their *pratling Eyes* would say.

The speciousness of this counterfeit coin is neatly pinpointed by the word "Puppet-play"; the speaker completes the game by playing mock pander for the "waggish *Nymphs*": "But here thou must remember to dispurse, / For without money all this is a Curse."

Similarly, in "FIDA: *Or The Country-beauty*" (Martin, p. 638), the woman's body, so carefully inventoried, is merely the cynosure of an obsessive gaze. The catalogue of her "charming *Sweets*"—hair, eyes, cheeks, lips, teeth, tongue, skin, neck, breasts—is summarized by the word "piece": "A piece so full of *Sweets* and *bliss*." She is the moral equivalent of a cookie jar or a candy-store window, all the more desirable for being labeled "Do Not Touch." Her "prudent Rigor" adds the spice of challenge to the fascination engendered by her physical attributes: "A face, that hath no Lovers slain, / Wants forces, and is near disdain." Addressed "*to* Lysimachus," the poem implies a dramatic situation: the speaker has been sceptical of Lysimachus's reports of the wondrous beauty of his mistress, but one look at her has infatuated him equally, and now he can do nothing but confirm his friend's account. The speaker's "stupid" infatuation is reflected in the exuberant agility with which he compiles similitudes to prove that she is the paragon of animals. The organization of the poem is simple, loose, and free: the speaker merely begins at the top of her head and proceeds anatomically with breathless speed, eagerly skipping from detail to detail as sensations crowd upon him. Vaughan always handles octosyllabic couplets with dexterity; here, by often varying the basic measure with lines of nine syllables, he creates an effect of spontaneous improvisation which is further heightened by numerous feminine rhymes and an occasional near-rhyme. The chief difference between this poem and others of its kind, such as Carew's "The Complement," is that Vaughan does not descend below the waist. This restraint, together with the poem's liveliness and lightness in rhythms and sound effects, makes it a fine example of the Cavaliers' ideal of delicate grace:

> Her *Hair* lay'd out in curious *Setts*
> And *Twists*, doth shew like silken *Nets*,
> Where (since he play'd at *Hitt* or *Miss*:)
> The God of *Love* her pris'ner is,
> And fluttering with his skittish Wings
> Puts all her locks in Curls and Rings.

The poems to Etesia and Amoret are less concerned with the woman's attributes and more with her effect upon the lover and with his relationship to her. The central image in the Fida poem is the image of the woman's body as a pastoral paradise—"a rich and flowry *Plain*." The woman in the Etesia and Amoret poems is usually expressed by images of the sun or a star, and the relationship between her and the lover is most often defined in terms of stellar or planetary influence. The central topic in each sequence is the relation of love to freedom of the will. The thematic contrast between them may be explained by examination of the different ways this topic is worked out.

The Etesia poems define the lover's plight in terms of astrological determinism, expressing by these means the traditional Christian-Platonic idea of the power of passion to enslave the whole personality. The clearest, though not the best, example is "To Etesia *looking from her Casement at the full* Moon" (Martin, p. 645). The speaker declares his lifelong subjection to the capricious influence of the moon, his natal star. Though his "constant mind" is "fix'd" in its affections, his fortunes are "humorous as wind." His life is full of *"Sorrows"* and "sad *Eclipses*" because it is his fate to pursue with constancy objects that are fickle and unstable. He is trying to overthrow the "Laws of Fate" and gain his freedom by reasoning himself out of vain passions when he suddenly falls in love with Etesia. The implication at the end of the poem is that Etesia has supplanted the moon as the capricious manipulator of his fortunes. Similar language of compulsion is characteristic of *"To* Etesia *(for* Timander,*) the first Sight"* (Martin, p. 643). It is her natal star that "Made me the *Subject*: you the *Queen*"; now that "sparkling *Planet*" works on him from her eyes with "nearer force, and more acute"; her eyes "controul" him, he "must adore" her. Undone with one bright glance, his loss of liberty is sudden and complete. Of course she can predominate in this way only because she is a miracle of nature, formed "that we might see / Perfection, not Variety." Passionate enslavement to perfection is pleasant pain.

We have seen that in some poems Vaughan presents reciprocated love as an aspect of an ideal natural order and that in others he presents the woman as an ideal natural object for man's possession or use. In some of these poems to Etesia the balance is tipped the other way, and the woman is presented as part of an ideal, supranatural order from which the man is separated by a vast moral gulf. His terrestrial passions have no counterpart in her world and he inevitably becomes the sport and plaything of his own desires. He is frustrated not so much by her indifference to his desires—the celebrated cruelty of the courtly mistress—as by their incompatability with the exalted conception he has of her. Seeking to justify his passions in terms of the Platonic theory of love as a desire for the beautiful and the good, he finds himself on the horns of a dilemma. The logical consequence of that theory, strictly followed, is that the highest form of love is an act of pure contemplation, an entirely intellectual act devoid of passional elements. This consequence is presented in *"The importunate Fortune"* (Martin, p. 634), where the soul's ascent to comprehension of "the Deitie" is accomplished through a purgation of all earthly faculties:

> First my dull Clay I give unto the *Earth*,
> Our common Mother, which gives all their birth.
> My growing Faculties I send as soon
> Whence first I took them, to the humid *Moon*.
> All Subtilties and every cunning Art
> To witty *Mercury* I do impart.
> Those fond Affections which made me a slave
> To handsome Faces, *Venus* thou shalt have.
> . . . .
> Get up my disintangled Soul, thy fire
> Is now refin'd & nothing left to tire,
> Or clog thy wings. Now my auspicious flight
> Hath brought me to the *Empyrean* light.
> I am a sep'rate *Essence*, and can see
> The *Emanations* of the Deitie.

The lover of Etesia might solve his problem, in accordance with the ethical implications of lady-service in medieval romance, by a similar purgation of base affections. He would then be capable of the act of pure contemplation which is alone consistent with the exalted conception of her expressed in "*The Character, to Etesia*" (Martin, p. 644). At least he could then meet her on her own level, from which they both might "descend / T'affections, and to faculties."[13] But it is the dilemma of the Platonizing lover to desire the best of both worlds and to be satisfied with neither. Desire and admiration fuse at the level of worship rather than of love, and the verse assumes the incantatory grandeur of a ritual act:

> Thou art the dark worlds Morning-star,
> Seen only, and seen but from far;
> Where like Astronomers we gaze
> Upon the glories of thy face,
> But no acquaintance more can have,
> Though all our lives we watch and Crave.
> Thou art a world thy self alone,
> Yea three great worlds refin'd to one.
> Which shews all those, and in thine Eyes
> The shining *East*, and *Paradise*.

The chief difference between Vaughan's audacity here and Donne's audacity in such poems as "The Canonization" and "The Sunne Rising" is that Donne makes such claims as this for both lover and mistress, whereas Vaughan exalts only the woman. As S. L. Bethell remarks, the poem expresses "a virtual adoration of the lady as not merely representing but really participating in the divine glory."[14] The morning star is to the sun what the Son of God is to God the Father; this is the language that Vaughan would use later in his sacred poems to express a love with nothing earthly for its object. She is the cynosure of the universe and its epitome, the source of the dark world's light and happiness, the origin and end of its creative energy:

> Thy Soul (a *Spark* of the first *Fire*,)
> Is like the *Sun*, the worlds desire;

And with a nobler influence
Works upon all, that claim to sense.

According to the Christian concept of the *imago Dei* and the Neoplatonic theory of creative emanation, every natural creature participated, to some degree, in the divine glory; every soul was a spark of the divine fire. But few were like the morning star or capable of nobler influence than the sun.[15] The hyperboles at the center of the poem are prepared for by the opening conceits; echoing the fantastic errands of Donne's "Goe, and catche a falling starre," they declare the impossibility of making an adequate "character" of Etesia with even the most prodigious of natural materials. She is ultimately beyond even the extraordinary dispensation of nature to which phoenixes and rivers of milk belong: "Such objects and so fresh would be / But dull Resemblances of thee." Her place is with the Platonic Ideas or Forms of the most superlative things of the natural world, as a contemporary comment acknowledges:

> Nor does thy other softer Magick move
> Us less thy fam'd *Etesia* to love;
> Where such a *Character* thou giv'st that shame
> Nor envy dare approach the Vestal Dame:
> So at bright Prime *Idea's* none repine,
> They safely in th' *Eternal Poet* shine.[16]

The paradox for the Platonizing lover is that passion dare approach "bright Prime *Idea's*" no more than envy and shame. But her charms nevertheless "seize" his heart and "oblige" him to admire her. He barely stops on this side idolatry:

> O thou art such, that I could be
> A lover to Idolatry!
> I could, and should from heav'n stray,
> But that thy life shews mine the way,
> And leave a while the *Diety*,
> To serve his *Image* here in thee.

The idea that spiritual love of the angelic mistress prepared the soul for the love of God was the solution of the problem for Dante and Petrarch. But the speaker in this poem has given vent to a dual passion, based as much on what she has in common with the "Rich *odours* . . . and *Sweetnesses*" of earth's flowers as on her morning-star qualities. The conclusion does not reconcile these diverse elements; it is an attempt to escape from the problem by ignoring one side of the speaker's nature. Only by self-delusion does he escape the ambiguities of the self-imposed dilemma with which courtly sonneteers had prevaricated in similar fashion many times before.

The character of Etesia changes with the fourth poem in the series, "*To* Etesia *parted from him, and looking back*" (Martin, p. 646). No longer the remote, capricious, untouchable paragon of the early poems, she reciprocates his passion or, at the least, responds with human kindness. She remains unattainable, and he remains in torment, because of an ordinary, irreducible situation: an apparently enforced separation. The poem dramatizes the way this situation transfigures all, converting even the manna of her kindness to gall:

> Strange *Art* of Love! that can make sound,
> And yet exasperates the wound;
> That *look* she lent to ease my heart,
> Hath pierc't it, and improv'd the smart.

These lines catch the very moment when she is parted from him and looking back. Their paradoxical healing-wounding motif runs through the whole poem, creating, with some lesser oxymora, an intense statement of the strangeness, the mystery, of love's contrarieties. Only gradually does the speaker come to the final recognition that the contradictions which make up his misery are inherent in the experience of love under these particular circumstances. For a while he questions whether the woman is not willfully cruel:

> Hath she no *Quiver*, but my Heart?
> Must all her Arrows hit that part?

Beauties like Heav'n, their Gifts should deal
Not to destroy us, but to heal.

The conclusion of the poem, implicitly absolving the woman, answers these questions by confirming the first stanza's impassioned recognition that the strangeness of his experience is due to the very nature of love:

O Subtile Love! thy Peace is War;
It wounds and kills without a scar:
It works unknown to any sense,
Like the Decrees of Providence,
And with strange silence shoots me through;
The *Fire* of Love doth fall like *Snow*.

This treatment of love had been standard for centuries; Vaughan brings it to life by dramatizing it as a personal experience. S. L. Bethell's remark that the fifth line is marked by "the emotive use of language to convey experience qualitatively rather than by objective definition" might be extended to the poem as a whole.[17]

Between this poem and the more successful "Etesia *absent*" (Martin, p. 647), which ends the series, are placed two poems which further develop the situation of the parting itself. The description of her "charming grief" in the Latin "In Etesiam lachrymantem" tends to humanize her still more and to intensify the impression that she accepts as reluctantly as he the "ill fortune" of their parting.[18] The inferior "To Etesia *going beyond Sea*" bids her "Go, if you must!" but detains her long enough for him to swear to keep the regular schedule of pining lovers. The tone of "Etesia *absent*"—a poem that is decidedly superior to the much anthologized "To Amoret gone from him"—stems mainly from the serious use of philosophic, religious, and scientific concepts. The poem's basic proposition, tersely compressed in the opening invocation, is "the common Renaissance conception that divine love was immanent throughout the cosmos and was, basically, the force effecting universal order and harmony."[19] The recession of human love through the woman's absence is presented as an alienation from this universal principle and, therefore, as a spiritual death far more dreadful than the death of the body:

> Love, the Worlds Life! what a sad death
> Thy absence is? to lose our breath
> At once and dye, is but to live
> Inlarg'd, without the scant reprieve
> Of *Pulse* and *Air*: whose dull *returns*
> And narrow *Circles* the Soul mourns.

Vaughan's paradoxical development of the basic idea makes the poem a tissue of oxymora. What we ordinarily think of as death merely frees the soul from its physical privations to enjoy an enlarged kind of life. By contrast, the "sad death" which the lover lives in the absence of his beloved is a severe privation, a lapse of his soul from joyful participation in the animating spirit of the universe, the very source of life. Real death is redeemed by the Resurrection; for the lover's living death there is no redemption except the woman's return. The antithetical structure of thought in the poem's opening statement is underscored by the stark antitheses between words denoting life and love and the far more numerous expressions denoting death, loss, and privation. Beneath this antithesis is an implied analogy between the soul mourning the death-in-life of its physical imprisonment and the lover mourning the death-in-life occasioned by his beloved's absence. This may be more than analogy, and hence more than hyperbole: according to the poem's basic conception of universal love, the aim of the lover seeking reunion is essentially cognate with that of the soul seeking fulfillment.

The opening conceits establish a basic definition of the lover's predicament; the remaining lines amplify the basic definition by developing these antitheses and analogies still further. The frustration of the lover's quest for a more vital life is dramatized in a series of violent antitheses:

> But to be dead alive, and still
> To wish, but never have our will:

> To be possess'd, and yet to miss;
> To wed a true but absent bliss:
> Are lingring tortures, and their smart
> Dissects and racks and grinds the Heart!

The discrepancy between the goal of desire and the lover's actual condition is insistently underscored by the connectives: *and still, but never, and yet, but*. The analogous structure of the conflicting clauses further points up the antithesis. The periodic structure of the sentence holds back the most forceful images of the lover's condition while short, sharply conflicting clauses build up tension, finally releasing their energy in "Are lingring tortures, and their smart / Dissects and racks and grinds the Heart!" An effect of rhythmically swinging blows is created by the mechanical repetition of "and" and by the fall of the heavy stresses on the harsh, violent verbs and on the lover's "Heart."

In the poem's beginning the living and dead states of the soul are dichotomized and static, reflecting the idea that the lovers' separation brings death by dichotomizing a living whole. At the conclusion, the lover anticipates a desperately slow movement toward an eventual reunion, presented as a return to life through analogy with the reunion of soul and body at the Resurrection. The clogged, dragging movement of the lines reflects the massive inertia of "Times long *train*," through which the lover looks in vain. Time takes on the sense of an almost physical obstacle and weight, shutting out life and light and entombing the lover in a dark torpor of spirit:

> As Soul and Body in that state
> Which unto us seems separate,
> Cannot be said to live, until
> Reunion; which dayes fulfill
> And slow-pac'd seasons: So in vain
> Through hours and minutes (Times long *train*,)
> I look for thee, and from thy sight,
> As from my Soul, for life and light.

> For till thine Eyes shine so on me,
> Mine are fast-clos'd and will not see.

In the first five poems of the 1646 volume the mistress is presented as an irresistible, heartless beauty who aggrandizes herself at the expense of her admirers' brokenhearted deaths. The song beginning "*Amyntas* goe, thou art undone" (Martin, p. 6) is typical:

> This Cruell thou hast done, and thus,
>   That Face hath many servants slaine.
> Though th' end be not to ruine us,
>   But to seeke glory by our paine.

Here we are close to the first year's cycle of Spenser's *Amoretti* and to thousands of conventional love lyrics. But with "To Amoret, Walking in a Starry Evening" (Martin, p. 7) we get a different mood. As in the early poems to Etesia, the woman is associated with the stars and the sun; but the relation between her and the lover is not defined simply in terms of stellar influence on a passive terrestrial creature. Instead it is presented as a "sympathie" between "two conspiring minds." And whereas in "*The Character, to* Etesia" she was a distant star upon which he could gaze only like an astronomer, here "no distance" can disrupt their unity. Similarly, "To Amoret gone from him" (Martin, p. 8) argues by analogy with the sympathy between flowers and the sun that the lovers also "At such vast distance can agree." "A Song to *Amoret*" and "*To Amoret, of the difference* . . ." (Martin, pp. 8, 12) boast of the lover's worthiness to be beloved by insisting on the purity of his soul and the spiritual foundation of his affections. The latter poem defines true love by analogy with the "mutuall fire" of "Spirits and Stars."[20] In "To Amoret Weeping" (Martin, p. 13) the speaker tries to allay her distress over the mediocrity of their shared estate by boasting at length of the power of his soul to transcend misfortunes and by urging her to recognize their mutual love as more precious than gold.

In these poems the speaker muses, reflects, deliberates, confidently reasons with the woman, remonstrates with her, and cajoles her—all from a position of either equality or superiority. Love is presented as not merely compatible with spiritual freedom but as in large measure the very foundation of that freedom.

The equanimity of the lover in these poems is reflected in the equable temperament of the verse. This is a poetry of cool, deliberate statement and reasoned argument rather than of passionate ardors and hyperbolical enthusiasms. The imagery is not as profuse as in the Etesia poems, the studied development of a single image being sometimes sufficient for a whole poem. But an awkwardness in the development of thought and in the handling of the complex stanzaic patterns too often produces a heavy, turgid effect. "To Amoret gone from him" succeeds better than most, perhaps because Vaughan is more comfortable with the octosyllabic couplet. But the "Song to *Amoret*" is for me the most satisfying of these poems apart from "To Amoret Weeping," which will be discussed in chapter 5 as a satire on riches rather than as a love poem. The neat, precise symmetry of the song's quatrains makes it the perfect vehicle for the speaker's emotional repose. He holds in suspension until the last stanza his sober statement of sincere, unshakeable affection while he imperturbably hypothesizes the character of "Some fresher youth" who, if the speaker were dead, might try "To warme thee with new fires." His strategy is simple: he grants to his hypothetical supplanter all that can be granted of virtue and wealth and then puts in the opposite scale the simplest of things: "So rich a heart as mine."

> Fortune and beauty thou mightst finde,
>   And greater men then I:
> But my true resolved minde,
>   They never shall come nigh.
>
> For I not for an houre did love,
>   Or for a day desire,

> But with my soule had from above,
> This endles holy fire.[21]

As in "To Amoret Weeping," Vaughan counterbalances the weighty values of the world—fortune, beauty, greatness—with a simple, lightly touched affirmation of love. The declaration that such a constant, sincere, and pure devotion will not coincide with worldly glory could not be more lightly yet firmly and effectively made. It brings to a point the evaluation of this hypothetical suitor which the language of the poem has been making all along:

> Were he as faithfull as the Sunne,
> That's wedded to the Sphere;
> His bloud as chaste, and temp'rate runne,
> As Aprils mildest teare;
>
> Or were he rich, and with his heapes,
> And spacious share of Earth,
> Could make divine affection cheape,
> And court his golden birth ...

The effect of the anticlimactic "spacious share of *Earth*" (my italics) and of the derogatory "heapes" is obvious; the rest of the stanza insinuates that he is vainly proud of his wealth and arrogantly insensitive to the superiority of "divine affection." He is pictured as one who expects to be loved because of his money.[22] At first glance, the other stanza just quoted seems very much like the speaker's own protestation at the end of the poem. This is the standard rhetoric of the wooer; but here it is slightly exaggerated, the claim to constancy and temperance being twice buttressed with hyperbolical similitudes. The rhetoric is further made to parody itself by the way it is introduced:

> If I were dead, and in my place,
> Some fresher youth *design'd*
> To warme thee with new fires ... (my italics)

The word "Arts" insinuates hypocrisy more directly; and finally there is the mocking summation in the phrase "the mighty Amorist."

> For all these Arts I'de not believe,
>   (No though he should be thine)
> The mighty Amorist could give
>   So rich a heart as mine.

In these subtleties, as well as in its smooth, balanced progression, the poem foreshadows the accomplishment of "They are all gone into the world of light!"[23] It seems to me quite as attractive as the best-known songs of Carew and Lovelace.

Chapter
V
SATIRE

A. Anti-Puritanism

"HE IS INGENIOSE, but prowd and humorous"—this is the enigmatic "character" of Vaughan left us by his cousin, John Aubrey.[1] Cryptic as it is, however, it vividly suggests an affinity for the splenetic, captious muse of satire. Vaughan was a satirist from first to last.[2] His first book of verse was divided about equally between love poems and a translation of Juvenal's tenth satire directed specifically toward the political disturbances of the middle 1640s:

> For the *Satyre*, it was of purpose borrowed, to feather some slower *Houres*; And what you see here, is but the *Interest*: It is one of his, whose *Roman* Pen had as much true *Passion*, for the infirmities of that state, as we should have *Pitty*, to the distractions of our owne: Honest (I am sure) it is, and offensive cannot be, except it meet with such *Spirits* that will quarrell with *Antiquitie*, or purposely *Arraigne* themselves; These indeed may thinke, that they have slept out so many *Centuries* in this *Satyre*, and are now awaked; which, had it been still *Latine*, perhaps their Nap had been Everlasting. (Martin, p. 2)

Pity for the distractions of the state during the 1640s and 1650s was an abiding motivation of Vaughan's satirical writing. An abiding target was the rebel party—a broadly drawn stereotype

[85]

which conglomerated Puritans and Parliamentarians of every religious and republican stripe. For Vaughan, all were equally the enemies of the King and the oppressors of the Church; more than that, they were the Satanic conspirators of Antichrist, enemies of God and of religion itself, the devilish scourge of God's chosen people. Thus, in "L'Envoy" (Martin, p. 541), the last poem in *Silex Scintillans* (1655), the impassioned opening prayer for an apocalyptic purification of the world is predicated upon the current triumphs of the Puritans:

> Onely, let not our haters brag,
> Thy seamless coat is grown a rag,
> Or that thy truth was not here known,
> Because we forc'd thy judgements down.
> Dry up their arms, who vex thy spouse,
> And take the glory of thy house
> To deck their own.

Between these two passages lies a large body of satirical writing. Much of it is naturally to be found in the secular poems; but the religious prose treatises and the sacred poems themselves are thickly studded with satirical passages ranging in tone from the most detached irony to the most savage vituperation.[3] "Prowd and humorous," however applicable to Vaughan, aptly describes the temperament of his satirical persona: always loftily assured, his humors are scorn, ridicule, contempt, disgust, anger, hatred, revenge.

Vaughan's innocent disclaimer of any offensive intent in publishing Juvenal's satire in English should not deceive us: it is entirely ironical. His basic purpose in these prefatory remarks is to establish a parallel between the state of England and the state of Rome as presented by Juvenal. The pose of innocent naïveté is a traditional pose of satiric personae, illustrated, for example, by Erasmus's Folly, More's "speaker-of-divine-nonsense" (Raphael Hythlodaye), and Skelton's rude rustic, Colin Clout. The pose has more than the function of disarming counterattacks on the author by camouflaging his opinions; it is designed to win the reader's sympathy by assuring him of the persona's honesty, integrity, and disinterestedness. The implication that the satire is unlikely to "meet with such *Spirits* that will quarrell with *Antiquitie*" is similarly double-edged. In adopting Juvenal's work as a comment on the contemporary scene, these are the very spirits at whom Vaughan takes aim. In the England of 1646, a violent quarrel with antiquity had been going on for some years, in parliamentary attacks on the traditional authority and privileges of the Crown and in reforming Puritans' attacks on the discipline of the established Church. These are the spirits who, Vaughan ironically acknowledges, may find the satire offensive. The implication that they are lethargic, stupid, ignorant of Latin, and basely insensitive to things of venerable worth sets the tone of all Vaughan's attacks on the proponents of political and ecclesiastical innovation.

In learning, in religion, in social and political matters, Vaughan's spirit was as traditionalist and conservative as it was haughty. Addressing the "ingenious Reader" of *Hermetical Physick* (1655), he self-consciously defends his interest in this 1613 treatise of Henry Nollius:

> For my owne part, I honour the truth where ever I find it, whether in an old, or a new Booke, in *Galen*, or in *Paracelsus*; and Antiquity, (where I find it gray with errors) shall have as little reverence from me, as *Novelisme*. (Martin, p. 548)

Just a few years before the establishment of the Royal Society was to authorize the empirical, pragmatic mode of investigation represented by Harvey's discovery of the circulation of the blood some forty years before, the issue for Vaughan is still between Galen and Paracelsus, and it is a charge of novelism, not antiquarianism, that he anticipates for his translation of Nollius's Paracelsian discourse. Before defending his interest in such novelties, he wrings the withers of the conservative Galenists:

> If any will be offended with this *Hermeticall* Theorie, I shall but smile at his frettings, and pitty his ignorance. Those are

bad Spirits, that have the light; and such are all malicious despisers of true knowledge, who out of meere envie, scribble and rail at all endeavours; but such as submit to, and Deifie their rigid superstition, and twice sodden Colworts. (Martin, p. 548)

Vaughan's intellectual conservatism is truly reflected in a letter of 1680 expressing impatience with the contemporary scepticism of astrology; attribution of this scepticism to an "ill humour" is a characteristic touch:

That the most serious of our profession have not only an unkindnes for, butt are persecutors of Astrologie: I have more than once admired: butt I find not this ill humour amongst the Antients, so much as the modern physicians: nor amongst them all neither. (Martin, pp. 692-93)

The depth and strength of Vaughan's animosity for "such *Spirits* that will quarrell with *Antiquitie*" is suggested by one of his translations from Boethius:

> for all things (in the worlds prime)
> The wise God seal'd their proper time,
> Nor will permit those seasons he
> Ordain'd by turns, should mingled be.
> Then whose wild actions out of season
> Crosse to nature, and her reason,
> Would by new wayes old orders rend,
> Shall never find a happy End.   (Martin, pp. 79-80)

In a very Boethian poem, "To . . . Master *T. Lewes*" (Martin, p. 61), Vaughan takes a similar view:

> Let us meet then! and while this world
> In wild *Excentricks* now is hurld,
> Keep wee, like nature, the same *Key*,
> And walk in our forefathers way.

The association of a political and social order with the rational laws of nature implies a quietist political stance—an obedience to established authority, a desire for order and peace, with a horrified recoil from any radical innovation as essentially unnatural, irrational, lawless, and finally irreligious. In this view, disobedience of king, bishop, or magistrate is virtually synonymous with disobedience of God, the source of universal law. This was the grand synthesis of the Elizabethan Settlement, driven home with scores of sermons and treatises on the virtue of obedience and the evil of sedition. The conclusion of *Of Temperance and Patience*, Vaughan's translation of a discourse by Nierembergius, is typical of this line of thought:

> That Supreme, Eternall mind is the master and deviser of this worldly *Drama*: Hee brings on the *persons*, and assignes them their *parts*. Art thou called to be a servant? be not troubled at it: Hath he ordained thy life to be short? desire not to have it lengthned: If poor, desire not to be made rich. What *part* soever he hath appointed for thee, be contented therewith, and Act it faithfully. It is thy duty to represent the *person* thou wert chosen for, and not to choose; that is the prerogative of thy great master. (Martin, pp. 275-76)

The political, social, and ecclesiastical implications of such views as these are precisely what the Puritans and Parliamentarians were attacking. It is on this besieged ground that Vaughan takes his stand and from which he surveys and castigates the "wild actions" of his contemporaries who indeed "Would by new wayes old orders rend."[4]

The dominant theme of Juvenal's tenth satire is the vanity of ambition, especially of ambition for power, glory, and great wealth—"greatness" or "state." The stories of Sejanus and Hannibal are the main *exempla* of the violent ruin and unhappiness, for both the individual and the state, which follow from excessive pride and lawless ambition. The couplet which concludes this part of the satire summarizes its theme:

> O foolish mad ambition! these are still
> The famous dangers that attend thy will.
>
> (ll. 320-21)

This is the broad, general lesson that Vaughan is reading to the rebels, whom he considers, obviously, to be as suitable *exempla* of the theme as Sejanus and Hannibal. Concluding the story of Hannibal's disasters, he addresses his readers directly:

> Goe now ambitious man! new plots designe,
> March o're the snowie Alps, and Apennine;
> That after all, at best thou mayst but be
> A pleasing story to posteritie! (ll. 284-87)

The story of Sejanus is introduced to illustrate the dangers of envy. It is possible that Vaughan was thinking of Strafford and his enemies when he wrote:

> But envy ruines all: What mighty names
> Of fortune, spirit, action, bloud, and fame,
> Hath this destroy'd? yea, for no other cause
> Then being such; their honour, worth, and place,
> Was crime enough.[5] (ll. 91-95)

Vaughan consistently presented the rebels as malicious calumniators of everything good, noble, and fine in the Church and in the state. He was certainly thinking of them when he wrote in the *Life of Paulinus*

> some *great ones* in this later age, did nothing else but countenance *Schismaticks* and *seditious raylers*, the *despisers of dignities*, that covered their *abominable villanies* with a pretence of *transcendent holinesse*, and a certain *Sanctimonious excellencie* above the Sons of men. (Martin, p. 371)

The concluding reflections on the Sejanus story seem to point it toward the rebel leaders of the Parliament and the army as a grim warning against what Vaughan saw as their ambitious aspiration to usurp the kingdom in the people's name:

> So fals ambitious man, and such are still
> All floating States built on the people's will:
> Hearken all you! whom this bewitching lust
> Of an houres glory, and a little dust
> Swels to such deare repentance! you that can
> Measure whole kingdoms with a thought or span
> Would you be as *Sejanus*? would you have
> So you might sway as he did, such a grave?
> (ll. 159–66)

In Vaughan's mind the rebel leaders were always, as here, associated with a tumultuous, degenerate rabble. Recommending *The Mount of Olives* (1652) to the "Peaceful, humble, and pious Reader," he urges, "Presse thou towards the mark, *and let the people and their Seducers rage*" (Martin, p. 141). "To his retired friend, an Invitation to *Brecknock*" (Martin, p. 46) expresses unmitigated scorn for "th'obtuse Rout" of townsfolk who cooperated with the rebels; and in the poem addressed to Thomas Powell as his "*Loyal Fellow-Prisoner*" Vaughan begs for Powell's company as an antidote to "loose, loath'd men" (Martin, p. 624). It is likely that Vaughan was sympathetic as he translated Plutarch's remark about the responsibility of a prince "to sway a Commonwealth burthen'd with a various and vicious multitude" (Martin, p. 97) and the terse comment of Maximus Tyrius: "The people are in their anger *Merciless*, in their desires *vehement*, in their pleasures *dissolute*, in their troubles *abject*, and in their furie *Mad*" (Martin, p. 118). Maximus's explanation of popular sedition as a disease of the mind is so similar to Vaughan's characteristic expressions that it might almost be his own account of the Rebellion:

> those persons in the Citie, who had the charge of the Republick (as Popular government hath ever too many) so

burnt with hatred, ambition, and Covetousnes one towards another, that they seemed rather to be out of their witts, than rightly in them. These mentall diseases in a short time so increased, and dispersed, that all *Athens* was infected, and so prevalent was the Contagion that it took also the Common people. . . . O blessed Statesmen! this was your Reformation! Ruine, Confusion, prodigious Changes, nationall Miseries, and civill Inflammations were the religion, and liberty they had from you! (Martin, p. 120)

Commonly, as in the reference to *"the people and their Seducers,"* Vaughan sees the populace as the ignorant pawns of unscrupulous rebel leaders, to whom he consistently attributes lawless violence, duplicity, and essentially selfish ambition. The term "self-ends" recurs again and again in reference to the rebels. In the elegy on *"R. W."* (Martin, p. 49), for example, he contrasts the fallen Royalist with

> all those vast pretenders, which of late
> Swell'd in the ruines of their King and State.
> He weav'd not *Self-ends*, and the *Publick* good
> Into one piece, nor with the peoples bloud
> Fill'd his own veins.

"To the pious memorie of C. W. Esquire" (Martin, p. 629) makes the same point in even stronger language:

> though thy Course in times long progress fell
> On a sad age, when Warr and open'd Hell
> Licens'd all Artes and Sects, and made it free
> To thrive by fraud and blood and blasphemy:
> Yet thou thy just Inheritance did'st by
> No sacrilege, nor pillage multiply;
> No rapine swell'd thy state: no bribes, nor fees
> Our new oppressors best Annuities.

In "The Men of War" (Martin, p. 516), Vaughan ironically declares that he would not "for a temporal self-end / Successful wickedness commend." In "The Agreement" (Martin, p. 528), he contrasts the Bible with modern books of devotion in which "zeal lays out and blends / Onely self-worship and self-ends." And in his translation of the *Life of Paulinus* he observes: "There are no such persecutors of the Church, as those that do it for selfe-ends, and their private advantage" (Martin, p. 362).

The idea that the thought of ultimate death should cure mad ambition is presented in lines 294–95 of Juvenal's satire: "The highest thoughts, and actions under Heaven, / Death only with the lowest dust layes even" (Martin, p. 25). The theme of death as the great leveler and therefore as the guardian and teacher of moderation and peaceableness is the central theme of "The Charnel-house" (Martin, p. 41), where the pretensions of the rebels are again ridiculed from this point of view.[6] The poem is a dramatic soliloquy in which the speaker's moral reflections evolve from contemplation of the dead bodies actually before him. The poem's language consistently emphasizes the shocking, irreducible immediacy of death. The tone of someone musing aloud is expressed by the loose, irregular, repetitive progression of thought, with uneven clauses and great variation in the placement of line-end and midline pauses. The thematic tension between vast ambition and the ultimate handful of dust is underscored by rhythmic variations and the sharp juxtaposition of contrasting images. The opening evocation of the destined end is rhythmically confined by short, uneven exclamations, but as "shoreless thoughts" and "Ambitious dreams" which seek to transcend these limits are evoked the verse expands in weighty cadences which ironically comment on man's delusions, finally sinking again as the speaker relentlessly circles back to the reality before him:

> Where are you shoreless thoughts, vast tenter'd hope,
> Ambitious dreams, *Ayms* of an Endless scope,
> Whose stretch'd Excesse runs on a string too high
> And on the rack of self-extension dye?
> *Chameleons* of state, Aire-monging band,
> Whose breath (like Gun-powder) blowes up a land,

Come see your dissolution, and weigh
What a loath'd nothing you shall be one day.

The verse itself imitates both the "stretch'd Excesse" of which it speaks and the very action of falling from great height. The pattern is repeated as the speaker's reflections once more circle around the central antithesis:

> Think then, that in this bed
> There sleep the Reliques of as proud a head
> As stern and subtill as your own, that hath
> Perform'd, or forc'd as much, whose tempest-wrath
> Hath levell'd Kings with slaves, and wisely then
> Calme these high furies, and descend to men;
> Thus *Cyrus* tam'd the *Macedon*, a tombe
> Checkt him, who thought the world too straight a Room.[7]

The fall now envisaged, analogous to the descent into a modest grave, is a moral descent from pretentious self-inflation to the level and stature of moderate, peaceful men. The speaker has already presented himself as an *exemplum* of death's morally restraining action: "How thou arrests my sense? how with the sight / My *Winter'd* bloud growes stiffe to all delight?" At the beginning of the third paragraph and at the end of the poem he again presents himself as, in a sense, the poem's ideal reader. Meanwhile the scope of the central paradox is extended with graphic "characters" of a miser and a soldier, the latter being almost certainly a deliberate caricature of the republican army:

> That famish'd slave
> Begger'd by wealth, who starves that he may save,
> Brings hither but his sheet; Nay, th'*Ostrich-man*
> That feeds on *steele* and *bullet*, he that can
> Outswear his *Lordship*, and reply as tough
> To a kind word, as if his tongue were *Buffe*,
> Is *Chap*-faln here, wormes without wit, or fear
> Defie him now, death hath disarm'd the *Bear*.

Like the chameleons of state, these emblematic figures are presented as typical of failings that are common to mankind at large. All are traditional figures in satire, but Vaughan has combined the general and the particular in such a way that the contemporary case becomes a mirror of human nature and fate. The speaker's reflections move on from these particular cases to find the same nemesis at the end of a general vision of human frailty:

> Thus could I run o'r all the pitteous score
> Of erring men, and having done meet more,
> Their shuffled *Wills*, abortive, vain *Intents*,
> Phantastick *humours*, perillous *Ascents*,
> False, empty *honours*, traiterous *delights*,
> And whatsoe'r a blind Conceit Invites;
> But these and more which the weak vermins swell,
> Are Couch'd in this Accumulative Cell
> Which I could scatter.[8]

His mind returns again to the central fact: the stark immediacy of death. And as it does so it focuses the poem's central irony in the repulsive image of swollen vermin: men swell themselves only to swell worms.

Vaughan did not always tax the Puritans so harshly. He can relax at times, and banter them lightheartedly in the derisive catchphrases of the times. Commending the 1647 edition of Fletcher's plays, for example, he equivocates with the political connotations of "plot" in order to mock the Puritans' austerity and distaste for stage plays in a lightly ironical tone:

> But thou hast *plotts*; and will not the *Kirk* strain
> At the *Designes* of such a *Tragick brain*?
> Will they themselves think safe, when they shall see
> Thy most *abominable policie*?
> Will not the *Eares* assemble, and think't fit
> Their *Synod fast*, and *pray*, against thy wit?
>
> (Martin, p. 55)

The implication that the Puritans are the witless enemies of wit develops from the earlier remark that through the publication of Fletcher's plays England is "freed from that *dearth* of wit / Which *starv'd* the Land since into *Schismes* split." In similar vein, "To Amoret Weeping" (Martin, p. 13) correlates stupidity, wealth, and sedition:

> I (had I been rich) as sure as fate,
> Would have bin medling with the King, or State,
> Or something to undoe me; and 'tis fit
> (We know) that who hath wealth, should have no wit.

The terms in which the toast to Caligula is proposed in "A Rhapsodis" (Martin, p. 10) make a similar ironic point about the intelligence of the Parliament:

> Come, take the other dish; it is to him
> That made his horse a Senatour: Each brim
> Looke big as mine; The gallant, jolly Beast
> Of all the Herd (you'le say) was not the least.

The speaker in the Fletcher poem becomes less detached as he develops the conceit that Fletcher's plots are a threat to the Puritans' political cause and religious way of life. His humorous assertion that Fletcher's plays "kill" and "overthrow" only in a make-believe world glances ironically at the real killing and overthrowing which make up the *"abominable policie"* of his enemies. The game changes to earnest, and the tone deepens from scoffing ridicule of the Puritans to direct hatred as Vaughan insists on the superiority of Fletcher's imaginative conquests to their military:

> Thou doest but *kill*, and *Circumvent* in *Jest*,
> And when thy anger'd Muse *swells* to a blow
> 'Tis but for *Field's*, or *Swansteed's* overthrow.
> Yet shall these *Conquests* of thy *Bayes* outlive

Their *Scotish zeale,* and *Compacts* made to grieve
The *Peace* of *Spirits,* and when such deeds fayle
Of their foule Ends, a *faire name* is thy Bayle.

Besides "self-ends," the most striking leitmotifs of Vaughan's anti-Puritan satire are "zeal" and "Saint." They are often found together, invariably as part of a violent accusation of fraud, deceit, and hypocrisy. Juxtaposing caricatures of the Puritans' devotion and their actions, he finds them to be demonic parodies of true religion and faith, fraudulent wolves in the clothing of the Lamb, false prophets, servants of the Devil posing as the priests of Christ. Probably he had them in mind when he translated Juvenal's account of the people derided by Democritus:

> He knew their idle and superfluous vowes,
> And sacrifice, which such wrong zeale bestowes,
> Were meere Incendiaries; and that the gods
> Not pleas'd therewith, would ever be at ods.   (ll. 83-86)

He begins his address to the reader of *The Mount of Olives* by deriding the Puritans' emphasis on the engagement of the spirit in devotion without the aid of ritual or other external props:

> I know the world abounds with these Manuals, and triumphs over them. It is not then their scarsity that call'd this forth, nor yet a desire to crosse the age, nor any in it. I envie not their frequent *Extasies,* and raptures to the third heaven; I onely wish them real, and that their actions did not tell the world, they are rapt into some other place. Nor should they, who assume to themselves the glorious stile of Saints, be uncharitably moved, if we that are yet in the body, and carry our treasure in earthen vessels, have need of these helps. (Martin, p. 140)

He mocks their ecstasies by insisting on the word's literal meaning, opposing to the supposedly disembodied Puritans ("rapt," not into heaven, but "some other place") those mere mortals "that are yet in the body." The ironical "assume to themselves the glorious stile of Saints" hits Calvinism at its crucial center, the doctrine of election. The point is made without irony at the end of "St. Mary Magdalen" (Martin, p. 507): "Who Saint themselves, they are no *Saints*." The line implicates the Puritans' censorious self-righteousness with that of the poem's "Self-boasting *Pharisee*" who accused the Magdalen of sin. She is hailed as "Dear, beauteous Saint!" while he is instructed to "Go Leper, go; wash till thy flesh / Comes like a childes, spotless and fresh." In "White Sunday" (Martin, p. 485), referring to the Pentecostal baptism of the apostles with flames of the Holy Ghost, the speaker disingenuously asks "Can these new lights be like to those, / These lights of Serpents like the Dove?" The question is answered here—"I can discern Wolves from the Sheep" —and in many other places, often by just this sort of antithesis between the piety of more primitive men and of "these new lights." The irony of this device is enhanced by the fact that it turns against the Puritans their own claim to be restoring a more pristine, sincere devotion than could be found in the degenerate Anglican and Catholic communions. One of the most savage examples of this line of attack appears in *Man in Darkness*:

> It was a blessed and a glorious age the Primitive *Christians* lived in. . . . what *Zeale*, what powerful *faith*, what perfect *charity*, hearty *humility*, and true *holinesse* was then to be found upon the earth? If we compare the *shining* and *fervent piety* of those Saints, with *the painted* and *illuding appearance* of it in *these of our times*, we shall have just cause to fear. . . . This was the *old way*, and whether we are *in it*, or *out* of it, is not hard to be decided. A pretended *sanctity* from the teeth outward, with the frequent *mention* of the *Spirit*, and a presumptuous assuming to our selves of the stile of *Saints*, when we are within full of *subtilty, malice, oppression, lewd opinions*, and *diverse lusts*, is (I am sure) a convincing argument that we are not onely *out* of it, but that we have no mind to returne *into* it. (Martin, pp. 181–82)

Satire [99]

Similarly, in "Religion" (Martin, p. 404), Vaughan's adoption of the pastoral mode turns against the Puritans some of their sharpest swords: the argument that the Bible was a sufficient basis for devotion; the claim that their style of worship restored the pure devotion of patriarchal and apostolic times; their insistence on the need to purify the Church of the contaminations accruing through its temporal history. The poem is built on Vaughan's ironic adoption of all these points. He puns on "leaves" in the first stanza to present the basis of the poem's argument as a lesson learned from the Bible. That basis, the norm of religious devotion, is the familiarity of the patriarchs with God and angels. The account of the Church's degeneration through history is presented to explain why "We have no Conf'rence in these daies." This description of the Church's history in terms of staining an original purity, of poison, noxious chemicals, infection, corrupted matter, and a dead externality is a thorough parody of the language of the Puritans' anti-Episcopal propaganda. And so is the concluding appeal for a divine intervention in human affairs to purify these waters and restore their original vitality:

> Religion is a Spring
> That from some secret, golden Mine
> Derives her birth, and thence doth bring
> Cordials in every drop, and Wine;
>
> But in her long, and hidden Course
> Passing through the Earths darke veines,
> Growes still from better unto worse,
> And both her taste, and colour staines,
>
> Then drilling on, learnes to encrease
> False *Ecchoes*, and Confused sounds,
> And unawares doth often seize
> On veines of *Sulphur* under ground;
>
> So poison'd, breaks forth in some Clime,
> And at first sight doth many please,

> But drunk, is puddle, or meere slime
> And 'stead of Phisick, a disease;
>
> Just such a tainted sink we have
> Like that *Samaritans* dead *Well*,
> Nor must we for the Kernell crave
> Because most voices like the *shell*.

The poem's epigraph is a verse from the *Song of Solomon*, traditionally read as an allegory of Christ as Bridegroom and the Church as Spouse: "My sister, my spouse is as a garden Inclosed, as a Spring shut up, and a fountain sealed up." These words are echoed in *The Mount of Olives*: in the "Admonitions how to carry thy self in the Church" (Martin, p. 147), Vaughan speaks of "These reverend and sacred buildings (however now vilified and shut up)"; and in the "Prayer in time of persecution and Heresie" (Martin, p. 166), which is undoubtedly personal and topical in every word, he says: "The wayes of *Zion* do mourne, our beautiful gates are shut up. . . . Thy Service and thy Sabbaths, thy own sacred Institutions and the pledges of thy love are denied unto us." He is referring, here and in the verse from the *Song of Solomon*, to the Act for the Propagation of the Gospel in Wales of February 1649/50, and to several earlier measures, under which ministers who retained Episcopal forms of worship were removed from their livings and their pulpits often left empty.[9] Replacement of the ejected ministers by Puritans was not, for Vaughan, a satisfactory substitute. "Thy Ministers are trodden down, and the basest of the people are set up in thy holy place," he exclaims in the "Prayer in time of persecution" (Martin, p. 166). "We have seen his Ministers cast out of the Sanctuary, & barbarous persons without *light* or *perfection*, usurping holy offices" (Martin, p. 171). The basis of his strong feelings on this subject is revealed in the *Life of Paulinus*:

> The Priesthood is an Office belonging to the Kingdome of Heaven. It is an honour that is ranged upon holy ground,

and by it selfe. Worldly dignities . . . may be acquired (with lesse offence) by humane meanes, as bribery, ambition, and policie. But to take hold of this white robe with such dirty hands, is nothing lesse then to spit in the face of *Christ*, and to dishonour his Ordinance. He that doth it, and he that permits it to be done, agree like *Herod* and *Pilate*, to dispise and crucifie him. They that Countenance and ratifie such disorders, take care to provide so many *Judasses* to betray Christ, and then vote the treason to be lawfull. (Martin, pp. 347-48)

These passages provide a context within which we can respond to the demonic implications of the underground passage of the stream in "Religion" and of the "veines of *Sulphur*" there on which it seizes. Like these passages, the poem presents the Puritan priest and the Puritan church as demonic parodies of the true priest and the true Church. The antithesis is focused by "that *Samaritans* dead *Well*" and "the springing rock" prayed for in the last stanza. The allusions are to Jesus's answer to the woman of Samaria in John 4: 13-14: "Whosoever drinketh of this water shall thirst again: But whosoever drinketh of the water that I shall give him shall never thirst; but the water that I shall give him shall be in him a well of water springing up into everlasting life." In "the springing rock" there is also an echo of Exodus 17: 6, traditionally interpreted as a type of Christ's ministry and thus of the true Church: "Thou shalt smite the rock, and there shall come water out of it, that the people may drink."

A satiric attack on the "zeal" of these "Saints" is again the central theme of "The Constellation" (Martin, p. 469). The opening meditation on the order and obedience of the stars is often spoken of, not only as though it were the main point of the poem, but as an example of an alleged "personal response to Nature" on Vaughan's part. The idea that the stars exhibited an ideal divine order was a commonplace of medieval and Renaissance thought, going all the way back to Aristotle's idea that planetary motion was perfect (i.e., circular) motion. The poem's central antithesis between the order of the heavens and the disorder of the world is developed in several of Vaughan's Boethian translations[10] and in *The World Contemned,* his translation of a discourse by Eucherius:

> You see also how the dayes and the years, and all the bright Ornaments and Luminaries of Heaven, do with an unwearied duty execute the commands and decrees of their Creatour; and in a constant, irremissive tenour continue obedient to his ordinances. And shall wee (for whose use these lights were created, and set in the firmament,) seeing we know our Masters will, and are not ignorant of his Commandements, stop our ears against them? (Martin, p. 325)

The stars' order and obedience is elaborated in "The Constellation" as an ideal perspective, a standard by which to define and evaluate the reality of man's life. The development of the antithesis in the first seven stanzas refers to man in general, but as Vaughan recapitulates the antithetical pattern, returning to the image of the stars in the eighth stanza, the poem focuses on more specific, contemporary examples of the general theme:

> But seeks he your *Obedience, Order, Light,*
>   Your calm and wel-train'd flight,
> Where, though the glory differ in each star,
>   Yet is there peace still, and no war?
>
> Since plac'd by him who calls you by your names
>   And fixt there all your flames,
> Without Command you never acted ought
>   And then you in your Courses fought.
>
> But here Commission'd by a black self-wil
>   The sons the father kil,
> The Children Chase the mother, and would heal
>   The wounds they give, by crying, zeale.

Satire [103]

> Then Cast her bloud, and tears upon thy book
> Where they for fashion look,
> And like that Lamb that had the Dragons voice
> Seem mild, but are known by their noise.
>
> Thus by our lusts disorder'd into wars
> Our guides prove wandring stars,
> Which for these mists, and black days were reserv'd,
> What time we from our first love swerv'd.

The central antithesis between God's will and "black self-wil" is focused by the ironic echo of "Command" in "Commission'd." The antithesis between celestial order and a world "disorder'd into wars" is focused by the description of the world's guides as "wandring stars" and the insistence that in the heavens there is "peace still, and no war." The black self-will which brings on these "black days," contrasting with the "Fair, order'd lights" which obey God's will, is directly linked, by the last line quoted above, with original sin: this Rebellion is an antitype of man's first disobedience. Emphasizing the execution of the King and the persecution of the Church, the poem presents the Rebellion as the product of an autonomous lust for "glory" dissembled by hypocritical appeals to the authority of the Bible—the book of the very God whose Church the rebels afflict.[11]

The imagery of darkness is found in conjunction with similar charges of hypocrisy and oppression in Vaughan's note to the reader of *Flores Solitudinis* (1654): "I write unto thee out of a land of darkenesse . . . where destruction passeth for propagation, and a thick black night for the glorious day-spring" (Martin, p. 217). Translating *Of Life and Death*, he adds his own savage affidavit to Nierembergius's evidence of the miseries of life, speaking of people "plundered, tortured, murthered, and martyred; their murtherers in the mean time pretending Religion, Piety, and the Glory of God" whereas they are actually full of "tyranny, covetousnesse, & sacriledge varnished outwardly with godly pretences, dissembled purity, and the stale shift of liberty of Conscience" (Martin, p. 278). Again, in the *Life of Paulinus*, he declares that Paulinus "preferred the indignation and hatred of the multitude to their love, he would not buy their friendship with the losse of Heaven, nor call those Saints and propagators, who were Devills and destroyers" (Martin, p. 346). Earlier he had contrasted Paulinus, as one of the true "Saints of God," with the "prosperous tyrants of this world; which like noysome exhalations, moving for a time in the Eye of the Sun, fall afterwards to the earth, where they rot and perish under the *chaines of darkness*" (Martin, p. 339). And in the same work he finds historical precedent for the sufferings of the Church:

> It was a perillous dissolutenesse of some Bishops in that Century, to admit of Lay-men, and unseason'd persons into the Ministry. . . . which complying afterwards with all manner of Interests, have torne out the bowels of their Mother. Wee need no examples: Wee have lived to see all this our selves. Ignorance and obstinacie make *Hereticks*: And ambition makes *Schismaticks*; when they are once at this passe, they are on the way toward *Atheisme*. (Martin, p. 354)

Introducing his translation of Anselm's "Discourse of the blessed state of the Saints in the New Jerusalem," entitled *Man in Glory*, Vaughan puts special emphasis on the difficulties of the church in Anselm's time, glancing parenthetically at the contemporary scene: "Anselmus Archbishop of *Canterbury* lived here in *Britaine*, in the reigne of *Rufus*, and striving to keep entire the Immunities of the Church, (which the spirit of Covetousnesse and Sacriledge did then begin to encroach upon,) he was twice banished" (Martin, p. 192). The verse following this declares the persecution of the church in Vaughan's time to be far more severe than in Anselm's and mocks the Puritans' abolition of episcopacy by insisting on Anselm's episcopal rank: "Here holy *Anselme* lives in ev'ry page, / And sits Arch-bishop still, to vex the age" (Martin, p. 193). Translating a provocative passage in *Hermetical Physick*, Vaughan twice substitutes the word "Saints" for

Nollius's neutral Latin, obviously for the purpose of directing this account of barbarism and hypocrisy toward the Puritans:

> And what then is one man to another? who smiles, when he hates, salutes and embraceth, when he intends destruction, who under a serene smooth countenance hides poyson, violence and blood-shed. . . . they have (indeed) the complexions of men, but the conditions of Devils. . . . But thou wilt reply, that Salvages, Barbarians, and Canibals, may (perhaps) commit such villanies. Art thou no better acquainted with our Saints of *Europe*? that humane society and commerce, that godlinesse and sanctity, which we so much celebrate and commend our selves for, is nothing else but meere monopolizing, meere deceit, and a mutuall imposture. And amongst us Saints, who (in our owne opinion) are mighty righteous, tender-hearted and brotherly, there is nothing more usuall, then to have store of *Anthropophagi*, or Men-eaters. (Martin, p. 554)

These quotations from the prose works echo the language of Vaughan's most violent and powerful denunciation of the Puritans, "The Proffer" (Martin, p. 486). When we keep in mind how often Vaughan cites the Puritans as Satanic, hell-born enemies of God, religion, and the truly religious soul, and as the most prominent examples of a degenerate worldliness masquerading as piety, it seems more than coincidence that, addressing some "black Parasites" who exhibit all these characteristics, he should speak of "your Commonwealth" immediately after speaking of "my Crown." Hutchinson suggests that the poem may reflect Vaughan's refusal of an offer of profitable employment under the Commonwealth regime.[12] Referring to himself as on the brink of death,[13] the speaker refuses to contaminate his soul and endanger his hopes of Paradise by making a league with the Devil's followers:

> O poys'nous, subtile fowls!
> The flyes of hell

> That buz in every ear, and blow on souls
> > Until they smell
> And rot, descend not here, nor think to stay,
> > I've read, who 'twas, drove you away.
> . . . .
> > Shall my short hour, my inch,
> > > My one poor sand,
> > And crum of life, now ready to disband
> > > Revolt and flinch,
> > And having born the burthen all the day,
> > Now cast at night my Crown away?
>
> > No, No; I am not he,
> > > Go seek elsewhere.
> > I skill not your fine tinsel, and false hair,
> > > Your Sorcery
> > And smooth seductions: I'le not stuff my story
> > With your Commonwealth and glory.

As well as referring to the crown of immortality, the speaker's refusal to "Revolt" and cast away his "Crown" expresses Vaughan's refusal to surrender his political and religious allegiances after suffering so much for them. In his reading of the poem as an allegory of spiritual pilgrimage, in which the parasitic night birds represent the partisans of worldly temptation, R. A. Durr disregards its topical dimension, just as Hutchinson, on the other hand, disregards the archetypal, mythic dimension which Durr explicates.[14] These readings are not in conflict, and that is itself a central fact. Both are valid, and therefore neither is adequate without the other, for in this poem, as is characteristic of his sacred verse, Vaughan perceives and interprets historical circumstances (which include his personal circumstances) in terms of the archetypal patterns of Christian myth. He conceives of his own times and of his personal experiences in them typologically —that is, he sees history as the recurrent fulfillment of Biblical prophecy, the exfoliation through time of a timeless myth. Thus the image of the crown which he refuses to cast away in "The Proffer" is a synecdoche of both eternal salvation and the Royalist cause, and the point of his refusal is that the two are interdependent, that to abandon the one would be to abandon the other. The crown is also—and we can see the fusion of mythic and topical meanings most clearly when we see this—Christ's crown of thorns, which symbolizes the suffering servant, the last who shall be first. The crown is the "burthen" which the speaker refuses to cast away "Now . . . at night," having borne it "all the day." The burden, in topical terms, is the oppression which Vaughan suffered as a partisan of the defeated Royalist and Anglican cause; and *that* burden, expressed in mythic or symbolic terms, is the burden which Christ bade men take up and follow him, the suffering for his sake for which the sufferer will be blessed when, having been faithful unto death, his crown of thorns will be transmuted to a crown of immortality, his affliction transmuted to glory. The poem expresses Vaughan's acceptance of the advice which he gave the reader of *The Mount of Olives*: "running thy race with patience, look to JESUS the Authour and finisher of thy faith, who when he was reviled, reviled not againe. Presse thou towards the mark, *and let the people and their Seducers rage*; be faithful unto the death, and he will give thee a Crowne of life" (Martin, p. 141).

The corrupt reality beneath the "fine tinsel, and false hair," the "Sorcery / And smooth seducements" of "The Proffer" is powerfully expressed by violently antithetical language of physical infection and corruption in the first stanza quoted above. Most of all, what Vaughan saw beneath the specious surface was the guilt of innocent blood, associated in his mind with the crime of crucifying Christ. For example, in "The Men of War" (Martin, p. 516), he exclaims:

> seeing Soldiers long ago
> Did spit on thee, and smote thee too;
> Crown'd thee with thorns, and bow'd the knee,

> But in contempt, as still we see,
> I'le marvel not at ought they do,
> Because they us'd my Savior so;
> Since of my *Lord* they had their will,
> The servant must not take it ill.

Just as those men of war had killed not a mere man but the Messiah, so these had killed a man who was also a king. Vaughan was certainly thinking of the rebels when he wrote in "Abels blood" (Martin, p. 523):

> If single thou
> (Though single voices are but low,)
> Could'st such a shrill and long cry rear
> As speaks still in thy makers ear,
> What thunders shall those men arraign
> Who cannot count those they have slain,
> Who bath not in a shallow flood,
> But in a deep, wide sea of blood?

A few lines later, he begs God to "accept / Of his vow'd heart, whom thou hast kept / From bloody men!" In the "Prayer in adversity" he exclaims that his enemies have "washed their hands in the blood of my friends, my dearest and nearest relatives" (Martin, p. 167). The friends are identified by the elegies addressed to "R. W." and "R. Hall" in *Olor Iscanus*; as Hutchinson suggests, "my dearest and nearest relatives" may indicate that the death of the poet's brother William in 1648 was due to wounds received in the Civil War.[15]

The poisonous night birds of "The Proffer" reappear in Vaughan's elegiac eclogue on the death of his brother, "Daphnis" (Martin, p. 676).[16] "And is't not just to leave those to the night, / That madly hate, and persecute the light?" is the reaction of Menalcas to the fact of Daphnis's death. This figurative comment on the Puritan regime is continued in the same antithetical imagery as night comes on and the shepherds depart:

All creatures that were favourites of day
Are with the Sun retir'd and gone away.
While feral Birds send forth unpleasant notes,
And night (the Nurse of thoughts,) sad thoughts promotes.

Damon's lament for "A fatal sadness, such as still foregoes, / Then runs along with publick plagues and woes" is elaborated in unmistakeable terms by Menalcas:

Heaven's just displeasure & our unjust ways
Change Natures course, bring plagues dearth and decays.
This turns our lands to Dust, the skies to Brass,
Makes old kind blessings into curses pass.
And when we learn unknown and forraign Crimes,
Brings in the vengeance due unto those Climes.
The dregs and puddle of all ages now
Like Rivers near their fall, on us do flow.

Two of the "*holy and apposite* Ejaculations" in *The Mount of Olives* echo Vaughan's recommendation to the reader: "running thy race with patience, look to JESUS the Authour and finisher of thy faith, who when he was reviled, reviled not againe." "*Give thy peace unto thy servant, O God . . . In patience, O Lord, let me possesse my soul,*" is the proper response "When thou art provoked to anger"; and the proper exclamation "For thine Enemies" is "*Lord, lay not this sinne to their Charge; they know not what they do*" (Martin, p. 154). The patience in affliction and the love and forgiveness of enemies recommended so strongly in these places were Vaughan's moral ideals and the basic principles of his faith. A similar quietist philosophy, directed toward plucking the beam from one's own eye, is the central theme of Vaughan's translation from Plutarch, *Of the Benefit Wee may get by our Enemies*:

It is an easie matter to be wittie, lowd, and bitter in our revilinges, but to be the man upon whom those taunts cannot justly fasten, there lyes the difficulty. And truly it seemes that god by that divine Injunction *Nosce teipsum*, warnes none so much as those, who are the revilers and rebukers of others, lest happily, while they take the liberty to speak what they will, they may heare what they will not. (Martin, p. 102)

Plutarch's advice on how to carry oneself before an enemy is close to the supreme Christian example:

silence . . . in the presence of a rayling Enemie is full of majesty, wisedome, and fortitude. . . . there is nothing in the world hath more of worth and gallantrie in it, than to beare the *big browes* of a base, upstart foe with a calme and smiling carriage. . . . a kind of virtuous Contempt. . . . But to forbeare revenge upon an Enemie, when wee opportunely may, is the highest glory in all humanity. (Martin, p. 105)

Enough has been said in this chapter to show that Vaughan was one of "the revilers and rebukers of others." We owe the picturesque revilings which make up a large part of his anti-Puritan satire to the fact that he often failed in his faith, failed to possess his soul in patience or to entertain anything like forgiveness, let alone love, for his enemies. The success of the Rebellion—seen especially in the execution of the King and the persecution of the Church—was a severe trial of faith for Vaughan. This is shown not only by the lapses from that faith reflected in many of the satirical passages, but in the many places where he bases his prayers for the grace to be patient and forgiving precisely on the triumphs of his enemies. The bulk of his sacred verse expresses his struggles with *Nosce teipsum*. We can only speculate that this turning of his gaze inward upon his own soul was in large part motivated, in the manner recommended by Plutarch and by Christ, by his intense awareness of the evil of his enemies. It seems likely, in view of the frequency with which his consciousness of sin, his repentance, and his prayers for grace and strength are expressed in relation to his awareness of an abundance of evil all about him in the world.

Stoic resignation and Christian patience and love are alike inimical to the satiric spirit, which thrives rather in those of us who feel free to be "wittie, lowd, and bitter in our revilinges." Vaughan's agonizing struggles to overcome this spirit in himself are part of the story of his anti-Puritan satire. There is the anguish of intense personal grief, and a violent struggle to overcome the hatred proceeding from that grief, in the "Prayer in adversity, and troubles occasioned by our Enemies":

> Thou seest, O God, how furious and Implacable mine Enemies are, they have not only rob'd me of that portion and provision which thou hadst graciously given me, but they have also washed their hands in the blood of my friends, my dearest and nearest relatives. . . . Keep me . . . O my God, from the guilt of blood, and suffer me not to stain my soul with the thoughts of recompense and vengeance, which is a branch of thy great prerogative, and belongs wholly unto thee. Though they persecute me unto death . . . yet Lord, give me thy grace, and such a measure of charity as may fully forgive them. Suffer me not to open my mouth in Curses, but give me the spirit of my Saviour, who reviled not again, but was dumb like a Lamb before his shearers. (Martin, p. 167)

In "Misery" (Martin, p. 472), Vaughan reflects upon the severe difficulty of stamping out "thoughts of recompense and vengeance" and of resisting the temptation to open his mouth in curses. He is "wilded by a peevish heart" because

> The Age, the present times are not
> To snudge in, and embrace a Cot,
> Action and bloud now get the game,
> Disdein treads on the peaceful name,
> Who sits at home too bears a loade
> Greater than those that gad abroad.

In "The Men of War" (Martin, p. 516), he lessons himself by paraphrasing Revelation 13:10: "He that leadeth into captivity shall go into captivity: he that killeth with the sword must be killed with the sword. Here is the patience and the faith of the saints." This is both a lesson for himself and an accusation and dire warning for the Puritans, the men of war to whom he applies Luke 23:11: "And Herod with his men of war set him at nought, and mocked *him*, and arrayed him in a gorgeous robe, and sent him again to Pilate." The false saintliness of the men of war is opposed to the patience of the true saints as Vaughan expresses his struggle to choose aright:

> Were not thy word (dear Lord!) my light,
> How would I run to endless night,
> And persecuting thee and thine,
> Enact for *Saints* my self and mine.
> But now enlighten'd thus by thee,
> I dare not think such villany;
> Nor for a temporal self-end
> Successful wickedness commend.
> For in this bright, instructing verse
> Thy Saints are not the Conquerors;
> But patient, meek, and overcome
> Like thee, when set at naught and dumb.

The hypothesis of his own wickedness is in part a device for ironically exhibiting the villainy of the Puritans as well as an expression of actual temptation. The conclusion of the poem emphasizes the latter:

> Give me humility and peace,
> Contented thoughts, innoxious ease,
> A sweet, revengeless, quiet minde,
> And to my greatest haters kinde.

Vaughan's anti-Puritan satire is a hypothetical destruction, a metaphorical tearing and rending, of his foes. He is constantly torn between giving vent to his hatred in thoughts of vengeance and the sort of sublimated vengeance described in *Of Temperance and Patience*:

> The conflicts of a good man with calamities are sacred: he is made a spectacle to the world, to Angels and men, and a hallowed *Present* to the Almighty. Let him in this state overcome his Enemies! A more glorious garland then the *Olympick* Olive-branches shall crown an enduring Patience, which by an humble, but overcomming Sufferance wearies the hands of those that beat us. It is the part of a wise man, to tire and weare out the malice of his Enemies. I say not by Suffering, but by Patience, which makes him neither their Patient, nor trampled upon, but a trampling overcomer. (Martin, pp. 232-33)

The sublimation of enmity in patience leads away from satire. The final phase of Vaughan's anti-Puritan satire is a vision of their literal, absolute destruction in an apocalyptic, divine act through which the vengeance denied Vaughan by his principles (and the military fortunes of his party) is finally wrought by God. He has the greatest difficulty in reconciling himself to the fact that "thoughts of recompense and vengeance" are part of God's great prerogative and that he must leave judgment to the Lord. But it is his final satisfaction to do just that, and to rehearse to himself the revenge of an angry God upon the enemies of Henry Vaughan. Ironically, the prayer for "A sweet, revengeless, quiet minde, / And to my greatest haters kinde" in "The Men of War" is immediately followed by the poet's anticipation of their eternal perdition:

> That when *thy Throne is set*, and all
> These *Conquerors* before it fall,
> I may be found (preserv'd by thee)
> Amongst that chosen company,
> Who by no blood (here) overcame
> But the blood of the *blessed Lamb*.

The central figure in these apocalyptic visions is *Christus victor*, the archetype of the Christian warrior-hero, who conquers Satan and all his crew forever. He is both Vaughan's personal champion and the champion of the Royalist cause. In "The day of Judgement" (Martin, p. 530), for example, the prayer for God to exercise his judgment rather than his mercy is predicated on the ravages of the Puritans:

> Sin every day commits more waste,
> And thy old enemy, which knows
> His time is short, more raging grows.
> Nor moan I onely (though profuse)
> Thy Creatures bondage and abuse;
> But what is highest sin and shame,
> The vile despight done to thy name;
> . . . .
>
> O God! though mercy be in thee
> The greatest attribute we see,
> And the most needful for our sins;
> Yet, when thy mercy nothing wins
> But meer disdain, let not man say
> *Thy arm doth sleep*; but write this day
> Thy judging one: Descend, descend!
> Make all things new! and without end!

Similarly, in the passage from "L'Envoy" quoted at the beginning of this chapter, the prayer for the apocalypse is based on the Puritans' persecution and desecration of Anglican churches and their multiplication of novel doctrines and forms of worship. "Corruption" (Martin, p. 440) is often discussed as though its central point were the long opening account of the spiritual affinity with God of "Man in those early days," as though its mood were merely one of nostalgia. But, as in "Religion" and "The Constellation," Vaughan adopts the pastoral mode here as a perspective for evaluating the contemporary scene; the evaluation leads to a generalized vision of human depravity and ends in another cry for divine vengeance on evildoers:

> Almighty *Love*! where art thou now? mad man
> Sits down, and freezeth on,
> He raves, and swears to stir nor fire, nor fan,
> But bids the thread be spun.
> I see, thy Curtains are Close-drawn; Thy bow
> Looks dim too in the Cloud,
> Sin triumphs still, and man is sunk below
> The Center, and his shrowd;
> All's in deep sleep, and night; Thick darknes lyes
> And hatcheth o'r thy people;
> But hark! what trumpets that? what Angel cries
> *Arise! Thrust in thy sickle.*

In Vaughan's very personal "Prayer in time of persecution and Heresie" (Martin, p. 166), he clearly prays God to take up the sword which he himself must lay down:

Arise O God, and let thine enemies be scattered, and let those that hate thee flee before thee. Behold, the robbers are come into thy Sanctuary, and the persecuters are within thy walls. We drink our own waters for money, and our wood is sold unto us. Our necks are under persecution, we labour and have no rest. . . . Wherefore dost thou forget us for ever, and forsake us for so long a time?[17]

Man in Darkness contains an equally militant, but more ironical, anticipation of judgment on sinners:

The *way* to heaven is *wet* and *slippery*, but it is made so with *teares* and not with *blood*. . . . It is ill coming to the *Lamb* of God in a *Wolfes* skin; They that do so, must be taught that he hath another *attribute*, and they shall finde him a *Lion*. (Martin, p. 182)

By far the most powerful of the apocalyptic visions in this final phase of Vaughan's anti-Puritan satire is to be found likewise in this discourse, as he anticipates a day of ultimate truth-telling in which God himself will be the irresistible satirist:

> Me thinks I see the remisse, lukewarme *professour*, and the *hypocritical, factious pretender* of *sanctity* looking up to the *Clouds*, and crying out, O *that throne! that flaming, white, and glorious throne! and he that sits thereon, with the sharp sickle in his hand and the crown of pure gold upon his head!* ... *Is he the Prince of life that was crown'd with thornes, scourged, spit upon, crucified, pierced through, and murthered, and comes he now to judge the world? Oh! It is he! It is he! miserable wretch that I am! What shall I do, or whither shall I go?*
>
> Such will be the *dreadful agonies* and *concertations* in that *day* betwixt the *Hypocrite* and his *conscience*, betwixt the *enemies* of Gods truth and their *gasping undone souls.* When the people that forget God shall go down quick into hell, and the secrets of all hearts shall be disclosed and laid open before Angels and men; For in that day all their dark and private *lusts,* their *closet-sins, bosome-councels, specious pretences,* and *bloody machinations,* which now (like so many *foul spirits*) lurk in their *gloomy breasts,* shall be forced out, and will appear as visible to all *mankind,* as if they were written with the *beams* of the *Sun* upon the pure and unclouded *firmament.* (Martin, p. 180)

B. Classical Themes

Sometimes, as in "A Rhapsodis" and the "Invitation to *Brecknock,"* the Puritans are the immediate objects of attack, but most of the satirical writing in Vaughan's secular verse is more general in scope, more detached from his immediate experiences and conflicts, than is the anti-Puritan satire discussed in the first section of this chapter. The translation of Juvenal's tenth satire is at the core of these poems, for most of them develop aspects of Juvenal's general satiric themes: the baseness of ambition, the destitution of riches, the squalor of "state," and, underlying all of these, pretension, self-delusion, and the unhappiness of a happiness vested in externals.[18] The Stoic conception of true happiness which provides the base and norm of Juvenal's satire is repeatedly echoed:

> Pray for a wise, and knowing soule . . .
> . . . .
> That starts not at misfortunes, that can sway,
> And keep all passions under locke and key;
> That covets nothing, wrongs none, and preferres
> An honest want before rich injurers;
> All this thou hast within thy selfe, and may
> Be made thy owne, if thou wilt take the way;
> What boots the worlds wild, loose applause? what can
> Fraile, perillous honours adde unto a man?
> What length of years, wealth, or a rich faire wife?
> Vertue alone can make a happy life.
> To a wise man nought comes amisse: but we
> Fortune adore, and make our Deity. (Martin, p. 31)

Vaughan chooses the failings of human nature, rather than topical events, circumstances, or personages, as his prime targets. His subjects are the general, perennial follies and obsessions of mankind which the Romans, with their broad ethical vision derived from Stoic philosophy, had made the central concerns of their satire. The key moral idea is the irrelevance of life's externals to human happiness; the folly of an excessive concern with externals is the central theme. The basic technique in this satire is to reveal or expose, to turn the fair surface of reality inside out to exhibit it as corrupt. This process of penetrating behind a false surface to a hidden reality is double, for the initial revaluation of externals which constitutes the satiric attack is followed or accompanied by a renewed penetration behind the corrupt exterior of life to a private interior of health and happiness. Paradox is the characteristic form of these poems; the speaker consistently leads us to truth by violating our ordinary sense of truth, usually by exhibiting, in a highly dramatic way, the incongruity between violently juxtaposed, contradictory entities.[19] The poems are packed full of topical allusions and concrete details, but this is not merely topical or descriptive poetry. Sometimes concretions fill out fictional *exempla* of the general theme, and these *exempla* are, usually, broadly drawn typical cases closely resembling in form the verbal emblems and "characters" then in vogue. More often the general theme arises from the speaker's passionate reflections upon a particular, dramatically conceived situation in which he is personally involved. The speaker's firm ethical vision creates a sense of distance between the reader and the phenomena of experience. With their colloquial diction and energetic prosody, the poems give us a sense of deep involvement with experience controlled and directed by an encompassing vision of its meaning and purpose.[20]

A poem that does not fit these generalizations, except in terms of style—a poem that shows Vaughan's satiric verve at its lightest and most humorous—is "Upon a Cloke lent him by Mr. J. *Ridsley*" (Martin, p. 52). Conceived dramatically as an epistle or speech accompanying the cloak's return to its owner, the poem is a brilliant parody of the contemporary style of extravagant compliment and effusive personal tribute. It caricatures the cloak as a stiff, shaggy, voluminous, burdensome monstrosity, dramatizing the speaker's discomforted resentment of it through a tone of excited speech marked by staccato ejaculations, a hurly-burly of remembered sensations—all preposterously unpleasant—and a breathless, irregular pace which builds several times to a crescendo of exasperation. That this is a mock-serious attack rather than a serious one, ironic rather than real vilification, is shown by the change in tone at the end. The speaker drops his mask and expresses sincere gratitude for the loan in direct language, excusing his exuberant fantasies by the ambition of his muse:

Satire [119]

> But I have done. And think not, friend, that I
> This freedome took to Jeere thy Courtesie,
> I thank thee for't, and I believe my Muse
> So known to thee, thou'lt not suspect abuse;
> She did this, 'cause (perhaps) thy *love* paid thus
> Might with my *thanks* out-live thy *Cloke*, and *Us*.

The freedom of his muse is clearly distinct from his own feelings; that is, the poem is a pure play of the imagination creating ironic hyperboles out of the hints of experience, and not a description of experience. As literary parody, a mock-serious tribute, it is an example of the ironic banter exchanged between intimate friends in the liberty of mutual confidence. The attack on the cloak is humorous because it contains a degree of truth which, directly expressed, would be improper in this situation. The attack disarms this truth by exaggerating it, thus rendering it untrue in one sense and reconciling it with a different kind of truth—the truth of the speaker's feelings for the lender. But we are constantly aware of both kinds of truth: the poet's friendship for Ridsley does not obliterate his discomfort with the cloak, nor does the extravagant expression of that discomfort render his gratitude insincere. The poem is unified by Vaughan's creation of an ironic balance between its conflicting elements. Like Catullus, Skelton, and Pope, he could write well on a trivial and humorous subject as well as on important and serious ones.

Campaigners are reputedly prone to reminisce. When the natural rigors of the campaign have been aggravated by such an incommodious garment as Ridsley's cloak, it seems natural for the hapless borrower to exclaim at once upon his experiences with it:

> Here, take again thy *Sack-cloth*! and thank heav'n
> Thy Courtship hath not kill'd me; Is't not Even
> Whether wee dye by peecemeale, or at once
> Since both but ruine, why then for the nonce
> Didst husband my afflictions, and cast o're

Me this forc'd *Hurdle* to inflame the score?
Had I neer *London* in this *Rug* been seen
Without doubt I had executed been
For some bold *Irish* spy, and crosse a sledge
Had layn mess'd up for their *foure gates* and *bridge*.

The qualities of this protective garment, designed to ward off colds and agues, are ironically inverted so that the cloak embodies all of the potential threat to the soldier of the war itself. His whimsical speculations on the fateful consequences of being seen in it near London hypothetically bring him to the death he has evaded at the hands of his enemies. The vigor and extravagance of these opening conceits establish the tone of the poem. They are developed in four well-defined phases which make up the poem's main structural components. Three episodes from the campaign are recalled and recounted in abundant detail, illustrating the intensity and plenitude of the cloak's discomforts (lines 11-18, 19-36, 37-64). In these there is a progressive increase in the concreteness and density of details and similitudes and a corresponding intensification of the speaker's excitement. The vividness of these episodes is amplified by repeated prods to the reader's imagination through the person of Ridsley: "Hadst thou been with me on that day . . ."; "O that thou hadst been there next morn . . ."; "Thou wouldst have ta'ne me. . . ." After the climax of the third episode, a new direction is signaled by the speaker's relieved "But (thanks to th' day!) 'tis off." The sense of pure fantasy, pure fun, is perhaps strongest in the fourth phase (lines 65-92), as the speaker ironically recommends a variety of incongruous uses for the cloak, his exuberant reflections culminating in the suggestion that it might well have served for armor "when this Jugling fate / Of Souldierie first seiz'd me":

I doe not doubt but (if the weight could please,)
'Twould guard me better than a *Lapland-lease,*
Or a *German* shirt with Inchanted lint
Stuff'd through, and th'devils *beard* and *face* weav'd in't.

The return to thoughts of the campaign in these final lines rounds out the body of the poem by providing a connecting link with the first three phases.

The consonantal thicket of lines 83-84—"I think't weav'd upon / Some stiffneckt *Brownists* exercising loome"—epitomizes the cloak's "*Horn'd* obstinacie," the speaker's mood, and Vaughan's capacity to embody meaning organically in the qualities of sound and rhythm. The headlong rush of the speaker's ideas and impressions overrides the formal pattern of meter and rhyme as enjambment and varied placement of the caesura create the irregularly stressful rhythm of impassioned speech. The formally constrained and even measure of the heroic couplet is made free and versatile, capable of the most varied effects, from precise, compressed definition to the surging, spacious energy of Shakespearian blank verse. A similar freedom, flexibility, and versatility is characteristic of Vaughan's many poems written in heroic couplets.[21] These qualities are revealed perhaps nowhere more fully than in this poem's exuberant ridicule of his fantastic appearance after sleeping naked in this absurd cloak:

> O that thou hadst been there next morn, that I
> Might teach thee new *Micro-cosmo-graphie*!
> Thou wouldst have ta'ne me, as I naked stood,
> For one of th' *seven pillars* before the floud,
> Such *Characters* and *Hierogliphicks* were
> In one night worn, that thou mightst justly swear
> I'd slept in *Cere-cloth*, or at *Bedlam* where
> The mad men lodge in straw, I'le not forbear
> To tell thee all, his wild *Impress* and *tricks*
> Like *Speeds* old *Britans* made me look, or *Picts*;
> His villanous, biting, *Wire-embraces*
> Had seal'd in me more strange formes and faces
> Than *Children* see in dreams, or thou hast read
> In *Arras*, *Puppet-playes*, and *Ginger-bread*,
> With *angled Schemes*, and *Crosses* that bred fear
> Of being handled by some *Conjurer*,

And neerer thou wouldst think (such *strokes* were drawn)
I'd been some rough statue of *Fetter-lane*,
Nay, I believe, had I that instant been
By *Surgeons* or *Apothecaries* seen,
They had Condemned my raz'd skin to be
Some walking *Herball*, or *Anatomie*.[22]

The gaiety of "To his retired friend, an Invitation to *Brecknock*" (Martin, p. 46), also in the epistolary form, is heavily shaded with grimmer impressions of the war—disorder, oppression, "black deeds." Just as the Stoics saw the possibility of virtuous public action smothered by the corruption and disorder of society, and pointed instead toward the cultivation of private virtue in the intimate society of friends, so this poem develops the antithesis pinpointed by lines 75-76: "let us / 'Midst noise and War, of Peace, and mirth discusse." The fact that the speaker derides "the times ridiculous miserie" with Democritean contempt does not mean, as John Greenleaf Whittier took it to mean, that Vaughan was indifferent to the tribulations of his society;[23] intentional fallacies aside, it means, as Democritus's laughter meant, that he has abandoned hope of stemming the tide of corruption that swirls about him, that he sees no honorable course of action save to preserve his own innocence and maintain in himself the values which society at large has surrendered:

> This portion thou wert born for: why should wee
> Vex at the times ridiculous miserie?
> An age that thus hath fool'd it selfe, and will
> (Spite of thy teeth and mine) persist so still.
> Let's sit then at this *fire*, and while wee steal
> A Revell in the Town, let others seal,
> Purchase or Cheat, and who can, let them pay,
> Till those black deeds bring on the darksome day;
> Innocent spenders wee![24]

The poem's mirth is the ironic, bitter kind that is only one step from despair. It expresses a nonheroic sort of resistance to social corruption that is essentially similar, in its view of the relation between the self and society, to the resistance that Vaughan would develop, in terms of Christian sanctity and devotion rather than of mirth, virtue, or happiness, in his sacred poems and prose. The poem's basic idea that a virtuous man should remain cheerful amidst tribulation and adversity as an antidote to wickedness in others and despair in himself is found over and over again in Vaughan's Boethian translations. It is an aspect of the general idea, central in Plato's *Phaedo* and in Stoic philosophy, that the soul preserves its original virtue by remaining aloof from the contaminating influences of the corrupt temporal world and indifferent to its vacillating conditions. Aspects of this idea are central in a number of Vaughan's sacred poems, notably "The Retreate" and "The Night." The idea that adversity is disarmed by cheerfulness is the explicit point of "To my worthy friend Master *T. Lewes*" (Martin, p. 61):

> Sorrows and sighes and searches spend
> And draw our bottome to an end,
> But discreet Joyes lengthen the lease
> Without which life were a disease,
> And who this age a Mourner goes,
> Doth with his tears but feed his foes.

The speaker's extravagant, whimsical speculations about his friend's long absence, expressing a free, vigorous play of the mind, establish the festive mood at the base of the poem. This mood is self-generating, an expression of a natural vitality, and not a response to external stimuli. It is the perspective through which external conditions in the town are observed and evaluated, and those conditions are directly antithetical to the speaker's mood—cause for grief, disgust, and scorn rather than joy. The disarming of adversity by cheerfulness, a function of the mind's superiority to temporal conditions, is expressed by the speaker's facetious presentation of these conditions as symptoms of the town's distress for her absent friend:

> The Town believes thee lost, and didst thou see
> But half her suffrings, now distrest for thee,
> Thou'ldst swear (like *Rome*) her foule, polluted walls
> Were sackt by *Brennus*, and the salvage *Gaules*.
> Abominable face of things! here's noise
> Of bang'd Mortars, blew Aprons, and Boyes,
> Pigs, Dogs, and Drums, with the hoarse hellish notes
> Of politickly-deafe Usurers throats,
> With new fine *Worships*, and the old cast *teame*
> Of Justices vext with the *Cough*, and *flegme*.
> Midst these the *Crosse* looks sad, and in the *Shire-*
> *-Hall furs* of an old *Saxon Fox* appear,
> With brotherly Ruffs and Beards, and a strange sight
> Of high Monumentall Hats ta'ne at the flight
> Of *Eighty eight*; while ev'ry *Burgesse* foots
> The mortall *Pavement* in eternall boots.

In its imitation of the hectic stresses of excited speech, the passage is typical of the poem as a whole. The rhythm is heavy with monosyllables and alliteration, and the violent tone of the language, reflecting the speaker's excitement and the disorder of the scene, is accentuated by harsh sounds and a dense accumulation of details. Though the Puritans are implicated as agents of the town's violent disruption, the townsfolk themselves are more directly involved, for it was in fact they who sacked the walls of Brecon to avoid a military siege.[25] Their degeneracy and barbarism are expressed by the passage's animal imagery, by the comparisons with savage Gauls and the sacking of Rome—symbol of civilization itself—and by the emphasis on their preoccupation with usury and trade. Their pretentiousness is ridiculed by "high Monumentall Hats" and the incongruous "eternall boots." The passage vividly conveys impressions of civil and moral disorder effected by men who are as ludicrously arrogant as they are successful in their "abominable" activities.

The antithetical festive mood of the speaker is developed further by the continuation of his whimsical speculations in the

Satire [125]

second paragraph. The grotesque asceticism hypothetically attributed to the friend parodies the Puritans' austerity in a manner which we have encountered before. The constraint and affliction of his supposed penance, as he sits like a badger "In the dark hole . . . rooting up of books," is parallel to the quality of life in the ruined town.[26] This "sullen state," which the friend is exhorted to abandon in favor of vinous revelry, is cognate with the blighting conditions of dullness, dishonesty, baseness, and barbarity which afflict the speaker. The furtiveness of "steal / A Revell in the Town" implies the speaker's defiance of those conditions, the effects of which are further expressed by the frozen immobility of nature "while the slow Isicle hangs / At the stiffe thatch, and Winters frosty pangs / Benumme the year." As S. L. Bethell says of these lines, "the stiffness of the frost has got into the words";[27] the thick mesh of consonants and the sluggish rhythm enact the meaning, as in "the dull *Market-landlord* with his *Rout* / Of sneaking Tenants durtily swill out / This harmlesse liquor." The speaker's defiance of this "sullen" state of things is fully developed in the antithetical theme of freedom, joy, inspiration, and friendship, conveyed by the invitation to saturnalia, the conceit of wine's inspirational powers, the delight in love poetry, and the Cavalier affectation of amorous gallantry and moral imprecision. The third paragraph, in which this festive theme is most fully conveyed, is even more hectic and passionate than earlier passages. The lines have a vigorous thrust and sweep, with spacious rhythmical units created by enjambment and by great flexibility in clause length and placement of the caesura. The rapid swirl of declamation embodying the invitation is fitly accentuated by assonant sounds and by consonants that speak trippingly on the tongue:

> Come! leave this sullen state, and let not Wine
> And precious Witt lye dead for want of thine,
> Shall the dull *Market-land-lord* with his *Rout*
> Of sneaking Tenants durtily swill out
> This harmlesse liquor? shall they knock and beat

For Sack, only to talk of *Rye*, and *Wheat*?
O let not such prepost'rous tipling be
In our *Metropolis*, may I ne'r see
Such *Tavern-sacrilege*, nor lend a line
To weep the *Rapes* and *Tragedy* of wine!
Here lives that *Chimick*, quick fire which betrayes
Fresh Spirits to the bloud, and warms our layes,
I have reserv'd 'gainst thy approach a Cup
That were thy Muse stark dead, shall raise her up,
And teach her yet more Charming words and skill
Than ever *Coelia*, *Chloris*, *Astrophil*,
Or any of the Thredbare names Inspir'd
Poore riming lovers with a *Mistris* fir'd.
Come then!

The sort of celebration anticipated in this poem is dramatized in "A Rhapsodis" (Martin, p. 10). As Marilla points out, the poem is "an attempt to catch in imagery and rhythm the progressive effects of 'royall, witty Sacke' and thus to dramatize the act of losing one's cares in a traditional alcoholic way."[28] The festive mood, the expression of "honest mirth," becomes increasingly self-absorbed, more remote from the world outside the speaker and his small group of friends. That is, the poem dramatizes the withdrawal from the world into a more limited society urged in the "Invitation to *Brecknock*." The drinking song at the end of the poem marks the completion of that withdrawal, as the revelers become totally absorbed in their "merry, mad mirth." As in the Brecknock poem, the satiric theme is developed through the interaction between the speaker's mirth and the objective world.

The extravagant development of the opening conceit—"Darknes, & Stars i'th' mid day! they invite / Our active fancies to beleeve it night"—has the effect of substituting the artificial order of the painting for the regular order of nature. The speaker's energetic fancy compels that chamber in the Globe Tavern to become the world. His description of the painted scene activates and animates it, endowing this imaginary order with principles of operation analogous to those of the real world, from which, presented as the speaker's real environment, it becomes indistinguishable:

> That artificiall Cloud with it's curl'd brow,
> Tels us 'tis late; and that blew space below
> Is fir'd with many Stars; Marke, how they breake
> In silent glaunces o're the hills, and speake
> The Evening to the Plaines; where shot from far,
> They meet in dumbe salutes, as one great Star.
>   The roome (me thinks) growes darker; & the aire
> Contracts a sadder colour, and lesse faire:
> Or is't the Drawers skill, hath he no Arts
> To blind us so, we cann't know pints from quarts?
> No, no, 'tis night; looke where the jolly Clowne
> Musters his bleating heard, and quits the Downe.
> Harke! how his rude pipe frets the quiet aire,
> Whilst ev'ry Hill proclaimes *Lycoris* faire.
> Rich, happy man! that canst thus watch, and sleep,
> Free from all cares; but thy wench, pipe & sheep.

This pastoral idyll, charged with light and moving in the orderly rhythms of peace and happiness, thus becomes an embodiment of the speaker's feelings and values. This imaginative absorption of the real world into a work of art epitomizes the power of fancy over externals and also makes the painting an objective, living symbol of the speaker's "mirth." Vaughan has ingeniously "varied" the traditional fiction of a pastoral paradise and used it, as the writers of Renaissance pastoral tended to use it, as a satiric device. The qualities of the world inhabited by the speaker within the tavern are juxtaposed to the violently antithetical qualities of life in the streets outside; the vigorous street scene which follows is similarly animated, but here the movement is violent, harsh, and chaotic:

> Should we goe now a wandring, we should meet
> With Catchpoles, whores, & Carts in ev'ry street:

> Now when each narrow lane, each nooke & Cave,
> Signe-posts, & shop-doors, pimp for ev'ry knave,
> When riotous sinfull plush, and tell-tale spurs
> Walk Fleet street, & the Strand, when the soft stirs
> Of bawdy, ruffled Silks, turne night to day;
> And the lowd whip, and Coach scolds all the way;
> When lust of all sorts, and each itchie bloud
> From the Tower-wharfe to Cymbelyne, and Lud,
> Hunts for a Mate, and the tyr'd footman reeles
> 'Twixt chaire-men, torches, & the hackny wheels.[29]

Within the tavern, the speaker draws into his mirth Caligula, Julius Caesar, and Sulla, whose common bond is some form of enmity for republican government. Specific acts of contempt and defiance of the Roman Senate are singled out for eulogy in the toasts to Caligula and Julius Caesar. These toasts obliquely pour scorn on the English Parliament and express the speaker's defiance of it, implicating the Parliament in the moral chaos and degeneracy which the previous paragraph has presented as the predominant qualities of London life. Particularly expressive details are the animal imagery for the Parliament in the first toast and the suggestions of stupidity, cowardice, dishonesty, and paltry cunning in the second. The power of the Parliament in London society is the culminating point of its corruption, the decisive element in the speaker's contemptuous withdrawal from that society into a joyful communion with intimate friends, represented by the peace, order, and contentment of the pastoral. Finally he imagines them, through the inspirational powers of wine, friendship, and mirth itself, moving "Equally with the gods above"—an apotheosis which places them far above the pastoral world and still farther above the chaos of London.

The pretentious affectations of "blood and state," as illustrated by London's fops, are the subject of "*To Lysimachus, the Author being with him in* London" (Martin, p. 632). Again the poem is dramatically conceived as an address to a particular person on a particular occasion. We are repeatedly made aware of the presence of Lysimachus through the speaker's adoption of direct address, the major satiric points of the first paragraph being introduced by a series of six rhetorical questions. The positive values and satiric viewpoint of the speaker are expressed through a development of his friend's character, as the public display and social arrogance which constitute the pride of the "trim'd *Gallants*" are contrasted with the simplicity, obscurity, and privacy of Lysimachus's life. The last line employs imagery of light and darkness paradoxically to pinpoint a satiric reversal of the world's ordinary values: "Thy darkest nights outshine their brightest dayes." The same imagery is used straightforwardly to develop the normative qualities of the inner life in terms of virtue and divine knowledge:

>   Wonders my Friend at this? what is't to thee,
> Who canst produce a nobler Pedigree,
> And in meer truth affirm thy Soul of kin
> To some bright *Star*, or to a *Cherubin*?
> When these in their profuse *moods* spend the night
> With the same sins, they drive away the light,
> Thy learned *thrift* puts her to use; while she
> Reveals her firy Volume unto thee;
> And looking on the separated skies
> And their clear Lamps with careful thoughts & eyes
> Thou break'st through Natures upmost rooms & bars
> To Heav'n, and there conversest with the Stars.

Lysimachus's enlightened soul is in opposition to the "blind discourse" of worldly pride. The fops' fantastic, affected gait, gaudy dress, and arrogant demeanor are topped by a flaunting of ancestry that is set off against Lysimachus's "nobler Pedigree":

>   What blind discourse the *Heroes* did afford?
> This *Lady* was their Friend, and such a *Lord*.
> How much of *Blood* was in it? one could tell
> He came from *Bevis* and his *Arundel*;

Morglay was yet with him, and he could do
More feats with it, than his old Grandsire too.

The dramatization of an intellectual ascent "through Natures upmost rooms & bars / To Heav'n" is the central structural principle of *"The importunate Fortune"* (Martin, p. 634). Though *"written to Doctor* Powel *of* Cantre," the poem is a dramatic monologue, directly protesting the enticements of a personified Fortune, rather than an epistle. Fortune's presence as an interlocutor in a dramatic situation is constantly stressed by the speaker's remonstrations: "For shame desist . . ."; "Leave off . . ."; "But thou wilt urge me still. Away, be gone"; "Why do'st thou tempt me . . . ?"; "I'le to my Speculations"; "Then leave to Court me. . . ." The speaker's dramatization of an imaginary "progress into ev'ry Sphere" arises out of this basic situation as an expression of the values on which his resistance to the deceptive and inferior amenities of Fortune is based. The basic metaphor of a royal progress imports the notion of the soul's kingliness—its dominion over the entire realm commanded by Fortune and more besides. The central point of the satiric attack on Fortune is neatly made by the play of antitheses in

> Is't best
> To be confin'd to some dark narrow chest
> And Idolize thy Stamps, when I may be
> Lord of all Nature, and not slave to thee?
> The world's my Palace. I'le contemplate there,
> And make my progress into ev'ry Sphere.
> The Chambers of the *Air* are mine; those three
> Well furnish'd *Stories* my possession be.
> I hold them all *in Capite* . . .

The connotations of freedom, sovereignty, and plenitude in this passage are further developed in the succeeding series of conceits which parallel the speaker's possession with the gifts of Fortune and dramatize his elevation to the uppermost regions of the terrestrial sphere. The Hermetic *Libellus* adapted for the account of his progress through the celestial spheres describes, as L. C. Martin says, "the processes which succeed the dissolution of the material body."[30] But the speaker here is dramatizing ecstasis, demonstrating that "though my Body you confined see, / My boundless thoughts have their *Ubiquitie*." The process is one of purgation and purification correlated with a progressive increase in spiritual freedom, sovereignty, and fullness of being. Among other things, the passage conveys the Aristotelian definition of motion as an entity's realization of its nature. It does not merely assert the speaker's superiority to Fortune; it demonstrates it through a *narratio* which dramatizes his progressive liberation from Fortune's world of natural accidents and from the moral impairments produced by the soul's involvement in that world. His apotheosis, the culmination of his "auspicious flight," places him close to the divine source of creativity and intelligent guidance in the universe—a position from which, like God, he looks down upon a cosmic panorama which easily comprehends the "great World" of Fortune's dominion. Thus he both proves the absurdity of her efforts to enthrall him and effects the immunity from her that he so vigorously seeks:

> First my dull Clay I give unto the *Earth*,
> Our common Mother, which gives all their birth.
> My growing Faculties I send as soon
> Whence first I took them, to the humid *Moon*.
> All Subtilties and every cunning Art
> To witty *Mercury* I do impart.
> Those fond Affections which made me a slave
> To handsome Faces, *Venus* thou shalt have.
> And saucy Pride (if there was ought in me,)
> *Sol*, I return it to thy Royalty.
> My daring Rashness and Presumptions be
> To *Mars* himself an equal Legacy.
> My ill-plac'd Avarice (sure 'tis but small;)
> *Jove*, to thy Flames I do bequeath it all.

. . . .

    Get up my disintangled Soul, thy fire
Is now refin'd & nothing left to tire,
Or clog thy wings. Now my auspicious flight
Hath brought me to the *Empyrean* light.
I am a sep'rate *Essence*, and can see
The *Emanations* of the Deitie. . . .

    Satire on riches is the most common theme of these poems. It is touched upon in most of those we have looked at, and is central in "To his friend ———," "*In Amicum foeneratorem*," and "To Amoret Weeping." The first of these (Martin, p. 44) attacks the unjust distribution of wealth, concentrating on the imbalance between spiritual and material riches, desert and reward. The poet, though "stor'd within," is outwardly a beggar, while "soules of baser stamp shine in their store." The speaker, identifying himself with "the wittie score," rebels with intense personal indignation against the "*Entailes* of povertie" which are "layd on Poets." The idea of an intractable perpetuity, conveyed by "*Entailes*," is amplified by the historical consistency of the poet's "thredbare, goldless genealogie" through "all the pilgrimage of time." The intransigence of this condition is further amplified by the expression of the poet's relationship to society in terms of oppression, confinement, and humiliation:

                When I by thoughts look back
Into the wombe of time, and see the Rack
Stand useless there, untill we are produc'd
Unto the torture, and our soules infus'd
To learn afflictions, I begin to doubt
That as some tyrants use from their chain'd rout
Of slaves to pick out one whom for their sport
They keep afflicted by some lingring art,
So wee are meerly thrown upon the stage
The mirth of fooles, and Legend of the age.

The poet's lot begins to take on something of the ineluctable force of natural law, though Nature, since she "Spent so much of her treasure in the birth / As ever after niggards her," is pardoned with the wry "Wofull profusion! . . . all hope of thrift and state / Lost for a verse." The extreme disproportions conveyed by the tyrant-and-slave analogy are developed as a portrait of the doleful, tattered poet is juxtaposed to lavishly dressed "*French apes*" and "th'earthly Usurer" lustfully obsessed with his sterile hoard. Though the speaker's language constantly suggests the inevitability of the injustices he perceives, he willfully persists in rebelling, complaining, and pouring out his frustrations, naïvely unaffected by the implication of futility residing in the very terms in which he defines the problem: "I'm mad at Fate, and angry ev'n to sinne, / To see deserts and learning clad so thinne." The remedy for the fated injustice of the poet's lot lies in the hands of men of wealth, but they are insensitive to the worth of poetry and preoccupied with baser things. His vigorous indictment of their obtuseness and niggardliness culminates in a frustrated excoriation of the patronage system:

> A Curse upon their drosse! how have we sued
> For a few scatter'd *Chips*? how oft pursu'd
> Petitions with a blush, in hope to squeeze
> For their souls health, more than our wants a peece?
> Their steel-rib'd Chests and Purse (rust eat them both!)
> Have cost us with much paper many an oath,
> And Protestations of such solemn sense,
> As if our soules were sureties for the Pence.
> Should we a full nights learned cares present,
> They'l scarce return us one short houres Content,
> 'Las! they're but quibbles, things we Poets feign,
> The short-liv'd Squibs and Crackers of the brain.

These malcontent railings finally exhaust themselves and bring the speaker to recognize a practical impasse. In form, the poem resembles Herbert's "The Collar," dramatizing the psychological stresses which lead finally to reconciliation and acceptance. The speaker's rebellion, by the very fullness with which it explores the external barriers to his contentment, inevitably produces the realization that the key to contentment lies in controlling his attitude to external circumstances. It would be inaccurate to say that the poem is based upon the Stoic values of patience and resignation, or that it states those values. Rather, it dramatizes their emergence from a discontented struggle of the will with material conditions and from a consequent recognition of ineluctable limitations on the will's freedom, thus demonstrating the necessity as well as the value of the attitude in which the speaker finally rests. The poem is one of Vaughan's most sustained and vigorous. Alliteration, heavily monosyllabic language, and versatile aural effects produce a rhythm and tone that is notably rough, harsh, and emphatic. Closed couplets are often used incisively to give sharp expression to the speaker's caustic strictures. Often the syntax and sound of the couplet give way to a headlong, declamatory rush of uneven clauses which accurately mirrors the irregularly stressful movement of excited speech:

> To think how th'earthly Usurer can brood
> Upon his bags, and weigh the pretious food
> With palsied hands, as if his soul did feare
> The Scales could rob him of what he layd there;
> Like Divels that on hid Treasures sit, or those
> Whose jealous Eyes trust not beyond their nose
> They guard the durt, and the bright Idol hold
> Close, and Commit adultery with gold.

By contrast, the calm resolution of the poem's conclusion is expressed in smooth, quiet, regular lines.

In "To Amoret Weeping" (Martin, p. 13), the speaker's dramatic self-revelation functions, as in *"The importunate Fortune"* and the "Invitation to *Brecknock*," as a technique of persuasion. His monologue is a speech of consolation aimed at reconciling the lady to the mediocre fortune which she shares with him.[31] But, though the basic situation is brought firmly into view at the beginning, the specific occasion of her distress evolves gradually and becomes fully evident only at the end of the poem. This fact defines the speaker's strategy. Seeking to win her over without exacerbating her mood by touching on specific contentious problems, he proceeds by way of rhetorical questions and moral reflections on such large general issues as the proper attitude toward Fortune, Fate, and adversity, expressing general propositions in which she cannot but acquiesce. The tender condescension of "Deare, idle Prodigall!" suggests a more relaxed mood than the abrupt opening command and implies that she is responding to his philosophy. Earlier, his repetition of short, cognate questions and comments suggested urgency and uncertainty, but now he elaborates his argument with confidence and witty gusto, fancying the disasters that might have ensued had he been born rich:

> But grant some richer Planet at my birth
> Had spyed me out, and measur'd so much earth
> Or gold unto my share; I should have been
> Slave to these lower Elements, and seen
> My high borne soul flagge with their drosse, & lye
> A pris'ner to base mud, and Alchymie;
> I should perhaps eate Orphans, and sucke up
> A dozen distrest widowes in one Cup;
> Nay further, I should by that lawfull stealth,
> (Damn'd Usurie) undoe the Common-wealth;
> Or Patent it in Soape, and Coales, and so
> Have the Smiths curse me, and my Laundres too;
> Geld wine, or his friend Tobacco; and so bring
> The incens'd subject Rebell to his King;
> And after all (as those first sinners fell)
> Sinke lower then my gold; and lye in Hell.

This hypothetical narrative, tracing the tragic fall of a great man led astray by greed, draws on the recent political uproar over monopolies and taxes to indict the moral and social evils of wealth, obliquely attributing the Rebellion to commercial greed and putting the rebels in their infernal place. Later, thanking the "blessed pow'rs" for delivering him from such a fate by "taking all away," he cites the Rebellion as a signal instance of the witlessness that may be expected in the rich:

> For I (had I been rich) as sure as fate,
> Would have bin medling with the King, or State,
> Or something to undoe me; and 'tis fit
> (We know) that who hath wealth, should have no wit.

These are all classic arguments in favor of a middle station in life. As he goes on musing over the course his life might have taken, the speaker becomes increasingly self-absorbed, finally praising his own "gallant soule" as a model for Amoret's emulation. But this egotism is mitigated by the conclusion, in which he simply assures her that their mutual love compensates for any material deficiency. Suggesting that "Content, and Love" have finally overcome Amoret's distress, the ending implies the happy resolution of this domestic drama.

In the last of these dramatic satires that we will consider, *"In Amicum foeneratorem"* (Martin, p. 43), the speaker mocks that most notoriously detestable character of Renaissance society, the usurer. Here there is none of the bitter and frustrated railing which characterizes his attitude toward the rich in "To his friend ———." As in *"The importunate Fortune,"* he has chosen his values, and his consistent stance of derisive contempt stems from a conviction of utter superiority. He is teasing "mighty *Silver*" and *"Og"* himself, indulging his sheer virtuosity in an imaginative play of wit. The effect of the poem is to make money itself and all who take it seriously look ridiculous; it is an assertion of total freedom from everything except the life of the imagination. The conceits of the first paragraph mock the usurer's greed through the absurd paradox of a man bribing his debtor to repay a loan: "how he doth dresse / His messages in *Chink*? not an Expresse / Without a fee for reading." The harsh, irreverent colloquialisms in which the speaker defies the usurer's demands contrast directly with the idealized, hyperbolical imagery in which he offers to repay the loan with an imaginary kingdom of pastoral erotica:

> Wilt rob an Altar thus? and sweep at once
> What *Orpheus*-like I forc'd from stocks and stones?
> 'Twill never swell thy *Bag*, nor ring one peale
> In thy dark *Chest*. Talk not of *Shreeves*, or gaole,
> I fear them not. I have no land to glutt
> Thy durty appetite, and make thee strutt
> *Nimrod* of acres; I'le no Speech prepare
> To court the *Hopefull Cormorant*, thine heire.
> Yet there's a Kingdome, at thy beck, if thou
> But kick this drosse, *Parnassus* flowrie brow
> I'le give thee with my *Tempe*, and to boot
> That horse which struck a fountain with his foot.
> A Bed of Roses I'le provide for thee,
> And Chrystal Springs shall drop thee melodie;
> The breathing shades wee'l haunt, where ev'ry leafe
> Shall *Whisper* us asleep, though thou art deafe;
> Those waggish *Nymphs* too which none ever yet
> Durst make love to, wee'l teach the Loving fit . . .

The mundane concerns of the usurer could not be more flatly rejected as brutish in comparison to the delights of poetry. But even this outrage to the usurer's belief in the relative value of money does not satisfy the speaker's puckish humor; his hyperbolical mood runs on, piling outrage upon outrage:

> But here thou must remember to dispurse,
> For without money all this is a Curse,
> Thou must for more bags call, and so restore
> This Iron-age to gold, as once before;
> This thou must doe, and yet this is not all,
> For thus the Poet would be still in thrall,
> Thou must then (if live thus) my neast of honey,
> Cancell old bonds, and beg to lend more money.

Chapter
VI
THE FORM OF NATURE

V AUGHAN, as we all know, was a "poet of Nature." When post-Romantic critics used the phrase, they conjured unhappy spirits, some of which still haunt us. If we have outgrown the nineteenth-century view of Vaughan as one who, in T. S. Eliot's curt phrase, "occupies himself in plastering nature with his own fancies,"[1] we have still not recovered from the habit of imputing a "passionate response to Nature" to him as though the phrase meant much the same then as it has since.[2] Vaughan knew from Psalm 19 that "The heavens declare the glory of God; and the firmament sheweth his handywork. Day unto day uttereth speech, and night unto night sheweth knowledge"; and he knew from Plato that the created world was an inferior copy of divine Ideas, and from Plotinus and other Neoplatonists that Nature embodied the divine Intelligence in varying degrees, having been created by the emanation or overflowing of Spirit into Chaos. All of these conceptions of Nature as an intelligible order flowed together in the Middle Ages and the Renaissance in the metaphor of Nature as a book to be read:

> There are two Books from whence I collect my Divinity; besides that written one of God, another of His servant Nature, that universal and publick Manuscript, that lies expans'd unto the Eyes of all: those that never saw him in the one, have discover'd Him in the other. This was the Scripture and

Theology of the Heathens. . . . Surely the Heathens knew better how to joyn and read these mystical Letters than we Christians, who cast a more careless Eye on these common Hieroglyphicks, and disdain to suck Divinity from the flowers of Nature.[3]

In Vaughan's time, it was quite consistent for a "bookish poet," as Frank Kermode has called him,[4] to be a "poet of Nature," for the study of the admirable, glorious, and eloquent order of God's creatures had nothing in particular to do with impulses from vernal woods or the beauties of the Welsh landscape. "Passionate response to Nature" reverses the relationship between subject and object and attributes it to the wrong faculty, for what is involved in Vaughan's "Nature poetry" is an intellectual search for knowledge of God in the Creation: "For the invisible things of him from the creation of the world are clearly seen, being understood by the things that are made" (Romans 1:20).

The post-Romantic habit of opposing natural to artificial is as inappropriate to Vaughan as the emphasis on emotion rather than understanding. "All things are artificial," said Browne, "for Nature is the Art of God."[5] And Sidney had compared the poet as maker with the divine Maker. As the witty invention of an omniscient Poet, Nature was not only the source of all poetic metaphor; it was itself metaphorical in form, the things that are made constituting secret and mysterious signs or hieroglyphs of the invisible things of God.[6] Tesauro in *The Aristotelian Telescope* and Reynolds in *Mythomystes* had used this view of Nature to justify a conceited style in poetry as a proper imitation of God's own dark conceit in the Creation. But Vaughan adapts it to the criterion of perspicuity in poetic style discussed in chapter 2. Echoing the Pauline phrase that the invisible things of God are *clearly* seen in the Creation, he speaks in his *Discourse of Death* of "very clear and inexcusable demonstrations . . . in *nature*" of Biblical promises of "the redemption of our bodies" (Martin, p. 175). "Here have we a clear type of the *resurrection*," he comments on one of these *exempla*, one of these "*prolusions* and strong *proofs* of our *restoration* laid out in *nature"* (Martin, pp. 176-77). The implication is that God's cosmic metaphors are plain and perspicuous rather than a system of riddles and enigmatical knots.

What then is the function of the poet in imitating Nature? The answer lies in Vaughan's belief that people are not equally able or willing to comprehend the plain truth of this Book. The parallel citation of Biblical and natural proofs of resurrection in the *Discourse of Death* indicates that study of the Book of the Creatures must be complemented and guided by study of that other Book, the Bible or Book of God's Word. The two Books will mutually illuminate one another; Nature must be read in the light of Scripture and must itself be attended to diligently: "There is no *object* we can look upon, but will do us the kindnesse to put us in minde of our mortality, if we would be so wise as to make use of it" (Martin, p. 174). "The Tempest" (Martin, p. 460) speaks again of man's willful or obtuse oversight of the evident significances of natural things:

> How is man parcell'd out? how ev'ry hour
>   Shews him himself, or somthing he should see?
>   This late, long heat may his Instruction be,
> And tempests have more in them than a showr.
> . . . .
> O that man could do so! that he would hear
>   The world read to him! all the vast expence
>   In the Creation shed, and slav'd to sence
> Makes up but lectures for his eie, and ear.
>
> Sure, mighty love foreseeing the discent
>   Of this poor Creature, by a gracious art
>   Hid in these low things snares to gain his heart,
> And layd surprizes in each Element.

(The word "surprizes," referring to the element of "suddenness" in formal gardening, intensifies the meaning of "gracious art" as well as the basic idea of Nature's eloquence.)

The Form of Nature [141]

"The Water-fall" (Martin, p. 537) makes it clear that the problem lies in the depravity of man's reason as well as in the depravity of his will:

> O useful Element and clear!
> My sacred wash and cleanser here,
> My first consigner unto those
> Fountains of life, where the Lamb goes?
> What sublime truths, and wholesome themes,
> Lodge in thy mystical, deep streams!
> Such as dull man can never finde
> Unless that Spirit lead his minde,
> Which first upon thy face did move,
> And hatch'd all with his quickning love.

The puns on the literal and figurative meanings of "clear" and "deep" import both the clarity and the profound significance of Nature's sublime truths. But the last four lines quoted transfer to the interpretation of this Book the traditional principle that the proper interpretation of Scripture required the illumination of human reason by the Spirit of God, understood as the third person of the Trinity and associated with the spirit of God which moved upon the face of the waters in Genesis 1:2. And this Spirit descends "but seldom, and then very sparingly, upon *men* of an ordinary or indifferent *holyness*," observed Vaughan in the preface to *Silex Scintillans*. There, in support of the idea that the sacred poet "must strive (by all means) for *perfection* and true *holyness*," because only then can he hope to receive the illumination of the Spirit necessary for him to write "A *true Hymn*," Vaughan had cited Revelation 4:1 as a proof text: "After this I looked, and, behold, a door *was* opened in heaven: and the first voice which I heard ... said, Come up hither, and I will shew thee things which must be hereafter."

"They are all gone into the world of light!" (Martin, p. 483) contrasts the perplexity of one who attempts to interpret Nature by the light of human reason alone with the assured grasp of Nature's sublime truths possible if the Spirit leads his mind:

> He that hath found some fledg'd birds nest, may know
>   At first sight, if the bird be flown;
> But what fair Well, or Grove he sings in now,
>   That is to him unknown.
>
> And yet, as Angels in some brighter dreams
>   Call to the soul, when man doth sleep:
> So some strange thoughts transcend our wonted theams,
>   And into glory peep.
>
> If a star were confin'd into a Tomb
>   Her captive flames must needs burn there;
> But when the hand that lockt her up, gives room,
>   She'l shine through all the sphaere.

The examination of Nature "at first sight" offers evidence of death, but not of immortality; but the emblem of the star confined in a tomb and released is offered as "a clear type of the *resurrection.*" The poetic invention or conceit is based equally on Nature and on the Biblical account of Christ's resurrection, which is the ultimate foundation of the speaker's faith in immortality. The passage succinctly illustrates Vaughan's interpretation of Nature in the light of Scripture and the Spirit. "Vanity of Spirit" (Martin, p. 418) provides a negative illustration of the same thing:

> I summon'd nature: peirc'd through all her store,
> Broke up some seales, which none had touch'd before,
>   Her wombe, her bosome, and her head
>   Where all her secrets lay a bed
>   I rifled quite, and having past
>   Through all the Creatures, came at last
>   To search my selfe, where I did find
>   Traces, and sounds of a strange kind.
> Here of this mighty spring, I found some drills,
> With Ecchoes beaten from th' eternall hills;
>   Weake beames, and fires flash'd to my sight,
>   Like a young East, or Moone-shine night,

> Which shew'd me in a nook cast by
> A peece of much antiquity,
> With Hyerogliphicks quite dismembred,
> And broken letters scarce remembred.
> I tooke them up, and (much Joy'd,) went about
> T' unite those peeces, hoping to find out
> The mystery; but this neer done,
> That little light I had was gone.

Here the speaker experiences the same perplexity as the rest of dull man, and for the same reason. Just as the man who found the fledged bird's nest could see only part of what it meant, so the speaker here, by the light of his own natural reason, can see only broken letters, not the truth in its natural wholeness and clarity. It is the function of the poet, as one endowed by God with superior *"spirits* and *qualifications,"* to serve God and mankind by uniting the fragments of truth, by interpreting or making plain those sublime truths and wholesome themes which are clearly seen when Nature is read by the light of Scripture and the Spirit.

This apostolic conception of poetry offered considerable latitude to the poet in "accommodating" divine truths to the capacities, experiences, and needs of his readers. But it also required that poetic invention should operate, not toward enfolding religious mysteries in verbal enigmas and riddles and esoteric notions, but toward *un*folding them, making them plainer and more evident. In relation to Nature and Scripture, the poem will be essentially exegetical. As Nature is an allegory of the invisible things of God, so the poem will "allegorize" Nature and Scripture, demonstrating the eloquent truth embodied in both by interrelating them and by applying this truth to the ordinary person's spiritual life. Vaughan's concern for perspicuity in poetic matter, form, and style would seem to have determined his avoidance, in general, of the esoteric allegorizing of Nature which constituted the Hermetic doctrines familiar to him through his brother's writings, and of the dialectical ingenuities, based often on out-of-the-way scraps of pedantic learning, so characteristic of the poetry of Donne. Vaughan's conception of his role as a sacred poet virtually requires the matter of his poetry to be a Christianized version of the *consensus gentium*, and such a preference for the "natural," for the great fundamentals of religious faith and experience, is reflected in his detestation of heresy and schism and his dedication to the "middle way" of the Anglican Church. Vaughan's heavy use of imagery drawn from the Book of the Creatures was a means of, literally, incarnating the truths of faith, of rendering them intelligible in a form accommodated to the terms of temporal experience and therefore capable of moving the reader's affections toward the love of God. Because Vaughan wishes to turn *many* to righteousness, his most common images of Nature are drawn from the most common aspects of Nature—light and dark, day and night, sunrise and sunset, the seasons, storms, stars, dew, streams, flowers and trees, etc. These are some of the aspects of Nature most frequently experienced and therefore indelibly imprinted in the memories and imaginations of most people. The prominence of this archetypal imagery in Vaughan's verse is largely responsible for its aura of simplicity as well as its evocative power.

It is not possible to distinguish here between images drawn from books and those drawn from Vaughan's direct observation of Nature, for his archetypal imagery is the predominant imagery of Biblical metaphor and part of a lingua franca of literature in general. Archetypal images are by definition phenomena which one is most likely to encounter both in books and in life. Vaughan could hardly have evaded them, but the popular image of him going about Brecknockshire absorbed in impassioned contemplation of stars and bedewed flowers is an unwarranted anachronism. And it blurs our reading of the poems by encouraging us to see the speaker's individual response or individual relationship to natural phenomena as central to the poem's meaning, whereas this is never central and is seldom unambiguously involved.[7] The central meaning of Vaughan's religious poems is always an aspect of common experience, a general truth about the Christian relationship to God and the things of faith as defined by Scripture and the Church. He prefers these particular images as modes of poetic incarnation because they are the most generally familiar to his audience, both through experience and through the Bible and other literature, rather than because they have (as far as we know) any special significance in his own experience. Nor can we describe images of the sort mentioned above as ideal, or otherworldly, or romantic, or mystical, and distinguish them from the "everyday" images which critics of thirty-five years ago thought distinctive of metaphysical poetry—for example, images of lamps and candles, wayfaring (roads, streets, paths, tracks, etc.), rooms and doors, domestic activities such as weaving, dressing and undressing, clothing and rags, afflictions, diseases and cures.[8] The Bible is full of such images, and the commonness of their associations is precisely what they have in common with the other group.

Vaughan's preference for a poetic language with a maximum potential of intelligibility can be seen also in the fact that his natural metaphors are usually organized in terms of the broadest, most salient concepts of popular science rather than in terms of the more abstruse and technical concepts which gave Donne a reputation for pedantry in his own day and for tough-mindedness in ours. The central principle by which most men organized their conception of the cosmos was still, as it had been in ancient and medieval times, the figure of the Chain of Being or Ladder of Creation—a figure made up by the coalescence of various aspects of ancient philosophy and mythology, Biblical exegesis, Ptolemaic cosmology, astrology, and popular scientific lore. The broad outlines of this conception of the cosmos as a unified, hierarchical system, a *discordia concors* which encompasses and disposes various plenitude with order and regularity, make up the "metaphysical" features of Vaughan's natural imagery: the concentric spheres, the immutability of the heavens, the flux of the elements, the supremacy of reason, man's primacy in the natural world, stellar influence, the decay and renewal of the cosmos, the correspondences between different orders of being. These ideas were basic components in the intellectual world-view of the time.

They occur with similar frequency in both Vaughan's early secular verse and his later sacred verse.[9]

It is difficult to speculate further about the motives which prompted Vaughan's powerful interest in imagery drawn from the Book of the Creatures. It may have been partly a reaction against dualistic and Manichean elements in Puritan polemics. Their attacks on the materialism or fleshliness of Anglo-Catholic ritual, iconography, and liturgical symbolism tended to emphasize the incompatibility of spirit and matter and thus to magnify and render crucial a philosophical problem which had always been dormant in Christian theology. Their attitude tended to minimize the possibility that matter was sanctified by pious uses and ultimately to weaken belief in God's love for the Creation. Among the potential consequences of these attempts to purify spirit from the contaminations of matter were the cancellation of man's responsibility for evil, the liberation of temporal affairs from the rule of God's law, and the undermining of faith in the temporal manifestation of God's goodness. Vaughan's natural metaphors present Nature in terms which had been developed by the Fathers and the Schoolmen to solve the problem, inherited from Plato, of the alienation of matter from spirit, and to rebut precisely such attitudes toward the flesh as those displayed by some Puritan factions in Vaughan's time. Their response was to emphasize the Biblical texts (e.g., Genesis 1, Psalm 19, Romans 1:20) which spoke of the Creation's goodness and of God's presence in it, to interpret the Fall in terms of the apostate will, and to emphasize the relation of spirit to matter by insisting on the concept of correspondence, which attributed anagogical and moral significance to material things.[10] The immanence of God in the Creation and the consequent mythologizing or allegorizing of Nature are the very foundation of Vaughan's natural metaphors, and the question of the temporal manifestation of Providence encompasses a great many of his poetic themes. Vaughan was no philosopher and no theologian, but his emphasis on the poetic treatment of these aspects of traditional thought may have been partly a reaction to the temper of the times. The violent contemporary attacks on the traditional liturgy may have contributed to the intensity of his interest in the traditional view of the relation of Nature to God on which the liturgy was based.

Vaughan may also have been reacting to Baconian science.[11] Whatever pious motives for the study of Nature Bacon professed, his insistence that inferences drawn from the study of material phenomena should be determined by the observations of the senses and not referred to first causes had the effect of driving yet another wedge between matter and spirit, the Creation and the Creator, human morality and the temporal environment. From the point of view represented by Vaughan this was idolatry of things, and Bacon's demand that mankind exploit its dominion over the natural world by applying knowledge to the amelioration of temporal existence, rather than to the glory of God, was a signal example of intellectual pride. Vaughan's stubborn recusance on the issue is suggested by an observation in the letter he wrote to John Aubrey in 1680:

> That the most serious of our profession have not only an unkindnes for, butt are persecutors of Astrologie: I have more than once admired: butt I find not this ill humour amongst the Antients, so much as the modern physicians. . . . I suppose they had not travelled so far, & having once entered upon the practise, they were loath to leave off, and learn to be acquainted with another world. (Martin, pp. 692-93)

And in the same letter he speaks of "my attendance upon (rather than speculations into) Nature." "The Constellation" (Martin, p. 469) condemns man for daring to "know Effects, and Judge them long before, / When th' herb he treads knows much, much more" rather than imitating the moral qualities of "*Obedience, Order, Light*" exemplified by the stars. This and the passage from "They are all gone into the world of light!" discussed earlier in this chapter seem to reflect exactly the distinction between attending upon Nature and speculating into it, to contrast the sacramental and the scientific approaches to Nature. And "The World" and "The Tempest" are only two of the many poems in which Vaughan condemns the idolatry and pride of those who regard the things of Nature as ends in themselves or who apply them solely to human use.

Another factor may have been the very confusion of contemporary society. The fate of the monarchy and the Anglican Church overwhelmed Vaughan with a sense of the alienation of human society from God, the fragility of even sacred institutions, and the opportunities which time provided for the exfoliation of corruption and error:

> We could not have lived in an age of more instruction, had we been left to our own choice. We have seen such vicissitudes and examples of humane frailty, as the former world (had they happened in those ages) would have judged prodigies. We have seen Princes brought to their graves by a new way, and the highest order of humane honours trampled upon by the lowest. We have seene Judgement beginning at Gods Church, and (what hath beene never heard of, since it was redeem'd and established by his blessed Son,) we have seen his Ministers cast out of the Sanctuary, & barbarous persons without *light* or *perfection*, usurping holy offices. . . . Suddenly do the high things of this world come to an end, and their delectable things passe away, for when they seem to be in their *flowers* and full strength, they perish to astonishment; And sure the ruine of the most goodly peeces seems to tell, that the dissolution of the whole is not far off. . . . Vain therefore and deceitful is all the pomp of this world, which though it flatters us with a seeming permanency, will be sure to leave us then, when we are most in chase of it. And what comfort then, or what security can poor man promise to himself? (Martin, pp. 170-71)

Vaughan's answer to the final question, of course, was "the knowledge and love of God." He may have turned to Nature as the medium of this knowledge, more than (as George Herbert had done) to the symbols and ceremonies of the now desecrated and banished Church, because Nature was the one temporal order uncontaminated by human corruption, a purer and more stable embodiment of the essential, eternal truths than human society or even the Church, for whose rehabilitation he hoped to bring new and better instruction from this divine source.

"One Almighty is, from whom / All things proceed, and up to him return, / If not deprav'd from good," Raphael tells Adam in *Paradise Lost* (V, 469-71).[12] The spatial and kinetic metaphor defines the traditional cosmos in terms of two great reciprocal motions of love and creative energy: a motion downward and outward from God into the Creation, and a movement of the Creation through space and time back to God by means of the creatures' reciprocation of his love. "If not deprav'd from good" reserves the possibility of a third motion, away from God, through a blocking or refraction of the creative cycle in self-love or love of inferior things. By the first motion the creature received its being, by the second fulfilled it, and by the third perverted it and destroyed itself. The great moving circle composed by the return of the creature to God was a perennial symbol of ideal harmony and perfect order. The breaking of the circle defined the difference between ideal and reality, between human potentiality and human actions.[13]

The Great Chain of Being was a fruitful imaginative scheme because it was comprehensive and therefore accounted for all of the possibilities in the same basic terms. It was not an inert, frozen pattern but a dynamic figure of contrary potentialities. The ideal form of life, the Creation's perfect manifestation of God's will, was portrayed as a chain which moved in perfect spatial harmony because each creature fulfilled the law of its own being. It existed no more, but its existence before the Fall and its renewal after the Day of Judgment could be imaginatively comprehended. Meanwhile some of its glory remained in the imperturbable wheeling of the immutable spheres, still perfectly obedient to the will of their Maker. Below the moon, innocence was lost, choice crucial, and motion more often violent and irregular. Achievement of the vertical circling movement required vigilant navigation to master the contrary pull of inertness, downward plunging, or directionless wandering in horizontal mazes. Since "God is Light, / And never but in unapproached Light / Dwelt from Eternity" (*Paradise Lost* III, 3-5), the Scale of Nature was also a vertical column of light, strong and steady at its source but fading and flickering where man dwells in willful exchanges with the dark.

Motion and light, and the motion of light, are the characteristic modes of Vaughan's natural metaphors. The symbols of perfect motion and perfect light are there, defining the ideal form of his nature which man has lost and must recover; but Vaughan's subject is the mixed condition of man in nature and time, the struggle to regain what was lost, to complete the circle and return to God and his own true self. The focal point of Vaughan's vision is the point at which light and darkness intersect, down distinguishes itself from up and direction from indirection. This is the point at which the choice is made and the conflict begins, and the progress of the struggle, the expansion of that point through the life of the soul, is the principal substance of Vaughan's sacred verse. The principal kinetic form of its metaphorical expression is the figure of the quest, and the fusion of this with light yields the figure of the night journey.[14] The principal metaphor of light is kinetic as well, an expansion of light which rolls back the dark, disperses mists and fogs, breaks through clouds and veils.[15] Vaughan's own consciousness of the centrality of these contrarieties and transfigurations in his sacred verse is suggested by his choice of the title *Silex Scintillans*—"the glittering flint." The dynamic swiftness of shifting and contrary motions and the rapid mutations of light give Vaughan's poetry an atmosphere in which sensuous and ethereal qualities are strangely fused. Probably this has much to do with its evocative power and fascination, with the sense of mystery which it communicates to the reader.

In this spherical universe, where God is the beginning and the end, going back and going forward are the same thing, for both prelapsarian innocence and apocalyptic purification are symbols of man's end and ideal form. They give temporal existence the meaning, form, and order without which it would be an absurd chaos. They define the state of grace, the potentiality in terms of which the failures of the state of nature are to be understood and overcome. They provide both the perspective by which the alienation wrought by man's sin is to be measured and the goal of the effort which should follow self-knowledge. It is the very nature of an ideal to be juxtaposed to the real, and the juxtapositions which we find in Vaughan—of eternity and time, stillness and motion, brightness and darkness, order and disorder, harmony and conflict, the One and the Many—are misrepresented by the critical overemphasis on his symbols of innocence and purity. It is necessary to insist that the soul of man must inevitably be moving either toward or away from its end, and that symbolizing that end is not the same thing as resting in exclusive contemplation of things outside of time and space. Vaughan's apocalyptic and romantic images speak of steady or strong light (stars, lamps, the sun), stillness, harmonious or rising motion (the spheres, dancing, birds or vapors or sighs or tears ascending), silence or harmonious sound (music, singing), pure or fructifying moisture (clear streams, dew, rain), gems and precious metals (gold, etc.), luxuriant vegetation (spicy aromas, germinating seeds, bright and perfumed flowers, green leaves, trees that grow straight and tall and full of sap). And his demonic or ironic images are antitheses of these: darkness or dim or fading light (caves, glowworms, untended lamps, obscuring clouds or veils), inertness or crabbed movement (heavy weights, transfixed bodies, confinement, staggering, falling, treacherous or hidden paths, restlessness, erroneous wandering), cacophonous noise, puddles, polluted streams, poisonous fluids, stones, dust, rocks, ashes, foul odors, stunted or wilted vegetation.[16]

Vaughan does not merely dichotomize these antithetical images. He does dichotomize them, because only if you know what things are can you know how they affect one another. But, to put it simply, he is less concerned with what Heaven is like than with what getting there is like. His central concern is with how one aspect of experience affects or modifies another in the soul's progress toward its end. Therefore he blends antithetical images, and the metaphors which result demonstrate how differing qualities act upon one another rather than describe the distinct qualities of different things. The metaphors function toward demonstrating a complex process rather than toward describing simple states of being. The process is multiform, yielding myriad resolutions in the soul's eddying fluctuations between opposites which will exist in separate purity only after the end of time. Its essential mode is conflict, for the soul's struggle to reach one condition involves the effort to free itself from or avoid succumbing to another. The condition of the soul is continuously mixed, for its life consists in a variable succession of temporary transfigurations, moments of insight or stability or balance which pass because time passes and everything in it changes. This is why the collection of short lyrics is an apt form for spiritual biography. His theme is the variable progress of the soul's efforts to transcend itself—the achievement or loss, rather than the possession, of the state of grace. That is why motion is his fundamental metaphor for the spiritual life. One suspects that Vaughan himself suspected as much:

> Beauty consists in colours; and that's best
> Which is not fixt, but flies, and flowes;
> The settled *Red* is dull, and *whites* that rest
> Something of sickness would disclose.
> Vicissitude plaies all the game,
> Nothing that stirs,
> Or hath a name,
> But waits upon this wheel,
> . . . .
> Thus doth God *Key* disorder'd man
> (Which none else can,)
> Tuning his brest to rise, or fall;

And by a sacred, needfull art
Like strings, stretch ev'ry part
Making the whole most Musicall.
("Affliction," Martin, p. 460)

The emblematic frontispiece of *Silex Scintillans* is itself a perfect example of the mobile blending of opposites characteristic of Vaughan's imagery. The flinty heart—heavy, hard, inert symbol of a reprobate will—is struck by a dart, the hand which holds it reaching down from a cloud. Flames rise up from the stone, which drops tears or blood. There are three reciprocal motions—one down, one up, and another down—and three transfigurations of quality: from cold stone to fire, from hard rock to moisture, and from dull flint to light. The verse legend facing the picture gives us Vaughan's own gloss:

You break through the *Rocky* barrier of my heart, and it is made *Flesh* that was before a *Stone*. Behold me torn asunder! and at last the *Fragments* burning toward your skies, and the cheeks streaming with tears out of the *Adamant*. Thus once upon a time you made the *Rocks* flow and the *Crags* gush, oh ever provident of your people! How marvellous toward me is your hand! In *Dying*, I have been born again; and in the midst of my *shattered means* I am now *richer*.[17]

The language coruscates with rapid movements, shifts in perspective, and transfigurations of meaning: flesh has become stone, but the stone is shattered and becomes flesh; flames rise toward the skies as fragments of stone burn and tears stream from rock; thus long ago rocks flowed; now I am dead, and have been reborn, enriched by destruction. The whole flickering pattern, but especially the two final oxymora, suggests yet another transfiguration of movement: the falling tears move upward with the rising flames —contrition is a form of love.

The focal point of Vaughan's language is a mobile moment, the point in space and time at which one condition overcomes another or is transformed into another. At the circumference of the language are the great antitheses of apocalyptic and demonic imagery. The point of transformation, choice, or conflict is sometimes defined by the rapidity with which the words glance from pole to pole:

> Heaven hath less beauty than the dust he spies.
> *Waters* that fall / Chide, and fly up.
> the Cloud / Sits on the Suns brow.
> to the dark world lend / These flames.
> keepe downe with thy light / Dust that would rise.
> cloath the morning-starre with dust.
> touch with one Coal / My frozen heart.
> It glows and glitters in my cloudy brest.
> Shining nowhere, but in the dark.
> A deep, but dazzling darkness.

These are particularly compact examples. The pattern is also found on a larger scale: it is the basic structural principle of Vaughan's poetry.

In the world view identified by the figure of the Great Chain of Being, everything is defined in relation to the opposite ends of the scale, and the opposites define one another: we know light by knowing darkness, good by knowing evil. Every creature has an infinite potential for transfiguration, an infinite capacity for motion: angels may become devils, the Son of God descended into hell and rose again to heaven, man's soul may become star or stone. The concept of correspondence or universal analogy defined this metaphysical volatility, and Vaughan's language, imitating Nature in these terms, derived a metaphorical volatility from it. This dynamic principle most commonly organizes the details of a whole poem. "The Tempest" (Martin, p. 460) is but one example of a poem which thus imitates the form of Nature and incidentally demonstrates how Nature is imitated in the life of the soul.

Vaughan's sacred poems were designed to supplement the private devotions of those who were dissatisfied, as he was, with public worship in the "purified" Church. Most of them are shaped in some measure by the art of formal meditation, and the Book of the Creatures is one of his principal sources for "some similitude, answerable to the matter."[18] The use of similitudes was one of several methods of "composing" or "seeing the place" by which spiritual truths were rendered incarnate and the senses and the will, as well as the understanding, involved in their apprehension. The dynamic quality which arises from the volatility of Vaughan's metaphors is enhanced by the actions of the soul in relation to the matter of the meditation and God, actions which shape the basic structure and pattern of meditative art:

> Meditation . . . is nothing els but a diligent and forcible application of the understanding, to seeke, and knowe, and as it were to tast some divine matter; from whence doth arise in our affectionate powers good motions, inclinations, and purposes which stirre us up to the love and exercise of vertue, and the hatred and avoiding of sinne.[19]

Dawson speaks of two kinds of mental action or spiritual motion: the first, roughly equivalent to the phases of composition and analysis, is a movement of the mind and senses outward to grasp "some divine matter" in the form of a metaphorical or historical (usually Biblical) representation; the second, the colloquy, is a movement of the affections toward God in the light of the knowledge gained in the first two phases. Because it is shaped fundamentally by these two kinds of mental action, meditative art often portrays, in a rapid and condensed way, an imaginative ranging through vast tracts of space and time: from the room in which the speaker sits to the places where Christ lived, from the Creation or patriarchal times to the Apocalypse. The presentation of these panoramas in an intensely conceived, present time and place yields a *discordia concors* which might be described as an imaginative imitation of the absorption of the Many by the One. Meditative art is marked by the simultaneous expression of opposites: the obtuseness of temporal conditions and their irrelevance, the alienation and disintegration of the spiritual life and its unity and freedom, time and timelessness, the swirling activity of the mind and the still point at which the soul meets God. The achievement or perception of unity or transcendence arises out of a full involvement in mundane contraries. Thus the central movement of the soul is through an understanding of conflicting variety to an understanding of the fusion or reconciliation of opposites in God.[20]

The italicized second stanza of "The Tempest" presents, as a similitude answerable to the matter, a hieroglyph or natural emblem of the spiritual truth contemplated—the reciprocal love between God and the soul.[21] The stanza is marked off from the rest by its length (three quatrains instead of one), by its substitution of alternating eight- and four-syllable lines for decasylabics, and by the use of italics. The first stanza expresses the underlying assumption of anthropomorphism and explicitly promises an exegesis of a natural phenomenon:

>   How is man parcell'd out? how ev'ry hour
>   Shews him himself, or somthing he should see?
>   This late, long heat may his Instruction be,
>   And tempests have more in them than a showr.

>   *When nature on her bosome saw*
>   *Her Infants die,*
>   *And all her flowres wither'd to straw,*
>   *Her brests grown dry;*
>   *She made the Earth their nurse, & tomb,*
>   *Sigh to the sky,*
>   *'Til to those sighes fetch'd from her womb*
>   *Rain did reply,*
>   *So in the midst of all her fears*
>   *And faint requests*
>   *Her Earnest sighes procur'd her tears*
>   *And fill'd her brests.*

The emblem expresses the ascent of prayer and the answering descent of grace. It is an exemplary model of the spiritual life, a representation of the ideal form of human response to human sinfulness. And it is a dynamic model, expressing a process of spiritual transfiguration in terms of upward and downward motion and natural fecundity or growth. The personification of Nature represents the rational soul, and her insight into her barren condition exemplifies the self-knowledge which is the first duty of rational creatures. The dryness of her breasts and the withering of her flowers represent the sterility which is a condition of the fall into sin and the consequent privation of gracious acts of the spirit. In sum, the first quatrain expresses the first step on the path of regeneration, the crucial point of tension between downward and upward spiritual progress. The action of the soul at this point is the recognition of its alienation from God and the acknowledgment of its dependence.

The Earth represents the sensitive or appetitive soul, the faculties which are owed to the material body. The sovereignty of Nature over the Earth and the Earth's obedience to her commands expresses the subjection of the passions to the rule of reason, a relationship of the faculties essential to spiritual health. The sighing of the Earth toward the sky represents the turning of the affections, under the rule of reason, toward God in an attitude of supplication, humility, and love. This shift in the direction of the soul's attention, from the self to God, is a shift from the essential condition of sin—self-love or pride—to the essential condition of regeneracy—humility or love of God. This voluntary action of the soul in renewing its primeval direction moves a merciful God to respond with a reciprocal downward action and thus sets in motion the archetypal cycle of creative energy or love. The watering of the ground by rain, representing an infusion of grace into the soul, suggests "softening of the heart" and points to the future well-being of the "infants." Thus the conclusion adumbrates a further movement toward heaven in the upright growth of the healthy flowers.

Stanzas three and four (quoted earlier in this chapter) expand upon the principle of correspondence which underlies the poem's method of reading the Book of the Creatures. The principle presents the hieroglyphic tempest as a natural embodiment of truth, which the poet has discovered, rather than as an arbitrary invention of poetic fancy, thus implying that the poet's art consists in the discovery and interpretation of the art of God, the exegesis of Nature as a source of revelation. Like Nature, the poet's intelligence is subservient to God's intelligence; the poetic imitation of Nature which these stanzas propose is thus the use of Nature which God intended in creating it. The moral imitation equivalent to the poetic involves the perception of Nature as sacramental and its interpretation in terms applicable to the human "heart." This proper use of Nature is part of the proper response to the "mighty love" which lavished "all the vast expence / In the Creation" precisely to aid fulfillment of the end of human life by providing natural emblems of it in the obedience of other creatures. In contrast to the ideal of obedience expressed by the emblem of the tempest, sin is defined as a willful despising of God's love, a misuse of the things of Nature by perceiving them as mere things and by applying them solely to human gratification:

> all the vast expence
> In the Creation shed, and slav'd to sence
> Makes up but lectures for his eie, and ear.

These stanzas complete the composition phase of the meditative action and initiate the phase of analysis, which then proceeds by an amplification of the contrast between sinful man and the obedient creatures:

> All things here shew him heaven; *Waters* that fall
>   Chide, and fly up; *Mists* of corruptest fome
>   Quit their first beds & mount; trees, herbs, flowres, all
> Strive upwards stil, and point him the way home.
>
> How do they cast off grossness? only *Earth*,
>   And *Man* (like *Issachar*) in lodes delight,

The Form of Nature [159]

> Water's refin'd to *Motion*, Aire to *Light*,   * *Light,*
> Fire to all *three, but man hath no such mirth.   *Motion,*
>   *heat.*
>
> *Plants* in the *root* with Earth do most Comply,
>   Their *Leafs* with water, and humiditie,
>   The *Flowres* to air draw neer, and subtiltie,
> And *seeds* a kinred fire have with the sky.
>
> All have their *keyes*, and set *ascents*; but man
>   Though he knowes these, and hath more of his own,
>   Sleeps at the ladders foot; alas! what can
> These new discoveries do, except they drown?

The speaker revolves the terms of the contrast several times in his mind, circling flexibly from the creatures to man, back to the creatures, and back again to man, pausing now for a moment, now for longer, at each point. This flexible movement of the speaker's mind has the effect of weaving man and the creatures together in a single pattern, so that the basic unity proper to the Creation becomes part of the poem's form as well as of its theme. As the speaker's mind moves outward from the single example of the tempest to range more widely over the creatures, he finds in all of them the same tension of contrary potentialities, expressed as the contrary pull of downward and upward movement. The words "down" and "up," with their cognates, weave a leitmotif which defines the spiritual life in terms of motion on a vertical scale. The difference between man and the other creatures is not simply that he slips down the scale and they rise up it. It is that they cast off grossness and he does not, that they resist and master the baser potentialities of their natures and he succumbs to them. The difference is not that man's nature alone is divided so that he suffers conflict while the other creatures do not. The difference lies in the way the creatures and man resolve the conflicts to which their mixed natures subject them. Like Nature and Earth in the hieroglyphic tempest, the creatures actively choose and struggle for the return to God which is Nature's responsibility in the creative cycle; they vigorously seek to realize their potentiality for greater purity. But man passively sleeps at the ladder's foot, allows himself merely to be acted upon, so that when he wills he wills the love of things inferior to his own best part rather than the love of God. Waters "fall," but then "Chide, and fly up"; corrupt mists "Quit their first beds & mount"; "all / Strive upwards stil." The transfiguring ascents thus laboriously produced are expressed by the refinement of water, air, and fire, and by the hierarchical description of plants and of the four elements with which their parts "Comply." By contrast, man's alienation, his transfiguring *de*scent, is a voluntary surrender.[22]

The two final stanzas are occupied by the final phase of the meditative action, the colloquy, in which the affections are moved "to the love and exercise of vertue, and the hatred and avoiding of sinne." The latter passion moves this speaker first. As he energetically sums up the case against man, his language is dominated by sharp juxtapositions of apocalyptic and demonic imagery; the brevity of the contrasts vividly expresses, in little, the enormous distance between the end of one motion and the end of the other:

> O foolish man! how hast thou lost thy sight?
>   How is it that the Sun to thee alone
>   Is grown thick darkness, and thy bread, a stone?
> Hath flesh no softness now? mid-day no light?

Here the speaker is the accuser of man; but suddenly, without warning or transition, he becomes one of the accused, self-accusing. Teacher becomes pupil as he begins to imitate the tempest and the other creatures from whom he has read lectures for man. In prayer to God, knowing that his own powers are insufficient, he begins the struggle to reverse in his own soul the demonic transfigurations of light to darkness and flesh to flint:

> Lord! thou didst put a soul here; If I must
>   Be broke again, for flints will give no fire
>   Without a steel, O let thy power cleer
> Thy gift once more, and grind this flint to dust!

"The Book" (Martin, p. 540) is a poem that is clearly shaped by the pattern of formal meditation on death.[23] The analysis of the problem proceeds by amplification of a conceit based on the identical functions of the Book of God's Creatures and the Book of God's Word—the Bible, or *the* book—as revelations of God's will. The conceit consists in identifying the physical book as a microcosm of Nature. The subject of the meditation is death; its object, or the image which the mind frames in order to relate understanding and the senses, ideas and affections, is the Bible perceived as a material thing. The whole poem is cast in the form of direct address to God, characteristic of the third and final phase of meditative action, the colloquy. Nevertheless, within this framework, the development of the poem may be seen in terms of the three phases normal in meditation.

The poem opens with a simple proposal of the subject and of the main idea which will be developed—the solution of the problem of death gleaned (we shall later learn) from the study of both books:

> Eternal God! maker of all
> That have liv'd here, since the mans fall;
> The Rock of ages! in whose shade
> They live unseen, when here they fade.

The stanza simultaneously presents the problem and its solution in the simultaneous decay and preservation of the natural world, the one proceeding from man, whose Fall invented death and decay, the other from God. God is presented as Creator, "maker of all / That have liv'd here," and the epithet "Eternal" heightens this emphasis on creativity and life, besides importing a contrast between the fragility of temporal existence and the stability of its timeless source and end. The mind moves from eternity and life to time and death and back to eternal life again, tracing the transfigurations wrought in Nature first by man's sin and then by God's mercy.

With the second stanza, the mind moves from contemplation

of abstract doctrine or summary generalization to apprehend the Bible as a physical object:

> Thou knew'st this *papyr*, when it was
> Meer *seed*, and after that but *grass*;
> Before 'twas *drest* or *spun*, and when
> Made *linen*, who did *wear* it then:
> What were their lifes, their thoughts & deeds
> Whither good *corn*, or fruitless *weeds*.
>
> Thou knew'st this *Tree*, when a green *shade*
> Cover'd it, since a *Cover* made,
> And where it flourish'd, grew and spread,
> As if it never should be dead.
>
> Thou knew'st this harmless *beast*, when he
> Did live and feed by thy decree
> On each green thing; then slept (well fed)
> Cloath'd with this *skin*, which now lies spred
> A *Covering* o're this aged book,
> Which makes me wisely weep and look
> On my own dust; meer dust it is,
> But not so dry and clean as this.
> Thou knew'st and saw'st them all and though
> Now scatter'd thus, dost know them so.

Here the mind in meditation effects transfigurations of its own, moving back and forth in time as it imaginatively recreates or restores the Book of the Creatures which has been reduced by death to the inanimate object before him. This action of the mind destroys as well as creates, exemplifying the simultaneous operation of the cosmic principles expressed in the first stanza. The book is a human artifact, a product—like sin and death—of human wit. The speaker destroys this, analyzing it into its parts, and imaginatively imitates the action of God in creating Nature out of Chaos and restoring the dead to life. As his mind flickers from book to "Book" and back again, he comprehends decay and preservation, the continuous transfiguration of life to death and death to life, by contemplating simultaneous images of God's living works and of the miniature charnel house which they have become, and by imaginatively participating in the process by which these transformations are wrought.

The consideration of death in this poem gains its peculiar poignancy from this sharp juxtaposition of expanded and contracted images, this simultaneous presentation of Nature in aspects of prosperity and privation. The well-being of the creatures as they flourished once amidst the plenitude of Nature is balanced by the sharp contrast of their present condition. But the contrasts do not stop there. The order of the natural world is expressed by presentation of the creatures in the ascending sequence of the Chain of Being, and our sense of Nature's symmetry is enhanced by the author's symmetrical reservation of a separate stanza for each order of creatures and by his orderly repetition of the verbal formula "Thou knew'st" to introduce each stanza. This insistence that the creatures are comprehended by God and sustained in life by his providential care jostles against the insistent presence of their crumbled remains, which starkly hint of God's withdrawal, final cessations and relapses. But the friction finally yields the joyful recognition that God's knowledge of his creatures *is* comprehensive, that death modifies but does not destroy the form of Nature. The unfolding of the knowledge that Nature is united by God and with God in death as well as in life is marked by a shift from "knew'st" to "know"; earlier, the shift from past to present had been from life to death, but now this is transformed:

> Thou knew'st and saw'st them all and though
> Now scatter'd thus, dost know them so.[24]

The speaker himself is the last of the creatures to be named. As his knowledge of God's sustaining love unfolds, so too does the knowledge that he is subject equally with the other creatures to the fate induced by human sin. The realization prompts questions about his fitness to receive God's love. This moral concern is applied first to the wearers of the linen from which the paper of the book was made: "What were their lifes, their thoughts & deeds / Whither good *corn*, or fruitless *weeds*." The vegetal imagery points to mankind's union with the rest of Nature; and, by associating the moral life with the book, it points to the book's function as a moral emblem. He sees the book as a *memento mori* and turns his attention to his own moral condition, realizing that he shares in the decay of all creatures and the sinfulness of mankind. The first recognition might have made him weep in self-pity, but its combination with the second makes him weep "wisely"—that is, in repentance. The "natural fear" of death is joined with the "holy fear" of judgment. But at the same time as he feels the need for God's mercy he realizes fully God's omnipotence and love, and these recognitions issue in the impassioned colloquy with which the poem ends. With a final pun on "works," his mind leaps forward to envisage an ultimate transfiguration and to pray for a part in it:

> O knowing, glorious spirit! when
> Thou shalt restore trees, beasts and men,
> When thou shalt make all new again,
> Destroying onely death and pain,
> Give him amongst thy works a place,
> Who in them lov'd and sought thy face!

Chapter
VII
ARCHETYPE AND WIT: THE BED-GRAVE IMAGE

THE FIGURATIVE ASSOCIATION of sleep and death is an archetypal or primitive metaphor. Employed consciously for literary purposes, it has produced myriad elaborations and applications, forms and meanings. Socrates cured himself of the natural man's fear of death by comparing it to dreamless sleep, seeing both as obliterations of sense and consciousness, one temporary, the other permanent. Through several centuries the imitators of Petrarch sought relief from unrequited love in the oblivion of sleep, or, if they were very desperate, of death. Christian devotional writers, meditating intensely on death in prose and poetry, developed the metaphor fully and purposefully, elaborating many specific parallels between the two states. One of the most common and most fully developed of such images was an image of the grave as a bed.[1]

The simple, archetypal form of the sleep-death figure may be viewed as a metaphorical expression of the Greeks' philosophical view of the death of the body and of the Stoic solution to the problem that view presented. To fear death is both natural and absurd, since it is fearsome only in prospect. The solution is therefore to cultivate a passive courage by enuring the senses to the prospect of oblivion; it is in expressing this solution that Socrates, to give one example, makes use of the sleep-death figure. Since death is merely a sleep from which we do not awaken, to die is only a little harder than to go to sleep; and it will be as easy if we conquer natural fear by "practicing" death in going to bed. The commonplace allusions to sleep as the shadow or brother of death are associated with these views and these usages of the figure, which remain as one element in Christian devotional literature of the seventeenth century. They remain because a Christian is a natural creature who suffers the same natural fate as any brute or pagan; but they cannot retain their simple form because a Christian is precisely not a *mere* natural creature. He suffers a more complex fate than brute or pagan, a fate which includes natural death but in which natural death loses its simplicity.

The elaborations and applications which the archetypal sleep-death figure underwent in the sixteenth and seventeenth centuries were not merely academic products of a doctrine of imitation and invention with its attendant emphasis on wit, though they do illustrate the achievement of novelty, surprise, and new significance through the rehandling of inherited material and thus illustrate various kinds of wit. But they were not controlled by a frivolous love of ingenuity for display, nor by an academic theorem conceived as an imperative. They were produced by the intermingling of cultural streams at the Renaissance, by a regard for tradition coupled with a desire for present relevance. Imitation preserves the material of ancient experience, wit transforms it and endows it with contemporary relevance by relating it to newer material, newer experiences; and so a new medium is forged which is neither inherited nor original in any of the simple senses of those words.[2] The process is seen on the largest scale in Aquinas's fusion of Aristotelian metaphysics with Christian theology, in the fusion of classical with Christian ethics in Christian Humanism, or in Milton's typological use of classical myth. On the smaller scale of my subject, the sleep-death figure was inevitably transformed when it became embedded, together with the Stoicism of which it was an expression, in a Neoplatonic and Christian world view and writers employed it in a medium expressing truths unknown to the Stoics.

What happened may be seen in Hamlet's famous "To be, or not to be" soliloquy. For a while this contemplation of the shocks that flesh is heir to and the prospect of suicide follows traditional Stoic lines. "To be, or not to be" formulates the nature of reality and the problem facing the hard-pressed soul in the simplest of Stoic terms, and the essence of Stoic nihilism is distilled in

> To die: to sleep;
> No more; and by a sleep to say we end
> The heart-ache and the thousand natural shocks
> That flesh is heir to, 'tis a consummation
> Devoutly to be wish'd.

But when the ground of this resolution is displayed in the digest of the "whips and scorns of time," it has already ceased to be a resolution, for both the problem which it resolved and the conception of reality on which the problem was based have been changed by a subtle modulation of the image of sleep:

> To die, to sleep;
> To sleep: perchance to dream: ay, there's the rub;
> For in that sleep of death what dreams may come
> When we have shuffled off this mortal coil,
> Must give us pause.

The question is no longer to be or not to be, but to be in one condition or another. The dubiety of "perchance" is quickly replaced by assurance, for it is what dreams may come, not whether dreams will come, that gives us pause. And Hamlet has learned from his father's spirit that bad dreams after death will be real enough. The soliloquy imitates imaginatively the enlargement of pagan wisdom by revelation or the enlargement of reason by faith. The crux of the imaginative process is the modulation of the sleep-death figure. Shakespeare does not simply embroider the archetypal image, though by enlarging it with one detail he might be said to realize a potency latent in it. By making the enlarged image the vehicle of a truth excluded by its primitive form he makes of it a new image, basically the same only in the superficies of associated terms. But it cannot be subsumed by the primitive image. Rather the old is revaluated as it is absorbed to a larger structure and reconstituted in a new medium.

Vaughan inherited all three of the traditions—Stoic, Petrarchan, Christian—which fostered the sleep-death figure, and the metaphor occurs frequently, assuming a variety of forms, both in his secular verse and in the religious verse of his maturity. Like the sleep-death figure, many of Vaughan's figures are, basically, simple archetypal metaphors; but he does not usually give them to us in simple form. The bed-grave image, for instance (his favorite form of the sleep-death figure), is ingeniously elaborated in a variety of complex ways and intricately related to other images.

The bed-grave image in Vaughan, besides the terms of the primitive figure, usually carries with it the most effective "invention" of Christian writers in enlarging those terms: awakening. This enlargement was of course produced by the pressure of the doctrine of Resurrection for metaphorical as well as conceptual expression. The essential structure of the resulting figure may be observed in two of those "*prolusions* and strong *proofs* of our *restoration* laid out in *nature*" with which Vaughan illustrates and supports "the promise of the *God* of nature" in his *Discourse of Death*:

> There are in *nature* many *creatures* which at certain *seasons*, that their *spirit* is inconsistent with, fall into a *dormition*, or *dead sleep* which differs little from *death*, and convey themselves into *secret places*, as *hollow trees*, or some *desolate ruines*, where they may rest in safety during that *season*, as being taught by some *secret informant* that they shall *awake* again. . . . do not we see that these *birds* and inferiour *creatures* which in the *spring* and *summer* continue here very merry and *musical*, do on a sudden leave us, and all *winter*-long suffer a kind of *death*, and with the *Suns* warmth in the *youth* of the year *awake* again, and *refresh* the world with their *reviv'd notes*? . . . How much more then shall *Jesus*

Archetype and Wit: The Bed-Grave Image [169]

Christ the *Sun of righteousnesse rising with healing under his wings*, awake those that sleep in him, and bring them again with a joyful resurrection? (Martin, pp. 176-77)

Here we are still close to a purely archetypal pattern of imagery, and can see it clearly in the expression of a death-resurrection cycle in terms of the annual cycle of the seasons and the sun. This archetypal pattern at the base of the imagery is focused by the identification of Christ as "the *Sun of righteousnesse."* The poet's "invention" consists in the construction of an analogous sleep-awakening pattern, and in the suggestion of the implicit analogies that *"secret places,* as *hollow trees,* or some *desolate ruines,"* in this context, have to both beds and graves. The beginning of a prayer for *"When thou dost awake"* assimilates the archetypal pattern further into the world of natural experience, and accordingly the element of poetic invention is more noticeable and more important:

O God the Father! who saidst in the beginning, *Let there be light,* and it was so; *Inlighten my Eyes that I never sleepe in death.* (Martin, p. 143)

Creation, regeneration, and final salvation are presented analogously under a figure of light. The logical relation of the last two —the contingency of salvation after death on the achievement of sanctity before—is expressed by the common ground of *"Inlighten"* and *"never sleepe"* as muted figures of awakening. The common ground consists in the relation of each to the literal awakening from sleep which is the occasion of the prayer, and which thus becomes a part of the imagery as a figure of both regeneration and redemption.

At its first appearance in Vaughan's poetry, the bed-grave image is merely tacked on as the poet addresses the tyrant of his heart:

> If when I'm gone, you chance to see
> That cold bed where I lodged bee:

> Let not your hate in death appeare,
> But blesse my ashes with a teare:
> This influxe from that quickning eye,
> By secret pow'r, which none can spie,
> The cold dust shall informe, and make
> Those flames (though dead) new life partake.
> Whose warmth help'd by your tears shall bring,
> O're all the tombe a sudden spring
> Of Crimson flowers.   ("Les Amours," Martin, p. 4)

The image is not properly articulated, and besides making a dead spot in the poem it becomes involved in irresolution and ambiguity. The associations of "bed" are not developed, and the image is not related meaningfully to its context. It is completely irrelevant to the developments which purport to depend on it. Vaughan's failure to make use of the bed-grave image is unhappily emphasized by his wrenching of the figure in accordance with the flower emblem to present the grave as a flower bed. A vestige of the initial figure appears in "curtaine," but dislocated from its proper context into the new flower-bed image it loses its expressive potential (thoroughly realized in later usages) and becomes a mere decorative fancy. The dissipation of the image's potential is manifested by the ambiguity of the poem's conclusion. The climax of the figurative resurrection conveyed by the development of the images is an advertisement of the proposition "That you kill'd me, 'cause I lov'd you." The figurative resurrection at the center of the poem is reduced to a contrivance by which this proposition receives the sanction of "Heaven." The apparent contradiction between means and ends reflects Vaughan's failure to fuse the chosen theme with the implications of the images by which he purports to convey it. His failure to realize the bed-grave image and his adventitious wrenching of it are aspects of this larger disharmony.

Both beds of "Les Amours" figure the charnel house in the poem of that name (Martin, p. 41), with the difference that they do not jar because they appear further apart and contribute differently to the theme. Instead of blurring the central term within a unit of thought, they present different aspects of the same theme, different perspectives from which it is approached. Irrelevant and conflicting associations of both beds are kept out, and both are so related to the second term of the figure that they repose together in the unity which they help to establish. The flower-bed figure occurs first, as one of a number of similitudes by which Vaughan describes the charnel house in an apostrophe:

> *Kelder* of mists, a second *Fiats* care,
> Frontspeece o'th' grave and darkness, a Display
> Of ruin'd man, and the disease of day;
> Leane, bloudless shamble, where I can descrie
> Fragments of men, Rags of Anatomie;
> Corruptions ward-robe, the transplantive bed
> Of mankind, and th'Exchequer of the dead.

The "transplantive bed" image carries the principal suggestion of growth amidst images conveying corruption and decay. The total meaning of the passage is growth in, or through, or from, decay. The charnel house is an emblem of the second Chaos to which death reduces the forms of nature. This aspect of the apostrophe's meaning is clarified later in the poem:

> As th'Elements by Circulation passe
> From one to th'other, and that which first was
> Is so again, so 'tis with you; The grave
> And Nature but Complott, what the one gave,
> The other takes.

This second Chaos must be "a second *Fiats* care" like the first. The relation between the anticipated second fiat and the Creation is essentially the same as in Vaughan's prayer: "O God the Father! who saidst in the beginning, *Let there be light*, and it was so; *Inlighten my Eyes that I never sleepe in death*." Satisfaction of the need expressed by "a second *Fiats* care" in this context is affirmed by the transplantive bed image. The flowers of the world have been transplanted hither, and in this new bed they lose what Nature gave. But the charnel house is not merely a rubbish heap; paradoxically, it is also a fertile bed, from which, under similar care to that which first produced them, the transplanted seedlings will grow to mature blooms. Or it is a seedbed from which seedlings reincorporating the forms of the decayed earthly flowers will be transplanted to grow to maturity in the richer soil of a heavenly garden. These are genuine paradoxes, not contradictions or confusions, not lapses in expressiveness: the paradoxical imagery expresses a paradoxical meaning. The point of view from which death appears as a new beginning conditions the rest of the apostrophe, where concern for the outcome of the first beginning is expressed in relation to death:

> *Torpedo* to the Eye! whose least glance can
> Freeze our wild lusts, and rescue head-long man;
> Eloquent silence! able to Immure
> An *Athiests* thoughts, and blast an *Epicure*.
> Were I a *Lucian*, Nature in this dresse
> Would make me wish a Saviour, and Confesse.

This point of view, derived from revelation of God's purposes, is subordinated to a natural or rational point of view from which death appears as an end. Vaughan's primary concern in this poem is with human behavior within the natural world (especially political behavior, as E. L. Marilla has shown).[3] Interpreting his "sad library," Vaughan is drawing moral rather than anagogical significances from the text. His concern is with the conditions of men rather than with God's purposes for their souls. The contingency of the latter on the former is developed far enough to deepen the moral significance of the poem but not so far as to dislodge it from its moral context. Death as perceived from this perspective is expressed by an image of the charnel house as a bed which simply concretizes the archetypal form of the sleep-death figure:

> *Chameleons* of state, Aire-monging band,
> Whose breath (like Gun-powder) blowes up a land,
> Come see your dissolution, and weigh
> What a loath'd nothing you shall be one day,
> As th'Elements by Circulation passe
> From one to th'other, and that which first was
> Is so again, so 'tis with you; The grave
> And Nature but Complott, what the one gave,
> The other takes; Think then, that in this bed
> There sleep the Reliques of as proud a head
> As stern and subtill as your own, that hath
> Perform'd , or forc'd as much, whose tempest-wrath
> Hath levell'd Kings with slaves, and wisely then
> Calme these high furies, and descend to men.

In this and later passages sounds the note of Hamlet in the graveyard contemplating the devolution of imperious Caesar. Hamlet rests in apprehension of the horror; Vaughan turns the horror into an ethical motive. It is an old theme, the moral application of death much elaborated by the Stoics, in which the annihilation in prospect enforces moderation and all the constructive virtues. Of course the weakness of the ethic is that if all suffer the same indignity moderation may be just as absurd in the face of death as excess. The moral argument from the shortness of life and inevitability of oblivion may be subverted by an appeal to sensuous license as the best use of time—the *carpe diem* theme. Christian moralists converted folly into sin by abolishing annihilation as illusory, making virtue the revealed will of God as well as a law of reason, and sanctioning earthly morality with transcendent consequences. Virtue was transcended by blessedness, natural death by eternal life or eternal death, natural fear of dissolution by the "holy fear" of damnation, and the rational motives of virtue by love of the Redeemer and aspiration toward eternal enjoyment of his love.

Vaughan adumbrates elements of this larger structure in "The Charnel-house," but prevents them blurring his more limited perspective. One aspect of this careful control of point of view is his omission from the typical bed-grave image of the anagogical significances of which it was capable and his conveyance of them in muted fashion through a different image employing a different kind of bed. Clarity and consistency are achieved through a limitation of perspective rather than by a transcendence of complexities or their fusion. When Vaughan fused in a single image the elements of both bed images in this poem, he expressed through it a more complex awareness, avoiding both confusion and oversimplification.

In "An Elegie on the death of Mr. R. W." (Martin, p. 49), as in "The Charnel-house," the Parliamentarians are the foils of virtue. Vaughan extols the "loyall upright life, and gallant End" of this Royalist at the expense of his enemies. He was

> More forward in a royall gallantrie
> Than all those vast pretenders, which of late
> Swell'd in the ruines of their King and State.
> He weav'd not *Self-ends*, and the *Publick* good
> Into one piece, nor with the peoples bloud
> Fill'd his own veins; In all the doubtfull way
> *Conscience* and *Honour* rul'd him.

The bed-grave image functions partly toward expression of these contrasting values:

> Though thy lov'd ashes misse me, and mine Eyes
> Had no acquaintance with thy Exequies,
> Nor at the last farewell, torn from thy sight
> On the *Cold sheet* have fix'd a *sad delight*.
> Yet what e'r pious hand (in stead of mine)
> Hath done this office to that dust of thine,
> And till thou rise again from thy low bed
> Lent a Cheap pillow to thy quiet head,
> Though but a private *turffe*, it can do more
> To keep thy name and memory in store

> Than all those *Lordly fooles* which lock their bones
> In the dumb piles of Chested brasse, and stones.

The deathbed and the grave are here fused into a single image, which thus accumulates additional concrete details, furnished with a *"Cold sheet"* and a "Cheap pillow" as in "Les Amours" it was furnished with curtains. "Cheap pillow" and "low bed" are integrated with the moral context, suggesting the modest reticence of a virtuous character in contrast to the moral defects symbolized by funerary display. Through the image Vaughan transcends the limited moral context of "The Charnel-house"; the conjunction of "low bed" with "rise again" expresses resurrection through allusion to awakening and suggests the relation of virtue to redemption.

An even more successful example occurs in "An Elegie on the death of Mr. *R. Hall*" (Martin, p. 58), where Vaughan integrates the bed-grave image with another of his favorite figures, an image of light specifically related to the stars.[4] After praising Hall for the rational virtues of learning and valor, he distinguishes these from spiritual sanctity, conveyed by a star image which is then joined with the bed-grave image to express the spirit's transcendence of death:

> Those richer graces that adorn'd thy mind
> Like stars of the *first magnitude*, so shin'd,
> That if oppos'd unto these lesser lights
> All we can say, is this, *They were fair nights*.
> Thy *Piety* and *Learning* did unite,
> And though with *Sev'rall beames* made up *one light*,
> And such thy Judgement was, that I dare swear
> Whole *Counsels* might as soon, and *Synods* erre.
>   But all these now are out! and as some *Star*
> Hurl'd in Diurnall motions from far,
> And seen to droop at night, is vainly sed
> To fall, and find an *Occidentall bed*,
> Though in that other world what wee Judge *West*

> Proves *Elevation*, and a new, fresh *East*.
> So though our weaker sense denies us sight
> And bodies cannot trace the *Spirits* flight,
> Wee know those graces to be still in thee,
> But wing'd above us to eternitie.

The paradox of life in death, reflecting a paradoxical subversion of reason by faith and revelation, of what "wee Judge" by what "Wee know," is expressed by a pattern of minor juxtapositions: "fall" and "Elevation," "what wee Judge *West*" and what "Proves" to be "a new, fresh *East*." The pattern is easily recognized as one based on the archetypal image of the sun's daily cycle as a metaphor of death and resurrection. The imagery suggests awakening from sleep in the morning and Christ's subversion of the Old Law through the Resurrection, which of course provides the theological basis of the assurance expressed by the passage as a whole. Discernible at the base of the whole pattern of imagery is the Christian myth of man's fall into a world of death from Eden and his elevation out of that world by means of Christ's repetition of man's act on Calvary, both Eden and Calvary being of course in the East. The natural or rational perspective on virtue and death is there, but it is not primary as in "The Charnel-house." Its limitations are expressed as it is placed in a larger scheme and its relations to a point of view that transcends it are clarified. The paradoxical discoveries of wit provide the only adequate mode of conveying the complexities of appearance and reality involved. The logical structure of the imagery here is essentially the same as in "The King Disguis'd" and the elegy beginning "I walkt the other day," which will be discussed in later pages. But, though it does not involve the bed-grave figure, perhaps the most obvious parallel is offered by "They are all gone into the world of light!" (Martin, p. 483):

> Dear, beauteous death! the Jewel of the Just,
>   Shining nowhere, but in the dark;

What mysteries do lie beyond thy dust;
    Could man outlook that mark!

He that hath found some fledg'd birds nest, may know
    At first sight, if the bird be flown;
But what fair Well, or Grove he sings in now,
    That is to him unknown.

And yet, as Angels in some brighter dreams
    Call to the soul, when man doth sleep:
So some strange thoughts transcend our wonted theams,
    And into glory peep.

If a star were confin'd into a Tomb
    Her captive flames must needs burn there;
But when the hand that lockt her up, gives room,
    She'l shine through all the sphaere.

In "The King Disguis'd" and "To his . . . *Loyal Fellow-Prisoner*" Vaughan integrates the bed-grave figure with other images to convey a fictive resurrection with much more success than in "Les Amours." The "*Loyal Fellow-Prisoner*" poem (Martin, p. 623) is the less complicated. The situation is that Powell has not been responding to the poet's affection and manifesting his own with customary vigor.[5] Vaughan figures Powell's lethargy as death and his anticipated arousal from it by the poem as resurrection. He establishes the figure by interrelating a number of elements, of which the most important is an adaptation of Gilbert's magnetic theory. This provides the principal terms of the figure: the state of "senseless things" as death through the recession of love, the response of iron to the attractive power of the magnet as life manifested in action as love. Powell and the poet may be likened to "Such two hard things as *Iron* are and *Stones*" because they lack the "excess" of "such whose equal easie hearts" enable them to "mingle Souls" with a facility Milton reserved for angels. The mode by which their mutual love "both unites" is analogous to the mode by which the "kind Soul in *Magnets*" "attones" (i.e., makes one) iron and stone. Vaughan is the stone, exercising its power of "attraction" on the iron (Powell), sending forth its "Invitation" (specifically the poem) as a manifestation of love. But

> we cannot state
> A Commerce, unless both we animate.
> For senseless things, though ne'r so call'd upon,
> Are deaf, and feel no Invitation;
> But such as at the last day shall be shed
> By the great Lord of Life into the Dead.
> . . . .
> For were it otherwise (which cannot be,
> And do thou judge my bold Philosophie:)
> Then it would follow that if I were dead,
> Thy love, as now in life, would in that Bed
> Of Earth and darkness warm me, and dispense,
> Effectual informing Influence.

Vaughan posits the norm of their relationship to contrast present appearances with it. With good-humored exaggeration he suggests the possibility that on present evidence Powell may "feel no Invitation" until doomsday, and assures his clerical friend that there is no heresy in his use of Gilbert's theory: a man may be as responsive as a piece of iron without endangering his soul! The explicit invitation is expressed in terms of the response it hopes to elicit, through a figure of the "resurrection" which, unless Powell is literally inanimate, it has power to effect. The associations of the image link it with the bed-grave image through which the hypothesis of Powell's senseless state has been in part conveyed.

> But as the *Mary-gold* in Feasts of Dew
> And early Sun-beams, though but thin and few
> Unfolds its self, then from the Earths cold breast

Archetype and Wit: The Bed-Grave Image [179]

> Heaves gently, and salutes the hopeful *East*:
> So from thy quiet *Cell*, the retir'd Throne
> Of thy fair thoughts, which silently bemoan
> Our sad distractions, come . . .

A subtly allusive poem, "The King Disguis'd" (Martin, p. 625) achieves unity and imparts depth and weight to its subject through Vaughan's integration of allusions in an encompassing figure which may be regarded in two ways: as a figure of incarnation, and as a figure of life in death represented crucially as resurrection. The imaginative fusion of incarnation and resurrection in a single set of images is a masterwork of wit discovering similarity-in-difference and difference-in-similarity and thus endowing the images with a remarkable range and power. The best example in Vaughan of this particular fusion is offered by "The Incarnation, and Passion" (Martin, p. 415):

> Lord! when thou didst thy selfe undresse
> Laying by thy robes of glory,
> To make us more, thou wouldst be lesse,
> And becam'st a wofull story.
>
> To put on Clouds instead of light,
> And cloath the morning-starre with dust,
> Was a translation of such height
> As, but in thee, was ne'r exprest;
>
> Brave wormes, and Earth! that thus could have
> A God Enclos'd within your Cell,
> Your maker pent up in a grave,
> Life lockt in death, heav'n in a shell.

Both terms of the title are imported by each of the images; any image may be interpreted with equal validity in relation to either term—or, rather, each image must be related to both terms at once. Similarly, in "They are all gone into the world of light!" the star locked in a tomb and released (besides the underlying but central reference to Christ) must be interpreted as the soul confined in the body, the whole person confined in the world (both transcended through death), and as the soul and body lodged in death and transcending it through the consummate union of the resurrection.

Vaughan's method causes "The King Disguis'd" to transcend the immediate situation which it celebrates,[6] making the situation the nucleus of a larger body of meaning, the metaphorical core of the poem. The language of the poem consistently suggests associations with the Incarnation and Passion of Christ. The resonance of "Poor, obscure shelter! if that shelter be / Obscure, which harbours so much Majesty" results, at the most literal level, from the use of such language through centuries of meditation on the Nativity, on the majesty of the Babe poorly and obscurely sheltered in the stable at Bethlehem. And that image was itself metaphorical, a vehicle of the profound mystery of the Word made flesh; and the analogous mystery of man, dust infused with the breath of God, was expressed in similar language. This is not a mere fancy in Vaughan: to a Royalist who believed that the universe was disposed in interlocking hierarchies by divine decree, the King manifest as a servingman was strictly similar, without hyperbole or poetic license, to the Son of God manifest as a carpenter and his image as a bare forked animal. Only wit was required to see and express the similarity-in-difference. This conception of Image and Word meeting in the disguised king is expressed by analogous images of obscure majesty which run through the poem: light confined by clouds, the sun shining in and after storms, light in darkness, alive in a coffin, curtains around a bed, life in death, saint in sheepskin, "King and no King."

The incarnation meaning of these images is obvious; their death-resurrection meaning appears more clearly when we see how they express and support an interpretation of the suffering Charles as England's sacrificial lamb, redeeming the people's wickedness through patient suffering in righteousness and love. The "true white Prince," endowed with divine light, "Himself deposed his own Majesty," stealing alive into his coffin and ravishing death to save his enemies from the damnation toward which their wickedness would have propelled them. This is parallel to both the Son's willingness to assume flesh and to Christ's meek acceptance of his sacrificial, redemptive role. Pursued by "Wolves," this "Royal Saint" traduces the majesty of his spirit "in sheep-skin." Paradoxically, this humble guise is a magic shield, a "sacred cov'ring" or divine shade in which he rides safely, the eyes of his pursuers—the "vulgar" for whom the mystery of kingship in a servingman is too deep—"blinded" by the disguise. Here, as elsewhere ("The Constellation," for instance), Vaughan interprets the Rebellion metaphorically under the figure of the rebellion of the angels and of the human rebelliousness toward God involved in Christ's Passion. But here the impious have raised arms, not against "an inglorious man," but against divine majesty manifest, the Word seen plain. However, the King's incarnation as an inglorious man has frustrated instead of (as with Christ) abetted the impiety. The deceptive appearances lead them away from instead of toward their ultimate crime; the evasion saves the rebels from the consequences of their sinful aims by fulfilling those aims voluntarily. A partial victory, it prefigures their eventual redemption in spite of themselves through the saving punishment of defeat. The consequence of the Passion (redemption) is fused with the act of rebellion, for the rebellion entails the Incarnation (the king's disguise), and this is presented as itself a saving sacrifice. It is itself a death, but a death that happens and is transcended simultaneously. The King is "alive," still King, in the "Coffin" of his disguise. The image of curtains around the royal bed, parallel to the disguise, figures both the veil of common man drawn around sacred majesty and the grave enclosing the immortal spirit. Incarnate or interred, the Word submits itself to the shows of things: "When he was first obscur'd with this coarse thing, / He grac'd *Plebeians*, but prophan'd the King." The submission is actual, but the Word is not circumscribed by it; the modes of flesh and death are not ultimate: "But all these Clouds cannot thy light confine, / The Sun in storms and after them, will shine."

As in spiritual, so in political "salvation": in order to save, the sacrifice must complete itself in resurrection, its conditions must be transcended. Literally, the King must put on himself again. The political optimism of the poem is tempered by an apocalyptic interpretation of the Rebellion which links it with the depravity of man, as the contemplation of death—a narrower eschatology—links it in "The Charnel-house." The poem combines an assured awareness of the strength of righteousness and the efficacy of sacrifice with an apprehensiveness expressing the vulnerability of mere truth in "this sinful Isle." This latter mood dominates the conclusion, made intensely moving by its expression in terms of the King's personal safety, with a further poignancy added by the irony of subsequent events:

> O may they wander all from thee as farr
> As they from peace are, and thy self from Warr!
> And wheresoe're thou do'st design to be
> With thy (now spotted) spottles Majestie,
> Be sure to look no Sanctuary there,
> Nor hope for safety in a temple, where
> Buyers and Sellers trade: O strengthen not
> With too much trust the Treason of a Scot!

Christ's driving of the money changers from the temple, a parable of the righteous purging the impious from God's society, was a type of the apocalyptic purgation of all evil from God's works in the destruction of the Serpent by *Christus victor*. The apprehension that the sacrifice Charles has already made may not be enough, that the purgation of evil and reign of the "true white Prince" may be frustrated by his playing the lamb instead of the lion, expresses an estimate of the depravity which he must conquer. The poem interprets the total political situation metaphorically as a war of Christ with Antichrist, the outcome of which is uncertain. When we see this, we can see that only a shift in events was needed to deepen this apprehension to a profound pessimism. The dimensions which the allusive style gives this poem enable us to see something of how, when regicide had confirmed its doubts, political despair came to be integrated in a profounder pessimism, to provide a motive toward solution of a problem of cosmic proportions by means of a profounder apocalyptic vision.

The simplest examples of the bed-grave image in Vaughan are to be found in "Easter Hymn" and the elegy beginning "Come, come, what doe I here?" (Martin, pp. 457, 420). A figure of sleep-awakening as death-resurrection, the essential structure of the image in the Christian scheme, is simply associated with a concretion. There is no analysis or elaboration of the image, and no linking of it by association with analogous images to construct large encompassing figures, such as we have seen in some of the poems examined so far. There is a corresponding lack of comprehensive fidelity to the truth of experience; though in a different direction, truth is here simplified far more severely than in "The Charnel-house," for instance. The images function not toward complex, experiential truth, but toward an effect of tone abstracted from its medium, like a symphonic theme presented by a single instrument without variation. The essence of Christian attitudes to death is distilled out of the complex matter of Christian experience and conveyed pure instead of through its inherent relationships with that experience. The remoteness of the isolated abstract idea is mitigated by a tone of cosy familiarity achieved through the domestic associations of the imagery. But it is precisely this tone that marks the extreme of simplification. The conclusion of the elegy

> But I would be
> With him I weep
> A bed, and sleep
> To wake in thee

leaves out more of the truth than we customarily expect of poets. But it is saved somewhat by the context, by the first stanza's expression of the burdensomeness of bereaved existence and more especially by the adjacent image which posits a different attitude toward death:

> Perhaps some think a tombe
> No house of store,
> But a dark, and seal'd up wombe,
> Which ne'r breeds more.

This hypothesis, reflecting an aspect of the natural experience of death, is too weakly expressed and too easily transcended, thrust aside with "Come, come! / Such thoughts benum." They do benumb indeed—that is the point; and so does the experience of death which they express. Faith does not so easily transcend the torments of the spirit in the flesh and the illusions of experience. The rock that Dr. Johnson kicked to disprove Berkeley may have been an illusion of his mind, and so may the pain in his great toe, but it hurt nevertheless. He did not disprove Berkeley, but he demonstrated succinctly that a rock provides a different experience from a mathematical formula. It is by the former that poetry lives, but Vaughan here forsakes it rather than stub his toe. The spirit's shrinking from reality is shown in the poem's emotional escapism, the imagination's in the tenuity of the poetic images.

In "Easter Hymn" the subversion of "Death, and darkness" by the Saviour is even more crudely simplified. The design prevents the images from functioning as pure hyperbole, to which an eclectic concentration of experience is essential, and instead impels them to insist on their inadequacy to what they celebrate:

> Graves are beds now for the weary,
> Death a nap, to wake more merry;
> Youth now, full of pious duty,
> Seeks in thee for perfect beauty,
> The weak, and aged tir'd, with length
> Of daies, from thee look for new strength,
> And Infants with thy pangs Contest
> As pleasant, as if with the brest.

Even as hyperbole this would be inadequate, but it is not permitted to function as hyperbole, for the realities it excludes are imported earlier:

Archetype and Wit: The Bed-Grave Image [185]

> Death, and darkness get you packing,
> Nothing now to man is lacking,
> All your triumphs now are ended,
> And what *Adam* marr'd, is mended.

The reality of death and darkness, of all that is summarized as what Adam marred, is so attenuated in generalization that it lacks any imaginative force; the recovered bliss and glory of Heaven is only a little less attenuated in the incommensurate generalities of the other passage. Thus, on both counts, the transfiguration of the one to the other lacks the significance which the poem assumes and which it is designed to express: the celebration itself dissipates its own motive and meaning. Both terms of the basic formula—the state of things "before" and "after" the first Easter—are present in every part of the two passages quoted; that is, the total design is reflected in each detail. But this repetition of the paradox only enhances its inherent weakness, its sentimental facility and the crude generality of its terms. The mention of death's "pangs," reminding us of their reality, contradicts the facile statement of their conversion into pleasures, which does not take account of that reality. The differences between graves and beds, between death and a nap, are real; the poem declares the similarities alone to be real. The resemblances between the "before" and "after" are real too; the poem insists on the sole reality of the differences. What Adam marred was not mended with a facile finger snap, as this poem expresses it. By so doing it undermines the praise of the Saviour with which it ends, leaving the expression of reverence for him a mere pious gesture.

Elements of the bed-grave image which lie in cold obstruction in these poems are brought to imaginative life in "*Death. A Dialogue*" and the elegy beginning "I walkt the other day." The latter poem (Martin, p. 478) elaborates one of those "*prolusions* and strong *proofs* of our *restoration* laid out in *nature*," a natural emblem or hieroglyph of the spiritual truth of resurrection, "the promise of the *God* of nature." By his method of dealing with the image, Vaughan makes it the imaginative counterpart of a fusion of physical and metaphysical reality, a central part of his theme which emerges to full statement in the last three stanzas. The process by which the structure of thought comes to be manifested, not merely conveyed, by the image, is possible because it is subtle, and it is made subtle by the working of a single point of view upon a single image. The process is crucially aided by the bed-grave image.

For the first four stanzas the digging up of the bulb—the "other bowre" to which the "gallant flowre" has retired for the winter—is developed as an emblem, a natural analogy of spiritual truth. The introduction of the bed-grave image in the fifth stanza, consolidating the emblem by subtly drawing the parallel, actually draws the parallel levels together, acting as a catalyst back on the preceding stanzas and converting the emblematic digging into a symbolic exhumation. It enables the digging up of the bulb to function as a clear parallel to the digging up of a grave, and simultaneously enables it to transcend those limits and become a perspective whereby the viewer can "peep and peer" into "that other world" where "what wee Judge *West* / Proves *Elevation*, and a new, fresh *East*." The thing seen as illustration becomes a mode of seeing that which it illustrated; the actual object of vision, becoming a mode of viewing the real object, partakes in the latter's reality as the latter's form is determined by the perspective in which it is seen. Instead of illustrating a spiritual truth in a parallel construction, the image "Proves" the truth by manifesting it: the emblem becomes a symbol. Vaughan celebrates the emergence of the "poor root" from emblem to symbol as a prelude to a brilliant statement of the larger view of reality within which the symbol functions, from which it derives its form, and which it here serves to justify and express:

> And yet, how few believe such doctrine springs
>   From a poor root
> Which all the Winter sleeps here under foot
>   And hath no wings
> To raise it to the truth and light of things,
>   But is stil trod
> By ev'ry wandring clod.

Archetype and Wit: The Bed-Grave Image

> O thou! whose spirit did at first inflame
> And warm the dead,
> And by a sacred Incubation fed
> With life this frame
> Which once had neither being, forme, nor name,
> Grant I may so
> Thy steps track here below,
>
> That in these Masques and shadows I may see
> Thy sacred way,
> And by those hid ascents climb to that day
> Which breaks from thee
> Who art in all things, though invisibly.

The introduction of the bed-grave image in the fifth stanza converts the emblem into a symbol by "applying" it or clarifying its meaning without, however, drawing a parallel with something outside the image. That is, it does not introduce determinants of the truth external to the image, but releases the properties of the image adumbrated in the preceding stanzas to operate as determinants themselves. The integration of the bed-grave image with the flower image to produce this symbol succeeds by reason of its extreme delicacy:

> This past, I threw the Clothes quite o'r his head,
> And stung with fear
> Of my own frailty dropt down many a tear
> Upon his bed,
> Then sighing whisper'd, *Happy are the dead!*
> *What peace doth now*
> *Rock him asleep below?*

The soil dug out to uncover the root is replaced as clothes of the deathbed drawn over the head of the corpse. At this point the imagery begins to ramify in all directions, to operate on many levels at once. The flower bed becomes the deathbed, the grave, a cradle, and an ordinary bed, the symbol consisting in the interaction of these with each other and with the properties of the central flower image. The paradoxical contradiction of appearance by reality, which the image has hitherto expressed, is made the basis of a larger paradox which subsumes it: the paradox of appearance manifesting reality. The root is able, by contradicting the appearance of the flower's loss, to express the "higher" reality of resurrection while continuing to be its own appearing self —a poor root. That is to say, it is a reality only in relation to the flower, as part of the order of nature. In relation to the spiritual truth of resurrection, as part of a larger spiritual order, it is itself an appearance. But this appearance is not contradicted by reality, but manifests it—manifests it not in spite of being a poor root but *by* being such. It is a paradox, and "few believe" it, not because it is factitious or they have not investigated the "facts" about flowers and bulbs, but because it is a difficult mystery.

The contradiction of appearance by "reality" in the "facts" of nature is simply an exposure of the deceptiveness of one sense perception by another, and extends knowledge only along a single plane. Grasp of fact as mystery enlarges that plane, exposing the deceptiveness of the limitations expressed by the *"mere* root" perceived by the senses. In reality it is "poor root" and more— one of the "steps" of God implanted "here below." Contradiction, reflecting a limited awareness, is absorbed in a unity which expresses itself in paradox, mystery, symbol. The poem presents death, human life, and Nature as real, not in themselves, but as aspects of a total reality which also encompasses resurrection, eternal life, and God. The symbol holds these in poise, saving the poem from the distorting simplifications of transcendentalism at one extreme and naturalism at the other. Accordingly there is no facile glossing of the pain of death or the agony of loss, no escapist reaction against a world made barren by bereavement. Man is a poor creature in the grave, "stil trod / By ev'ry wandring clod," but yet "A gallant flowre"; Nature is a sorry affair of "Masques and shadows," but yet, seen aright, God's "sacred way"; life is a wintry field, but yet the sphere wherein "here below" God's steps may be tracked and we may

> by those hid ascents climb to that day
> Which breaks from thee
> Who art in all things, though invisibly.

The "hid ascents" are the "Masques and shadows" seen in full perspective; among them, of course, is death. It is through his death that the speaker prays God to

> shew me his life again
> At whose dumbe urn
> Thus all the year I mourn.

In "Death. *A Dialogue*" (Martin, p. 399), the bifurcation of viewpoint in the dialogue does not override unity or complexity, because it is subsumed by the unity of imagery. The basic terms in which the poem presents death are those of the epigraph from the book of Job: "A Land of darknesse, as darkenes is selfe, and of the shadow of death, without any order, and where the light is as darknesse." Obviously, images of oblivion after death have meaning only as negations of experience. Entirely dependent upon the senses' report of reality, they present a hypothetical prospect, an expression of death's appearance to the natural mind "Before I goe whence I shall not returne." So the grave is presented in the "*Loyal Fellow-Prisoner*" poem as a "Bed / Of Earth and darkness" which love cannot warm because "there is no *sence* . . . no *Passion*, nor *Intelligence*." As here the dead are "senseless things," so in "The Charnel-house" they are "a loath'd nothing" presenting "a Display / Of ruin'd man,'" and are described in terms of "dissolution." This view of death authenticates as real the experience of life in this world, and supports an elegiac tone which enhances the value of that experience.

In "Death. *A Dialogue*" this natural view of death is thoroughly integrated with a transcendental view. The Body's entertainment of the possibility that it may retain some "sence" in death expresses the reluctance of the senses to resign, the natural affection for this fleshly sphere. It is essentially elegiac. Moreover, it enables the idea of resurrection to be introduced as a part of the Body's awareness; the Body envisages a longing for release as the primary effect of its hypothetical experience. So presented, the idea of resurrection simultaneously intensifies the elegiac mood and points toward a reality beyond nature, especially by the images of the curtained bed and the obscured sun:

> But if all sence wings not with thee,
> And something still be left the dead,
> I'le wish my Curtaines off to free
> Me from so darke, and sad a bed;
>
> A neast of nights, a gloomie sphere,
> Where shadowes thicken, and the Cloud
> Sits on the Suns brow all the yeare,
> And nothing moves without a shrowd.

The Soul promptly confirms Body's view of death, thus endorsing the validity of sense experience and natural reason, which Body has assumed. This point is not altered by the fact that Soul explicitly denies Body's supposition that some sense may remain to it after death, sponsoring instead the Body's senseless sleep, as in "*To his . . . Loyal Fellow-Prisoner*":

> But thou
> Shalt in thy mothers bosome sleepe
> Whilst I each minute grone to know
> How neere Redemption creepes.

The truth of Body's elegiac view of life and death is endorsed and at the same time the elements of this view are enlarged to include their apparent opposites—the burdensome pain of life and the sweet relief of death's dreamless sleep. The recognitions that prompt virgins to make much of time and Hamlets to make their own quietus are fused in a single recognition. This is revealed most fully in the first three stanzas of Soul's speech, where Soul confirms and clarifies Body's explanation of death by employing the same images in a parallel explanation of life:

> 'Tis so: But as thou sawest that night
> Wee travell'd in, our first attempts
> Were dull, and blind, but Custome straight
> Our feares, and falls brought to contempt,
>
> Then, when the gastly *twelve* was past
> We breath'd still for a blushing *East,*
> And bad the lazie Sunne make hast,
> And on sure hopes, though long, did feast;
>
> But when we saw the Clouds to crack
> And in those Cranies light appear'd,
> We thought the day then was not slack,
> And pleas'd our selves with what wee fear'd;
>
> Just so it is in death. . . .

The bed-grave, light-darkness, sleep-waking images we have looked at are contained within a day-night image which organizes the poem. The basic figure of dawn, containing both night and day in the transformation of one to the other, is not simple in itself and is made more complex by multiple uses yielding a double vision of death. Both life and death are given seemingly contradictory values which do not cancel one another but are contained within a larger vision. Through his "witty" handling of the poem's basically simple imagery, Vaughan exceeds the limited simplicities of naturalism and transcendentalism, encompassing both in a complex vision revealed particularly by the poem's chiaroscuro imagery.

In the elegy beginning "Joy of my life!" (Martin, p. 422), as in the elegy on R. Hall, the integrity of the soul both before and after death is expressed by a star/light image associated with the bed-grave figure. Through this imagery both poems express the intimate relation of the natural to the transcendent order of reality as this relation is rendered crucial by death. It is seen to be crucial when death is considered in conjunction with redemption, and this is the pattern expressed by the conjunction of the star and bed images. "A life well lead," imaged as a star "of mighty use" to the pilgrim struggling through the world's night toward the "shining spires" of the Heavenly City, may be compared to those "steps" of God, spoken of in the elegy beginning "I walkt the other day," which the pilgrim following His "sacred way" must "track here below." The thesis demonstrated by the images in "Joy of my life!" is stated in conceptual language in the first stanza:

> A life well lead
> This truth commends,
> With quick, or dead
> It never ends.

The simplicity of diction, syntax, and prosody may, with a reader accustomed to Donne's style, discourage recognition of the actual intricacy of this statement. A good life does not end with the quick or with the dead. In the simplest sense: a good life does not end when the "quick" state of the person who lives it ends, since the immortal soul realizes its goodness eternally. This is the meaning when the good life is considered in itself. Considered in relation to others, as example ("How in thy absence thou dost steere / Me from above!"), the expression acquires further meanings: in life or death, the good soul continues to influence others, and the effects of this influence are seen after the deaths of those subject to it. Vaughan integrates these various meanings by punning on "well lead" so that it means "Well guided" as well as "good." The process of influence is a continuing cycle—a further enrichment of the meaning of "never ends."

The pattern expressed in these four "simple" lines is a facet of the interrelation of the natural and temporal order with the spiritual and eternal. The former fulfills itself in the latter through death; but the process of transformation is not simply forward, working toward sanctity or transcendence, but reciprocal. The higher state acts back on the lower, impelling that motion toward itself by which the lower is fulfilled. "Higher" and "lower" are not separate entities, but interdependent phases of a total process; they can be grasped as distinct phases only by an imaginative suspension of the process at a particular stage. The brilliance of this poem is that it expresses a distinct grasp of death as such a crux and simultaneously, through the same images, expresses the dynamic nature of the total process. This dynamism is expressed chiefly by the figure of pilgrimage which pervades the poem. Virtuous souls, whether abiding "With quick, or dead," are imaged as stars which "are of mighty use" to "guide a croud" through this lower world where "The night / Is dark, and long; / The Rode foul. . . ." The complex figure is expressed most powerfully in the third stanza, where the phantasmagoric, frightening passage lit by these "shining lights" is converted to the safe and familiar event of going to bed by candlelight:

> Gods Saints are shining lights: who stays
>   Here long must passe
> O're dark hills, swift streames, and steep ways
>   As smooth as glasse;
>   But these all night
>   Like Candles, shed
>   Their beams, and light
>   Us into Bed.

The unity of multiple experience comes through in powerful overtones, suggesting a mitigation of sin and death—of all the foul road and long dark night of the world—when seen as phases of a dynamic teleology.

APPENDICES

NOTES

BIBLIOGRAPHY

INDEX

Appendix

I

VAUGHAN'S ILLNESS

LITERARY LEGENDS die hard. The legend that Vaughan's turning to sacred verse in 1648 or 1649 may have been prompted in part by the onset of a severe illness has proven hardy indeed.[1] It began in 1847 when the Rev. H. F. Lyte observed: "He was at this time [ca. December 1647] visited by a severe and lingering illness, of what character exactly is not specified. It was however of a nature to bring him to the brink of the grave, and to keep him long in a state of solitude and suffering."[2] Lyte drew this inference from a passage in the preface, dated "Septem. 30. 1654," prefixed to the enlarged reissue of *Silex Scintillans* published in 1655:

> By the last *Poems* in the book (were not that *mistake* here prevented) you would judge all to be *fatherless*, and the *Edition* posthume; for (indeed) *I was nigh unto death*, and am still at no great distance from it; which was the necessary reason for that solemn and accomplished *dress*, you will now finde this *impression* in. (Martin, p. 392)

Vaughan clearly enough relates his illness to the poems added since the 1650 issue of *Silex Scintillans*, which make up part II of the 1655 volume—"the last *Poems* in the book." But in the 1655 issue the preface precedes the poems, reissued as part I of the enlarged volume, which had appeared in 1650, and Martin prints the preface in this position in both of his editions. Apparently his scholarly apparatus has not been sufficient to withstand a romantic propensity for tubercular genius fostered by the popular image of Keats, for Lyte was merely the first of a swarm of commentators who have taken this passage as referring to the period immediately before publication of the 1650 *Silex*.

As recently as 1960, for example, E. C. Pettet ruminates as follows over the inspiration of Vaughan's sacred verse:

> Poor physical health may have had something to do with the miracle, for we have A. E. Housman's testimony, valid perhaps for certain other poets, that "I have seldom written poetry unless I was rather out of health." True, the only certain evidence of Vaughan suffering from severe illness . . . comes from the period, probably in or about 1653, between the two Parts of *Silex Scintillans*. On the other hand, the onset of this illness, whatever its nature, and the privations experienced during his Civil War service . . . may have already undermined his health much earlier, in the year or two when he was composing the poems of the first Part of *Silex Scintillans*.
>
> Again, there is the possibility that he had suffered some kind of mental breakdown. Most of his prose translations of this period are obviously relevant to his own needs and condition, and it may not be an accident that two of the four published in 1651 (both entitled *Of the Diseases of the Mind and the Body*) argue the case that mental illness is far worse than physical.[3]

If A. E. Housman's testimony were to suggest anything about Vaughan (although there is no reason that it should), it would have to suggest that he was rather out of health for thirteen or fourteen years, for he wrote poetry somewhat more than seldom from about 1640 until 1654. And from that would follow that poor physical health may have had something to do with all of his poetry—which would be incompatible with the supposition that it had something special to do with "the miracle" of *Silex Scintillans*. As for "the privations experienced during his Civil War service," one should add "if any": in the poem on Ridsley's cloak (Martin, p. 52), Vaughan describes himself wearing the cloak while riding through a rainstorm, and sleeping naked in it (presumably on the ground), but that is all we know about his privations as a soldier, and may be all there is to know. And the distinction, fundamental in Pettet's reasoning, between *suffering* from severe illness and having one's health *undermined* by "the onset of this illness" some four or five years earlier, is a distinction which I, for one, am simply unable to grasp. As Pettet says, echoing Hutchinson, the only certain evidence about Vaughan's illness points to the period "in or about 1653." His attempts to suggest an earlier date, and thus to link illness with the inspiration of the sacred verse, are followed by a frank admission that "these speculations ... are guesswork." His fabrication of a "possibility" that Vaughan "had suffered some kind of mental breakdown" is Pettet's own contribution toward a new legend. The rest is venerable but equally irresponsible gossip.

Fifteen years earlier, E. L. Marilla had tried to scotch the legend, pointing out that "whereas none of Vaughan's expressions prior to 1652 ... contains mention of ill-health, the prefatory addresses (as well as the title-page) of *Flores Solitudinis* and the Preface of the 1655 *Silex* record an increasingly severe illness during 1653-4 and clearly testify to its influence on the poet's thinking during these years."[4] And only a pertinacious tenderness for gossip can account for the legend's survival of F. E. Hutchinson's remarks two years later:

> It has often been held that a grave and prolonged illness, threatening to be fatal, caused or precipitated Vaughan's conversion. But the only certain references to illness belong to the period between the publication of the first and second parts of *Silex Scintillans*. ... The dedication, dated 1 October 1651, and the undated preface of *The Mount of Olives* (1652) make no allusion to sickness, but the Epistle Dedica-

tory, dated 1653, of *Flores Solitudinis. Collected in his Sicknesse and Retirement* (1654) refers to "the incertainty of life, and a peevish, inconstant state of health".... Still more explicitly, in the preface, dated 30 September 1654, to the completed *Silex Scintillans* (1655), Vaughan warns his readers that they will misunderstand "the last *Poems* in the book" ... if he did not tell them how near he had been to death.... Vaughan's nearness to death in or about 1653 would doubtless have deepened his piety, but there is no sufficient evidence of his having had a similar sickness before writing the first part of *Silex Scintillans*.[5]

It may be possible to date Vaughan's illness more precisely than Marilla's "during 1653-4" and Hutchinson's "in or about 1653." Hutchinson notes, but rightly dismisses, the possibility of autobiographical reference in the prayer for use in sickness included in *The Mount of Olives* (1652).[6] This is a devotional manual or handbook intended for private use in the regular practice of a religious life. The prayers, all cast in the first person, are essentially dramatic fictions in which the relevant circumstances and conditions are imagined as present. It would be a misconception of genre to infer an autobiographical intent in the "Prayer when thou findest thy self sickly, or when thou art visited with any Disease," with its references to "this thy present *visitation*" and "this present *sicknesse*" (Martin, pp. 188-89), or in the succeeding "Prayer in the hour of Death." Vaughan places these set prayers, intended for use on these occasions, at the end of *Man in Darkness, or, A Discourse of Death*, which is a formal meditation on death as one of the Four Last Things. If this theme had possessed any immediate personal relevance Vaughan probably would have mentioned the fact in the preface; but he gives a quite detached description of the book's contents and emphasizes its didactic, utilitarian purpose:

Thou hast here sound directions and wholsome words....
Here are *Morning* and *Evening* sacrifices, with holy and ap-

posite *Ejaculations* for most times and occasions. And lastly, here are very faithful and necessary Precepts and Meditations before we come to the Lords Table. To which last part I have added a short and plaine Discourse of Death, with a Prayer in the houre thereof. And for thy comfort after thou hast past through that *Golgotha*, I have annexed a Dissertation of the blessed state of the righteous after this life. . . . And thus, Christian Reader, do I commend it to thy practise, and the benefit thou shalt finde thereby. (Martin, pp. 140-41)

The preface is undated, but we can infer an approximate date from the fact that the book was registered on December 16, 1651, and from the dating of the dedication, which likewise makes no mention of illness, on October 1, 1651.

The preface to *Flores Solitudinis*, dated April 17, 1652, indicates clearly that the translations which comprise the book had already been completed. The separate notices prefixed to *The World Contemned* and *Primitive Holiness* do not mention sickness at all, and the preface mentions it only as a figure for sin (Martin, p. 217). The earliest indication of any kind that Vaughan suffered a serious illness during his writing career is contained in the dedication of *Flores Solitudinis*. Dated simply "1653," it cannot be later than September 15, when the book was registered, nor earlier than March 25, when the year began by the Julian calendar. Vaughan excuses his "suddaine and small *Presents*," as he calls the book, upon the ground of severe sickness: "The incertainty of life, and a peevish, inconstant state of health would not suffer me to stay for greater performances, or a better season" (Martin, p. 215). Since he had finished the book and written a preface for it by the middle of April of the previous year, it seems likely that his illness began within a few months after this date. This is an earnest religious work dealing with moral and spiritual problems with which Vaughan was passionately concerned; only some very serious circumstance could have prevented him from delivering the manuscript to the printer very soon after he had it ready. It seems that he had been ill for a long time when he wrote the dedication; at least he was still extremely sick, and by no means confident of final recovery. Comparing the book to "some forward *flowers* whose kind hast hath brought them above ground *in cold weather,*" he declares that he dedicates it to Egerton now lest he never again have an opportunity to show his friendship in this way.

Vaughan's illness probably persisted throughout the greater part of 1653. The title page of *Flores Solitudinis* describes the book as "Collected in his Sicknesse and Retirement." An inference, from "collected," that the translations were actually made while Vaughan was sick, would not be supported by the prefatory addresses written in 1652, which indicate that the book was already finished but do not mention illness. But the literal meaning of "collected"—gathered, accumulated, assembled—is consonant with the inference that Vaughan was still seriously ill when he sent the manuscript to the printer, probably in the summer or early autumn of 1653.

Finally, the preface of September 30, 1654, to the augmented *Silex Scintillans* states clearly that Vaughan is writing during a period of convalescence after a nearly fatal illness: "*I was nigh unto death,* and am still at no great distance from it." And the last poems in the book do indeed speak in the voice of a man on the brink of death. "To the Holy Bible" (Martin, p. 540) is a formal leave-taking:

> Take this last kiss, and let me weep
> True thanks to thee, before I sleep.
> . . . .
> Living, thou wert my souls sure ease,
> And dying mak'st me go in peace.

"L'Envoy" (Martin, p. 541), with its impassioned prayer for the Second Coming, is the author's farewell to life as well as to the book.

Hutchinson gives the legend too much nourishment when he says there is not *sufficient* evidence of Vaughan's having had a serious illness before writing the first part of *Silex Scintillans*. There is, simply, no evidence whatever to suggest that Vaughan suffered a serious illness before April 1652. There are strong indications that he was seriously ill throughout the greater part of the period from that date to September 1654. His illness may have disposed him to translate Nolle's *General System of Hermetic Medicine*,[7] but the only part of his original writings which can, reasonably, be thought to have been influenced by sickness is the second part of *Silex Scintillans*. And the romantic faith in the power of physical illness to stimulate the creative faculties may be somewhat discouraged by the opinion of some critics, including this one, that the second part of *Silex Scintillans*, by and large, is decidedly inferior to the first.

Appendix

II
AMORET, ETESIA,
AND CATHERINE WISE

KATHERINE PHILIPS'S REMARK that Amoret was "twice crown'd by thee: / Once by thy Love, next by thy Poetrie" (Martin, p. 617) suggests that Amoret was real and (coupled with her insistence, and Vaughan's, on the innocence of this affair) opens the possibility of identifying Amoret with Catherine Wise, who became the poet's first wife. E. K. Chambers was noncommittal: "The Amoret of these *Poems* may or may not be the Etesia of *Thalia Rediviva*; and she may or may not have been the poet's first wife."[1] F. E. Hutchinson and E. L. Marilla give positive answers to both questions. They regard the *Poems* of 1646 as a memorial of Vaughan's courtship and marriage, after the example of Habington's *Castara*. "It is possible to discern a continuity of theme throughout the thirteen poems, from the rejection of the author's initial overtures, through a succession of changes in Amoret's attitude, eventually to marriage, and finally to a peaceful retrospect and reminiscence of the courtship," argues Marilla, fitting "To my Ingenuous Friend, *R. W.*" and "A Rhapsodis" into this autobiographical scheme as the temporary retreats of a thwarted suitor into masculine conviviality.[2] Hutchinson and Marilla are convinced that the Etesia poems also were addressed to Catherine Wise. Marilla finds the tone of some of them "much too fervent . . . to be considered as impersonal expressions,"[3] and Hutchinson argues that "the tone in the Amoret and Etesia poems is the same, and often even the circumstances are similar or identical, and the expression the same."[4]

"Upon the Priorie Grove" (Martin, p. 15) provides the only clear point of contact between the *Poems* of 1646 and any specific circumstance of Vaughan's life. Celebrating the grove as the first meeting place of the lovers, the poem was thought by Grosart and Beeching to refer to the Priory Cardigan, later the home of "the matchless Orinda" and her husband, James Philips.[5] But, following the suggestions of Chambers and Ernest Rhys, Hutchinson pointed to the grove of Brecon Priory near Vaughan's home and demonstrated the close connections between Brecon Priory and the family of Catherine Wise.[6] These facts, together with the poem's placement at the end of the series as a "peaceful retrospect and reminiscence of the courtship," make it conceivable that Vaughan designed the volume (apart from the translation of Juvenal's tenth satire, which occupies about half the space) as a compliment to Catherine Wise. But the chances are that the design was ex post facto: most of the poems have something to do with love, but only six are addressed to Amoret, and only "Upon the Priorie Grove" (which does not mention Amoret) is reasonably circumstantial. The rest are as likely to have been written without Catherine Wise or anybody else particularly in mind, being later gathered together and arranged to form the narrative pattern of successful courtship that Marilla describes. For the form of the narrative—initial despair, gradual development (despite some reversals) of mutual affection, finally a happy marriage—Vaughan might have found a model in Spenser's *Amoretti and Epithalamion* as well as in Habington's *Castara*.

The Etesia sequence tells a quite different story: three poems celebrating the lover's enslavement are followed by four expressing the anguish of the couple's separation. This is the familiar pattern of frustrated courtship thoroughly established in literary tradition by Petrarch and his imitators. How can both stories be true *and* both ladies be Catherine Wise? And if both ladies are Catherine Wise, why does Vaughan use different names? Marilla suggests that the Etesia poems were written after publication of the Amoret poems in 1646, and that "the author changed the poetic name in these later poems in order to avoid implying incompleteness in the volume which he wished to stand as a composite memorial."⁷ But what then happens to the autobiographical significance of the Etesia poems? Vaughan was married by this time, but, for example, the remote grandeur of the lady in *"The Character, to Etesia"* (Martin, p. 644) is not particularly suggestive of the relations of man and wife sharing a household together. And why should Vaughan, after marrying the lady of his heart, address poems to her lamenting her loss?

Hutchinson offers no explanation of the name change, nor does he suggest a reason for Vaughan's omission of the Etesia poems from the 1646 volume. He advances only two examples to support his claim that the sequences are closely parallel in tone, circumstances, and expression. The verbal parallel, a comparison of the lady's face and eye to a star, is a commonplace of medieval and Renaissance love poetry; and so is the lover's declaration that he first met his beloved among the shades of a wooded retreat, which comprises the circumstantial parallel. In the Amoret sequence we have, it seems, a particular place—the Priory Grove; but in the Etesia sequence we have only "those happy *Shades* . . . / Where first I saw my beauteous Foe" (Martin, p. 646). I have found a half-dozen additional parallels in phrasing and imagery, all similarly inconclusive.⁸ "To Amoret gone from him" and "Etesia *absent*" (Martin, pp. 8, 647) both deal with the separation of the lovers, but whereas the Amoret poem argues calmly, in the manner of Donne's "Valediction, forbidding mourning," that the spiritual unity of the lovers transcends space, the Etesia poem proclaims the lover's spiritual death amidst "lingring tortures." Hutchinson speaks of this poem as "addressed to a wife"; he gives no reasons, but probably had in mind the figurative use of the word "wed": "To be possess'd, and yet to miss; / To wed a true but absent bliss." The agonized mood of the whole poem hardly seems appropriate to a man temporarily parted from his wife; and the comparison of his state to that of the dead awaiting resurrection suggests that he does not expect reunion within the foreseeable future.

The fact is that the Etesia poems make no specific references to any known circumstances of Vaughan's life. The idea that they refer to Catherine Wise is pure speculation. Their fervency is beyond dispute, but I suppose we can grant Vaughan a fervent imagination. If we assume an autobiographical significance in the Amoret sequence (although that is itself highly questionable), then it seems most reasonable to suppose that the Etesia poems were written in the early 1640s, before Vaughan had met his future wife. As Chambers might have said, Etesia may or may not have been a real person. One might speculate that these were simply the poems that were left when, out of a sheaf of love poems that he had written with nobody particularly in mind, Vaughan chose the ones that best expressed his feelings for Catherine Wise, only later perceiving the possibility of arranging the remainder in a meaningful sequence, and only having occasion to publish them when, late in his life and long after his wife's death, his friends persuaded him to collect his unpublished work under the title *Thalia Rediviva*.

Appendix

III
IMMORALITY AND PROFANE LITERATURE

THE BULK of Vaughan's preface of 1654 to the enlarged reissue of *Silex Scintillans* published in 1655 is occupied by a strident denunciation of "idle books."[1] Describing the object of his attack, Vaughan mixes the comparatively mild epithets "idle" and "vain" indiscriminately with more pejorative terms: "*scurrilous conceits,*" "*lascivious fictions,*" "*vitious verse,*" "Obscene, vile fancies," "A dirty sink," "a dung-hill," "unclean *vermine,*" "lewd ware." The semantic muddle is particularly prominent in such phrases as "idle or sensual *subject,*" "*vain* and *vitious subjects.*" "Idle" and "vain" were commonly applied by zealous writers to the most innocent secular literature, and signified a lack of positive value rather than actual evil. Vaughan's use of these terms in conjunction with much stronger language gives ground for considerable uncertainty as to just what he means. He exhorts "the gifted persons" to follow the example of George Herbert—"the first, that with any effectual success attempted a *diversion* of this foul and overflowing *stream*—"by a wise exchange of *vain* and *vitious subjects,* for *divine Themes* and *Celestial praise.*" Most critical commentary on the preface tends to convey the vague implication that Vaughan means to denounce all secular literature as actually wicked. And, since none of his own published verse seems particularly scurrilous, lascivious, or obscene, this implication has been fortified by his "free confession . . . that I my self have for many years together, languished of this very *sickness*; and it is no long time since I have recovered." If such an interpretation were accurate, the preface would mark Vaughan's adoption of an extremely ascetic, almost Manichean position—the position that all writing not explicitly religious and Christian is evil.

It had always been a commonplace of Christian culture that knowledge of temporal and natural things was trivial in comparison to knowledge of God, and consequently that scripture, divinity, and sacred art were vastly superior to "profane" forms of knowledge such as natural philosophy and humane letters. But this theoretical position attributed considerable value, within a limited sphere, to secular learning, enabling devout Christians to study the writings of wise and virtuous pagans without perturbation and at the same time to distinguish some writings as harmful to morals. Ultimately, of course—that is, when weighed in the balance with salvation and faith—all such secular learning was idle and vain, but such comparisons were seldom more than rhetorical methods of promoting humility, for everybody knew that the things of faith were *above* the things of the world, not side by side, and were therefore beyond compare. Besides, having been put in their lowly place by God, the things of the world were above human contempt. In Vaughan's time, the morally extreme position that all literature not directly conducive to salvation was evil was more characteristic of radical forms of Puritanism than of the Anglo-Catholic tradition which he inherited.

If this is what the preface means, it represents a significant narrowing of his views, for he had expressed no such attitude before 1654. On the basis of his "it is no long time since I have recovered" and his reference to the "many pious *Converts*" of George Herbert, "of whom I am the least," critics date his alleged renunciation of secular literature from the time he came under Herbert's influence and began writing sacred verse—that is, about 1648.[2] The theory that Vaughan renounced secular literature at this time is part and parcel of the theory (it is difficult to distinguish cause from effect, evidence from inference in critical thinking on this point) that his composition of sacred verse was accompanied by a withdrawal from the temporal world into a private world of religious contemplation. This standard characterization of Vaughan's "conversion" is greatly fortified by the retroactive dating of the attitude toward secular literature supposedly expressed by the 1654 preface. The question is therefore of some importance.

Nobody is quite sure of the date of Vaughan's "conversion" or of his beginning to write sacred verse, but 1648 is the most popular year. He published a volume of secular poems in 1646, a volume of sacred poems in 1650, and in 1651 he published (or allowed to be published) another volume of secular poems for which he had written a dedication in December 1647. The delay in this book's appearance is usually ascribed to the author's sudden intolerance of secular literature, a symptom of the onset of his conversion, and it is sometimes suggested that the book was eventually published against his will or at least without his consent.[3] But the evidence that Vaughan felt no intolerance of secular literature during the period 1647–1651 is quite clear. In 1647, 1648, 1650, and 1651 he wrote commendatory poems warmly praising the work of Beaumont and Fletcher, William Cartwright, Ben Jonson, Katherine Philips, and Sir William D'Avenant. The poem on Cartwright was probably written in 1648, either shortly before or shortly after he began to compose the first part of *Silex Scintillans*. The poem to Katherine Philips was possibly written after *Silex* appeared in 1650, and the poem to D'Avenant was certainly written nearly a year later.[4] People who consider secular literature vicious, scurrilous, lascivious, obscene, vile, and lewd do not write poems in praise of its authors.

The 1650 *Silex* includes a poem which exhibits the same ambiguity in the use of "idle" that we find in the 1654 preface. The title is "Idle Verse" (Martin, p. 446), but the language of the poem is much more severe: "Lust in the Robes of Love," "Vice in a fairer name," "sugred sin," "rank poyson," "Blind, desp'rate *fits*"—but also "The idle talk of feav'rish souls." At about the time this was written and published, Vaughan was expressing enthusiasm for the work of William Cartwright and Katherine

Philips; and, about a year later, he commended the romantic theme of D'Avenant's *Gondibert*. In view of this, it seems impossible to interpret "Idle Verse" as an attack on all secular verse, or even as an attack on verse which treats of romantic love. It seems, rather, that Vaughan is not using "idle" as a synonym for "secular" or "romantic," but as a synonym for "scurrilous," "lascivious," "obscene," and "lewd." He is not condemning love poetry or secular poetry in general as corrupt; he is making a distinction between that which is corrupt and that which is either innocuous or positively good.

Vaughan had always made this distinction: there is nothing new about his intolerance of licentious verse. The preface to the 1646 *Poems* insists on the chastity of his muse:

> You have here a *Flame*, bright only in its owne *Innocence*, that kindles nothing but a generous *Thought*; which though it may warme the Bloud, the fire at highest is but *Platonick*, and the *Commotion*, within these limits, excludes *Danger*. (Martin, p. 2)

In the poem to Katherine Philips, Vaughan praised the "wittie fair one" for her avoidance of the indecency which often mars the poetry of the age:

> no Coorse trifles blot the page
> With matter borrow'd from the age,
> But thoughts as Innocent, and high
> As *Angels* have, or *Saints* that dye. (Martin, p. 62)

The measure of Vaughan's flexibility on this question is suggested by his admiration of Beaumont, Fletcher, and Jonson, whose works, to say the least, are sometimes rather indelicate. And occasionally he glances critically at censorious attitudes toward secular literature, as when he speaks of Cartwright's imitation of "those *grand Miracles* which *deifie* / The old worlds *Writings*, kept yet from the *fire*, / Because they *force* these worst times to *admire*" (Martin, p. 56). He praises D'Avenant for purifying love poetry and thus vindicating it against any general charge of immorality:

> Th'hast cleer'd the prospect to our harmless *Hill*,
> Of late years clouded with imputed Ill,
> And the *Soft, youthfull Couples* there may move
> As chast as *Stars* converse and smile above.
> Th'hast taught their *Language*, and their *love* to flow
> Calme as *Rose-leafes*, and coole as *Virgin-snow*,
> Which doubly feasts us, being so refin'd
> They both *delight*, and *dignifie* the mind,
> Like to the watrie Musick of some Spring,
> Whose pleasant flowings at once *wash* and *sing*.
>
> (Martin, p. 64)

The passage obliquely discredits those who indiscriminately condemn all love poetry, attributing to all the evil which may be found in some because of a failure to observe the positive value of the rest. In other words, the passage repudiates the attitude which modern critics have attributed to Vaughan at this time.

This was where Vaughan stood in 1651, about three years after his "conversion" and almost a year after the 1650 *Silex* appeared. His next statement on the subject is the 1654 preface. Did he develop a more intolerant, "otherworldly" attitude in the interim? Until 1651, his attitude had been a mild reflection of that expressed by Jonson in the epistle to *Volpone*:

> Now, especially in *Dramatick*, or (as they terme it) Stage-*Poëtry*, nothing but Ribaldry, Profanation, Blasphemy, al Licence of offence to God, and Man, is practised. . . . But, that all are embarqu'd in this bold adventure for Hell, is a most uncharitable thought, and, utterd, a more malicious slander. For my particular, I can (and from a most cleare conscience) affirme that I have ever trembled to thinke toward the least Prophanenesse; have loathed the use of such foule,

and un-washed Baudr'y, as is now made the foode of the Scene.[5]

This passage incidentally substantiates Vaughan's claim in the preface: "Divers persons of eminent piety and learning (I meddle not with the seditious and *Schismatical*) have, long before my time, taken notice of this *malady*; for the complaint against *vitious verse*, even by peaceful and obedient *spirits*, is of some antiquity in this Kingdom." And, since Jonson is not reputed to have been particularly "otherworldly," it is interesting to note that his tone is comparable to the vigorous tone of Vaughan's preface, one passage of which is similar to Jonson's:

> But an idle or sensual *subject* is not all the *poyson* in these Pamphlets. Certain Authors have been so irreverendly bold, as to dash *Scriptures*, and the *sacred Relatives* of *God* with their impious conceits. . . . Others of a later *date* . . . have stuffed their books with *Oathes*, *horrid Execrations*, and a most gross and studied *filthiness*.

Vaughan's feelings on the subject are obviously stronger, his attitude more severe and stern, than before 1651. One could confidently conclude that no other change has taken place, that there has been no real change in his thought, were it not for the passage in which he confesses his own guilt. This is the most problematical paragraph in the whole preface, and needs to be examined with great care:

> And here, because I would prevent a just *censure* by my free *confession*, I must remember, that I my self have for many years together, languished of this very *sickness*; and it is no long time since I have recovered. But (blessed be God for it!) I have by his saving assistance suppress my *greatest follies*, and those which escaped from me, are (I think) as innoxious, as most of that *vein* use to be; besides, they are interlined with many virtuous, and some pious mixtures.

What I speak of them, is truth; but let no man mistake it for an *extenuation* of faults, as if I intended an *Apology* for *them*, or my *self*, who am conscious of so much *guilt* in *both*, as can never be expiated without *special sorrows*, and that cleansing and pretious *effusion* of my Almighty Redeemer: and if the world will be so charitable, as to grant my request, I do here most humbly and earnestly beg that none would read them.

The most remarkable feature of the passage is the way the third sentence appears to contradict the second. He describes his published poems as inoffensive, virtuous, and pious, but nevertheless expresses profound guilt and penitence and begs that none would read them. For some critics, Vaughan's profession of penitence even for secular poems which are "innoxious . . . interlined with many virtuous, and some pious mixtures" has clinched the argument that the preface condemns as wicked all writing not expressly occupied with divine themes and celestial praise. And this conclusion has been encouraged by the inference that "I have . . . supprest my *greatest follies*" refers to the early love poems to Etesia, not published until 1678. These poems are as "innoxious" as the rest of Vaughan's work, but the theory that they were deleted for moral reasons from the volume planned in 1647 and published in 1651 as *Olor Iscanus* has never been seriously challenged.[6] "Idle Verse" makes it virtually certain that Vaughan did indeed suppress some of his work during this period:

> Go, go, queint folies, sugred sin,
>   Shadow no more my door;
> I will no longer Cobwebs spin,
>   I'm too much on the score.
>
> . . . .
>
> Let it suffice my warmer days
>   Simper'd, and shin'd on you,
> Twist not my Cypresse with your Bays,
>   Or Roses with my Yewgh.

But his admiration, at this time, for Beaumont, Fletcher, Jonson, Katherine Philips, and D'Avenant makes it inconceivable that he here renounces secular poetry in general or rejects the Etesia poems as immoral. It seems more likely that he had composed coarser pieces in his youth and that it is to these and their suppression before 1650 that he refers in the preface.[7] The second sentence of the paragraph quoted above expresses, by "escaped from me" and the implication that his published secular verses are his *lesser* follies, no more than a certain diffidence toward his published secular poetry. But these suggestions of coolness are overwhelmed by the defensive self-justification of the rest of the sentence, and Vaughan underlines this exemption of himself from blame with "What I speak of them, is truth." What can he mean by retracting all this in the next sentence? How can there be faults in innocuous, virtuous, and pious verses? How can he be conscious of so much guilt as can never be expiated without special sorrows? How can he fear that such verses will corrupt the reader?

Let us remember that the paragraph occurs in the midst of a vituperative denunciation of other writers for their "wilful despising of Gods *sacred exhortations*, by a constant, sensual volutation or wallowing in *impure thoughts* and *scurrilous conceits*, which both defile their Authors, and as many more, as they are communicated to." Then he implicates himself in their guilt, freely confessing that he too has defiled himself and others. Since he confesses to "prevent a just *censure*," presumably his greatest follies, although never published, had circulated in manuscript. But then he disclaims the degree of guilt which he imputes to others, dissociating himself from the full measure of the wrath poured out on them. Others "persist so to the end. . . . all their life time, and out of meer design," but he has persisted so only "for many years together." The vicious verse of others is "willingly-studied and wilfully-published," but he has suppressed his, and that which he has published is "innoxious . . . interlined with many virtuous, and some pious mixtures." He is beginning to sound like one who thanks God he is not as other men, and his next words suggest that he has suddenly become aware that he sounds self-righteous, hypocritical, and sanctimonious: "What I speak of them, is truth; but let no man mistake it for an *extenuation* of faults, as if I intended an *Apology* for them, or my *self*." What is this but "Let no man mistake it for what it is"? What he has just written cannot be interpreted as anything but an extenuation of faults, an apology for his published verse. The hyperbolic profession of penitence which follows, and the heroically self-effacing plea "that none would read them," seems mainly rhetorical, a grandly magnanimous gesture designed to assure the reader of the purity of his indignation—a gesture prompted, and partly justified, by the fact that he does have legitimate reasons for penitence. He has written poems which he considers obscene, and he has communicated them to others; but he has not published them. As far as his published work is concerned, he is guilty only of misusing his poetic talent by neglecting a higher good—"*divine Themes* and *Celestial praise*"—in pursuit of a lower good, verse which is merely harmless and merely "interlined" with virtuous and pious elements.

This is the traditional "retraction" penned by Christian writers who have followed the way of the world (Chaucer, for example), a recognition of ultimate values in the light of Christ's parable of the talents, and does not imply that secular literature is evil per se. Such diffidence toward writing not explicitly sacred is a new element in Vaughan's thought, a development from the position he expressed as late as 1651. Vaughan did not renounce secular verse in the late 1640s, when he began to write sacred poetry; that did not happen until 1654, long after publication of the first part of *Silex Scintillans*. And nowhere in the preface does he unequivocally denounce secular literature as actually wicked, in and of itself. His anger is more violent than before, but it falls where it had always fallen—on the "evil consequence" of *"lascivious fictions."* The intense, hyperbolical language of his retraction reflects the urgency of his desire to bring the persuasive potencies of verse to the aid of distressed religion.[8] To the extent that he does implicate himself and the other writers of "idle" and "vain" verse in the real guilt of those who publish "lewdness and impieties," that would seem to be a rhetorical stratagem—an *ad hominem* argument designed to muster all the forces of poetry for the relief of a beleaguered Church.

NOTES

Chapter I: Introduction

1. Richard S. Sylvester, ed., *The Anchor Anthology of Seventeenth-Century Verse*, II (New York, 1969). Similarly, Miriam K. Starkman, ed., *Seventeenth-Century English Poetry*, vol. II of *The Borzoi Anthology* (New York, 1967), does not include Vaughan with Jonson, Herrick, Carew, Waller, Cowley, Lovelace, Suckling, and Marvell. But generous selections from Vaughan's sacred verse appear in Starkman's first volume in the Borzoi series, and in Louis L. Martz, ed., *The Anchor Anthology of Seventeenth-Century Verse*, vol. I (New York, 1969).
2. E.g., S. L. Bethell, *The Cultural Revolution of the Seventeenth Century* (London, 1951), pp. 121–61; Robert Ellrodt, *L'Inspiration Personelle et L'Esprit du Temps chez Les Poètes Métaphysiques Anglais* (Paris, 1960), II, 173–260; Maren-Sofie Røstvig, *The Happy Man: Studies in the Metamorphoses of a Classical Ideal*, vol. I, *1600-1700*, 2nd ed. (New York, 1962 [1954]), pp. 201 ff.; D. J. Enright, "George Herbert and the Devotional Poets," *From Donne to Marvell*, vol. III of *A Guide to English Literature*, ed. Boris Ford (Baltimore, 1956), pp. 142–59; E. C. Pettet, *Of Paradise and Light: A Study of Vaughan's "Silex Scintillans"* (Cambridge, 1960), pp. 191–93.
3. *The Secular Poems of Henry Vaughan* (Uppsala, 1958).
4. "The Private Imagery of Henry Vaughan," *RES*, n.s. I (1950), 208.
5. These relationships are discussed by E. L. Marilla, "The Secular and Religious Poetry of Henry Vaughan," *MLQ*, IX (1948), 394–411; Kermode, "The Private Imagery of Henry Vaughan," pp. 206–25; Pettet, *Of Paradise and Light*, pp. 4–8; Margherita Leardi, *La Poesia di Henry Vaughan* (Firenze, 1967), pp. 10–48; Ellrodt and Røstvig in the essays cited in n. 2; and in my "Henry Vaughan and the Great Chain of Being," in *Studies in En-*

glish Renaissance Literature, ed. Waldo F. McNeir (Baton Rouge, La., 1962), pp. 149–67, and "Some Traditional Oxymora in Vaughan's Secular Verse," *Die Neueren Sprachen*, XII (1962), 569–73.

6. "The Religious Conversion of Henry Vaughan," *RES*, XXI (1945), 15–22, and "Henry Vaughan's Conversion: A Recent View," *MLN*, LXIII (1948), 394–97.

7. Cf. Pettet, *Of Paradise and Light*, pp. 51–52, 57–58, and Mary Ellen Rickey, "Vaughan, *The Temple*, and Poetic Form," *SP*, LIX (1962), 162–70. Rickey's essay is valuable, however, for its emphasis on the formal artistry of the sacred poems. And Pettet, with the exceptions noted, accurately defines the nature and extent of Vaughan's indebtedness to Herbert.

8. Bennett, *Five Metaphysical Poets* (Cambridge, 1964), pp. 71–74; Gardner, ed., *The Metaphysical Poets* (Baltimore, 1957), p. 321; Hutchinson, *Henry Vaughan: A Life and Interpretation* (Oxford, 1947), p. 99.

9. A similar view is expressed by Bethell, *The Cultural Revoluton of the Seventeenth Century*, pp. 133–34.

10. Hutchinson, *Henry Vaughan: A Life and Interpretation*, p. 84. ["Despite E. L. Marilla's worthy attempt to bring Vaughan's secular poetry into greater estimation, the artistic superiority of his religious verse is indisputable"] Esch, *Englische religiöse Lyrik des 17. Jahrhunderts* (Tübingen, 1955), p. 161. Unless otherwise noted, all translations are mine.

11. John Aubrey, *Brief Lives*, ed. Oliver Lawson Dick (London, 1949), p. 303. The remark does not appear in other editions.

12. Edmund Blunden, *On the Poems of Henry Vaughan: Characteristics and Intimations* (London, 1927), reviewed by T. S. Eliot, *The Dial*, LXXXIII (1927), 259–63.

13. See his remarks that Vaughan's political passions "even disturb the remote air of *Silex Scintillans*," and that "allusions to contemporary events . . . mar some of Vaughan's best poems" (*Henry Vaughan: A Life and Interpretation*, pp. 44, 121).

14. The quotations are from French Fogle, ed., *The Complete Poetry of Henry Vaughan* (New York: Doubleday, 1964; New York University Press, 1965), p. xii, but this is the lingua franca of Vaughan criticism, and I hope Fogle will pardon my thrusting this gratuitous notoriety upon him. Some of my remarks, here and elsewhere in this chapter, are adapted from my review of Fogle's edition, *MP*, LXIIII (1966), 355–57.

15. *Henry Vaughan and the Hermetic Philosophy* (Oxford, 1932), p. 4.

16. *Of Paradise and Light*, pp. 24–31, 40–47, 154.

17. [". . . between abandonment to intuition and the act of the will"; "the true Vaughan is to be sought between the lines of his poetry"; "a dualism always at the base of Vaughan's writings: a dualism between the themes of his poetry and the language in which he embodies them, between the quality

of his imagination and that of the literary tradition to which it is drawn."] *La Poesia di Henry Vaughan*, pp. 53, 57.

18. *On the Mystical Poetry of Henry Vaughan* (Cambridge, Mass., 1962), pp. xx-xxi.

19. "The Metaphysical Poets," Eliot's famous review (*TLS*, October 20, 1921, pp. 669–70) of Grierson's *Metaphysical Lyrics and Poems of the Seventeenth Century: Donne to Butler*, reprinted in Eliot's *Selected Essays* (London, 1932), pp. 281–91. The quotations are on pp. 286, 288.

20. [" . . . is not determined by the study of the language of the poetry"; "ciphers used to give an aura of rationality and orthodoxy to the magical world of his fantasy."] *La Poesia di Henry Vaughan*, pp. 53, 57.

21. *Of Paradise and Light*, pp. 8–11.

22. *Mystical Poetry*, pp. xv-xvi.

23. *Of Paradise and Light*, p. 19.

24. *The Mystical Element in the Metaphysical Poets of the Seventeenth Century* (Edinburgh and London, 1948), pp. 193–263 passim.

25. *Of Paradise and Light*, pp. 22–23; cf. Itrat-Husain, *The Mystical Element in the Metaphysical Poets*, and Helen C. White, *The Metaphysical Poets: A Study in Religious Experience* (New York, 1936), pp. 259–314, esp. pp. 305–06, 308.

26. *Mystical Poetry*, pp. xii, xviii, 8.

27. Kermode, "The Private Imagery of Henry Vaughan," pp. 206–25; H. J. Oliver, "The Mysticism of Henry Vaughan: A Reply," *JEGP*, LIII (1954), 352–60; Ross Garner, *Henry Vaughan: Experience and the Tradition* (Chicago, 1959), pp. 132 ff; Pettet, *Of Paradise and Light*, pp. 16–18; Durr, *Mystical Poetry*, p. xix.

28. *The Mystical Element in the Metaphysical Poets*, pp. 193–263.

29. *Mystical Poetry*, pp. xiii-xv.

30. *Henry Vaughan: Experience and the Tradition*, pp. 144–56.

31. *Mystical Poetry*, pp. xv-xvi, xx.

32. *Henry Vaughan: Experience and the Tradition*, p. 154.

33. L. C. Martin, ed., *The Works of Henry Vaughan*, 2nd ed. (Oxford, 1957), pp. 182, 278, 485. All quotations from Vaughan follow this edition, cited hereafter in the text as "Martin."

34. *Of Paradise and Light*, pp. 8–11, 22–23.

35. *Mystical Poetry*, pp. 29, 74–78.

36. [" . . . the true Vaughan"; "the rushing of his fantasy in cosmic visions, in a rarefied atmosphere beyond time and space"; "images of infinite and fabulous vastness"; "Vaughan thus renounces the external world, the world of appearance, but the better to master the world of eternal reality free from mortal veils; and exactly from this the true Vaughan arises free,

the subjective lyric, all by itself in his magical and visionary world."] *La Poesia di Henry Vaughan*, pp. 43, 46, 50.

37. *Of Paradise and Light*, p. 193.

38. Maren-Sofie Røstvig, *The Happy Man*, vol. I, pp. 206–11; Paul A. Olson, "Vaughan's *The World*: The Pattern of Meaning and the Tradition," *Comparative Literature*, XIII (1961), 26–32; my "Vaughan's Masterpiece and Its Critics: 'The World' Revaluated," *SEL*, II (1962), 77–93; and Leland H. Chambers, "Vaughan's 'The World': The Limits of Extrinsic Criticism," *SEL*, VIII (1968), 137–50. The older reading is revived by Earl Miner, *The Metaphysical Mode from Donne to Cowley* (Princeton, 1969), pp. 193–95.

39. Cf. E. L. Marilla, "The Significance of Henry Vaughan's Literary Reputation," *MLQ*, V (1944), 155–62, who argues that the reputation of the secular poetry in particular has suffered from "the inertia of literary criticism."

40. Trench, *A Household Book of English Poetry* (London, 1870), p. 411; McMaster, "Vaughan and Wordsworth," *RES*, XI (1935), 313–25; L. R. Merrill, "Vaughan's Influence upon Wordsworth's Poetry," *MLN*, XXXVII (1922), 91–96; Muriel Morris, "A Note on Wordsworth and Vaughan," *MLN*, XXXIX (1924), 187–88; Empson, "An Early Romantic," *The Cambridge Review*, 31 May 1929, pp. 495–96; Blunden, *On the Poems of Henry Vaughan*, reviewed by Eliot, *The Dial*, LXXXIII (1927), 259–63.

41. See Durr's concise survey of this criticism in *Mystical Poetry*, esp. pp. 3, 4, 17–20.

42. *Henry Vaughan: A Life and Interpretation*, pp. 20–25, 166–69.

43. *Of Paradise and Light*, pp. 86–98.

44. *Seventeenth-Century English Poetry*, vol. I of *The Borzoi Anthology* (New York, 1967), p. 15.

45. Quotations from Thomas Hutchinson, ed., *The Poetical Works of Wordsworth*, rev. Ernest de Selincourt (London, 1904), pp. 205–06.

46. A full listing through 1960, with annotations, may be found in E. L. Marilla, *A Comprehensive Bibliography of Henry Vaughan* (Tuscaloosa, Ala., 1948), and E. L. Marilla and James D. Simmonds, *Henry Vaughan: A Bibliographical Supplement, 1946-1960* (Tuscaloosa, Ala., 1963). More recent studies are those of A. W. Rudrum, "Henry Vaughan and the Theme of Transfiguration," *Southern Review* (Australia), I (1963), 54–68; "Henry Vaughan's 'The Book': A Hermetic Poem," *AUMLA*, XVI (1961), 161–66; "Vaughan's 'The Night': Some Hermetic Notes," *MLR*, LXIV (1969), 11–19; and "The Influence of Alchemy in the Poems of Henry Vaughan," *PQ*, XLIX (1970), 469–80. Garner, *Experience and the Tradition*, pp. 46–127, surveys the critical literature on Vaughan's Hermeticism in what seems to me the most satisfactory examination of the problem to have appeared so far.

47. "The Metaphysical Poets," cited in n. 19.

48. *Henry Vaughan: Experience and the Tradition*, p. 82.

49. *European Metaphysical Poetry* (New Haven and London, 1961), p. 16n.

Chapter II: Ben Jonson and the Craft of Poetry

1. E. L. Marilla, "The Significance of Henry Vaughan's Literary Reputation," *MLQ*, V (1944), 155–62, traces the nineteenth-century origins of this approach to the early Vaughan; see also his edition, *The Secular Poems of Henry Vaughan* (Uppsala, 1958), pp. 99–101.

2. E. C. Pettet, *Of Paradise and Light: A Study of Vaughan's "Silex Scintillans"* (Cambridge, 1960), p. 191, remarks in passing that some early verse "was no doubt chiefly inspired, if sometimes through more immediate channels, by 'Great Ben'." The affinities of Vaughan's secular poetry with that of Jonson and his "Sons" is explored by Margherita Leardi, *La Poesia di Henry Vaughan* (Firenze, 1967), pp. 10–22. In *The Meditative Poem* (New York, 1963), and the revised edition of that book, *The Anchor Anthology of Seventeenth-Century Verse*, vol. I (New York, 1969), pp. xxxviii–xxxix, Louis L. Martz sees Jonson's influence on the early secular poems as more important than Donne's, and states that *Silex Scintillans* reflects the combined influence of Jonson and Herbert. His position is congenial with my argument in this chapter and in chapter 3. These chapters were written before I had an opportunity to see Georgia B. Christopher, "A Study of the Jonsonian, Pastoral, and Apocalyptic Strains in *Silex Scintillans*," Diss. Yale 1967.

3. The quotations are from *Conversations with William Drummond*, "To the Memory of . . . Mr. William Shakespeare," and *Timber* respectively, as reprinted in Edward W. Tayler, ed., *Literary Criticism of Seventeenth-Century England* (New York, 1967), pp. 89, 94, 101. All quotations of Jonson, Drummond, D'Avenant, Hobbes, Bacon, and Reynolds in this chapter are from Tayler's collection, cited hereafter in the text as "Tayler."

4. See his letter of January 23, 1589, to Sir Walter Raleigh, "expounding his whole intention" in *The Faerie Queene* because he knows "how doubtfully all Allegories may be construed." J. C. Smith and E. de Selincourt, eds., *The Poetical Works of Edmund Spenser* (London, 1912), pp. 407–08.

5. On the relations between the metaphysical conceit and such "dark figures" as allegory, see Rosemond Tuve, *Elizabethan and Metaphysical Imagery: Renaissance Poetic and Twentieth-Century Critics* (Chicago, 1947), passim, and Helen Gardner's succinct statement in the introduction to *The Metaphysical Poets* (Baltimore, 1957). Among the various modern studies whose influence on my thinking about Renaissance poetics is reflected generally rather than specifically in this chapter (and in chapter 7), I am especially conscious of Tuve's and of George Williamson, *The Proper Wit of Poetry* (London, 1961).

6. I am not suggesting that the metaphysical style as reflected in Donne, for example, owes anything in particular to the sort of theories presented by Reynolds, but am comparing his views with Vaughan's because, if modern critics are right about Vaughan's "mysticism," we might expect him to be more in sympathy with Reynolds's position than with Jonson's—for example, Frank J. Warnke, *European Metaphysical Poetry* (New Haven and London, 1961), p. 17, speaks of "Vaughan's conception of the poet as a dealer in hidden mysteries." However, the importance of the social and intellectual coterie of the Inns of Court as a source of Donne's preciosity has been recognized by, for example, J. B. Leishman, *The Monarch of Wit: An Analytical and Comparative Study of the Poetry of John Donne* (London, 1951; 7th ed., 1965), and Robert Ellrodt, *L'Inspiration Personnelle et L'Esprit du Temps chez Les Poètes Métaphysiques Anglais* (Paris, 1960).

7. Cf. Milton, *An Apology Against . . . Smectymnuus* (1642): "He who would not be frustrate of his hope to write well hereafter in laudable things, ought him selfe to bee a true Poem, that is, a composition, and patterne of the best and honourablest things; not presuming . . . unlesse he have in himselfe the experience and the practice of all that which is praise-worthy" (Tayler, p. 195).

8. *Paradise Lost* XII, 306, in *John Milton: Complete Poems and Major Prose*, ed. Merritt Y. Hughes (New York, 1957).

9. Cf. my discussion of Vaughan's "mysticism" in chapter 1.

10. For substantiation of these remarks, see especially the texts adduced in the first section of chapter 5, and cf. E. L. Marilla, "The Religious Conversion of Henry Vaughan," *RES*, XXI (1945), 15–22, and "Henry Vaughan and the Civil War," *JEGP*, XLI (1942), 514–26, especially, in the latter, his discussion of "*Ad Posteros*" (Martin, p. 32).

11. Martin, p. 625. See my detailed analysis of this poem in chapter 7.

12. The political crises of the 1640s and 1650s are examined in relation to Vaughan by F. E. Hutchinson, *Henry Vaughan: A Life and Interpretation* (Oxford, 1947), especially in the chapters on "Military Service" and "The Puritan Régime," pp. 55-71, 109-26, and by E. L. Marilla in the articles cited above (n. 10) and the commentary of his edition, *The Secular Poems of Henry Vaughan*.

13. Marilla (see n. 10) emphasizes the influence of these events on Vaughan more than any other critic, but he too sees Vaughan's response as a reaction, retirement, or withdrawal from temporal problems into private contemplation and prayer, as does Herbert G. Wright, "The Theme of Solitude and Retirement in Seventeenth-Century Literature," *Études Anglaises*, VII (1954), 22-35, who likewise regards the political chaos of the times as an important influence on Vaughan, in contrast to Hutchinson, *Henry Vaughan: A Life and Interpretation*, pp. 99-108, who dismisses it as a relatively minor factor in inducing Vaughan's "conversion." R. A. Durr,

On the Mystical Poetry of Henry Vaughan (Cambridge, Mass., 1962), pp. 3-9, surveys the various external causes which scholars have adduced— Vaughan's illness (on this, see Appendix I), his Hermetic reading, the Bible, Herbert's influence, the deaths of his wife, brother, and friends, political events—but will have none of them, citing as conclusive Itrat-Husain's oracular pronouncement that the real stimulus was internal: "Vaughan seems to have early received some sign of favour from Christ, and this was really the cause of his conversion" (*The Mystical Element in the Metaphysical Poets of the Seventeenth Century* [Edinburgh and London, 1948], p. 205).

14. Except (and it is a major exception) that he does not emphasize the objective side of the equation, my formula here resembles (and is indebted to) Louis L. Martz's comparison of Vaughan's sacred verse to Augustinian "tumbling" meditation, in which the central action is a search of the memory. See the chapter on Vaughan in *The Paradise Within: Studies in Vaughan, Traherne, and Milton* (New Haven and London, 1964), and the earlier essay, "Henry Vaughan: The Man Within," *PMLA*, LXXVIII (1963), 40-49. Earl Miner, *The Metaphysical Mode from Donne to Cowley* (Princeton, 1969), passim, insists that Vaughan's poetry is essentially subjective, private, or "lyrical," and that he could not maintain a fruitful tension with the objective world, as Donne and Herbert could. Northrop Frye, *Anatomy of Criticism* (New York, 1966 [1957]), pp. 301-02, remarks that the central convention of Vaughan's poetry is the convention of "the recognition poem . . . which reverses the usual associations of dream and waking, so that it is experience that seems to be the nightmare and the vision that seems to be reality." A more accurate description of Vaughan, as I read him, is Frye's account of "the poem of expanded consciousness, where the poet balances the catharsis of his view of experience with the ecstasis of his view of a spiritual, invisible, or imaginative world. . . . not a direct mimesis of life but a spectacular mimesis of it, able to look down on experience because of the simultaneous presence of another kind of vision" (p. 301).

Chapter III: The Well-Ordered Poem

1. *Ben Jonson's Conversations with William Drummond*, in *Literary Criticism of Seventeenth-Century England*, ed. Edward W. Tayler (New York, 1967), pp. 83, 89.

2. The extensive critical commentary on the image of childhood in this poem is summarized by R. A. Durr, *On the Mystical Poetry of Henry Vaughan* (Cambridge, Mass., 1962), pp. 13-17, who rightly insists that the image is to be read symbolically, that its source is the Bible, and that it is

to be sharply distinguished from Wordsworth's view of childhood in the *Intimations of Immortality*.

3. Cf. the comments of Lowry Nelson, Jr., *Baroque Lyric Poetry* (New Haven and London, 1961), p. 39, on the importance of progressive and retrogressive time in the poem's structure.

4. *Timber*, in *Literary Criticism of Seventeenth-Century England*, ed. Edward W. Tayler, p. 115.

5. In its (now rare) sense of "dull" or "drab," "sad" may be read as contributing to the color imagery of these lines; cf. Milton, *Lycidas*, line 148: "every flower that sad embroidery wears."

6. An assumption that it does seems to underlie Pettet's criticism of the poem's organization, *Of Paradise and Light: A Study of Vaughan's "Silex Scintillans"* (Cambridge, 1960), p. 165: " 'Mysteries' in [the fourth] stanza suggests that the development of the poem might turn on something of a contrast, the hopes, the assurances of 'glory,' weighed to some extent against the unknown. Indeed, the following stanza on the fledged bird's nest does begin to develop this contrast; but in stanza seven, and still more in stanza eight, we are switched back to the intimations and assurance of heavenly glory, with the result that we have a sense of lost or arrested pattern and even of some obscurity in an otherwise transparent poem." And, in a related comment (p. 161): "It is easy enough, Vaughan is saying, to know when the soul . . . has departed from the body, just as it is obvious when the fledged bird has deserted its nest. What puzzles us is where the bird and the soul have gone." Pettet's reading does not attach enough importance to the distinction between the speaker and the finder of the bird's nest. The contrast which he speaks of is there, but this distinction makes it an aspect of a contrast between modes of knowledge; and that is itself an aspect of the basic contrast which *is* developed consistently throughout the poem—the contrast between temporal and eternal modes of being.

7. Pettet, *Of Paradise and Light*, p. 165, considers these stanzas "very repetitive in sentiment and idea. . . . slackly phrased and sometimes prosaic," and finds in them further support for the popular view of Vaughan as "the poet who does not know when or how to stop." Like Helen C. White, *The Metaphysical Poets: A Study in Religious Experience* (New York, 1936), p. 304, Pettet seems to miss the point that the last stanza does not pray twice for the same thing. As he specifies what the preceding stanza renders in general terms as "true liberty," Vaughan presents two alternatives and leaves the decision to God. Only the second alternative is death (cf. I Corinthians 13:12: "For now we see through a glass, darkly; but then face to face: now I know in part; but then shall I know even as also I am known"). The first alternative is illumination by the Spirit in this life (i. e., the achievement of perfect knowledge), the meaning of the "mists" which are to be dispersed being given by the first three stanzas of the poem. The

"then" of the Pauline text is "when that which is perfect is come" (I Corinthians 13:10); Vaughan's prayer implies a dual interpretation of that which is perfect and of when it may come.

8. Cf. Ezekiel 37:1-14, one of the principal proof texts for the resurrection of the body, memorably adapted also by T. S. Eliot in the second section of *Ash-Wednesday*.

Chapter IV: Love Poetry

1. On the question of their autobiographical significance and the identity of the ladies, if any, see Appendix II. A briefer version of this chapter appeared as "Vaughan's Love Poetry," in *Essays in Honor of Esmond Linworth Marilla*, ed. Thomas Austin Kirby and William John Olive (Baton Rouge, La., 1970), pp. 27–42.

2. C. S. Lewis, *The Allegory of Love: A Study in Medieval Tradition* (London, 1936), pp. 298, 360.

3. See the introductions to *The Poems of John Donne*, ed. H. J. C. Grierson (Oxford, 1912) and to Grierson's *Metaphysical Lyrics and Poems of the Seventeenth Century: Donne to Butler* (Oxford, 1921).

4. For example, Joan Bennett, "Henry Vaughan, 1622–1695," in *Five Metaphysical Poets* (Cambridge, 1964), pp. 71–74. This is a reprinting of the essay on Vaughan in Bennett's *Four Metaphysical Poets: Donne, Herbert, Vaughan, Crashaw* (Cambridge, 1934), to which E. L. Marilla replied in "The Secular and Religious Poetry of Henry Vaughan," MLQ, IX (1948), 394–411, and again in *The Secular Poems of Henry Vaughan* (Uppsala, 1958), pp. 135–36; Marilla further defends the Amoret poems, pp. 99–101.

5. S. L. Bethell, *The Cultural Revolution of the Seventeenth Century* (London, 1951), pp. 126, 128.

6. Helen Gardner, ed., *The Metaphysical Poets* (Baltimore, 1957), p. 321. Bennett, *Five Metaphysical Poets*, pp. 71–74, judges the secular verse as a whole by one of the weakest of the Amoret poems. As with Fogle (see chapter 1, n. 14), I cite Gardner and Bennett only for the typicality of their views.

7. Marilla, *Secular Poems*, p. 317, takes this to mean that "the children will marry distinguished persons"; my suggestion is compatible with his comment, pp. 315–16, that Morgan is associated with the sun in terms of "the traditional conception of the sun's light and heat as representing two aspects of the Trinity."

8. J. C. Smith and E. de Selincourt, eds., *The Poetical Works of Edmund Spenser* (London, 1912), p. 584.

9. Cf. Vaughan's inversion of this pastoral figure of the pure, fructifying stream in "Religion" (Martin, p. 404), discussed in chapter 5.

10. *The Faerie Queene*, III, vi, 41–51. The quotations follow Smith and Selincourt, *Poetical Works*, except that I have normalized *u* and *v*.
11. Like "The Retreate" (Martin, p. 419), this poem exhibits the structural use of progressive and retrogressive time. The ending points back to the beginning, speaking of a future state as a re-creation of the past, and thus the poem suggests the circularity of time as symbol of perfection. See Lowry Nelson, Jr., "Time as a Means of Structure," *Baroque Lyric Poetry* (New Haven and London, 1961), pp. 21–84, especially his comments on "The Retreate" (p. 39), and my analysis of "The Retreate" in chapter 3.
12. The text is from Grierson's 1912 edition of Donne.
13. John Donne, "The Extasie"; Grierson's text.
14. *Cultural Revolution*, p. 128.
15. Marilla, *Secular Poems*, p. 330, sees "nobler influence" as referring to "sense" in the following line. By this reading, the speaker is claiming only that her influence is spiritual rather than physical.
16. Martin, p. 620. This commendation of *Thalia Rediviva* is signed "I. W. A. M. Oxon." Marilla, *Secular Poems*, pp. 263–64, 267–68, cites various scholars' speculations about the identity of I. W.
17. *Cultural Revolution*, p. 130.
18. I quote from Marilla's prose translation, *Secular Poems*, p. 95.
19. Marilla, *Secular Poems*, pp. 333–34. Bethell, *Cultural Revolution*, p. 130: "Human love is spoken of in terms appropriate to the divine love of which it is an aspect."
20. These are some of the echoes of Donne which have so fascinated Vaughan's critics; see chapter 2, pp. 22–23.
21. Bethell, *Cultural Revolution*, p. 128, points to the poem's serious wit and notes the "finely controlled simplicity" of these stanzas.
22. The meaning is intensified, and so is our appreciation of Vaughan's wit, if we read "cheape" both adjectivally and in its archaic verbal sense, noted by Marilla, *Secular Poems*, pp. 123–24, of "bid" or "bargain for."
23. The formal similarities of the two poems are discussed in chapter 3.

Chapter V: Satire

1. Oliver Lawson Dick, ed., *Aubrey's Brief Lives* (London, 1949), p. 303. Some of the material in this chapter was originally presented, for a different purpose, in my "The Publication of *Olor Iscanus*," *MLN*, LXXVI (1961), 404–08.
2. The closest approach that I have seen to recognition of Vaughan as a satirist is a sentence by E. C. Pettet, *Of Paradise and Light: A Study of Vaughan's "Silex Scintillans"* (Cambridge, 1960), p. 191: "In much of Vaughan's early work . . . there is a strain of poetry that may perhaps be

described as rhetorical—objective, observational writing that is usually directed towards everyday and social life, that is explicit in statement, vigorous . . . colloquial, humorous, and often generally satirical."

3. Cf. F. E. Hutchinson, *Henry Vaughan: A Life and Interpretation* (Oxford, 1947), p. 44: "Vaughan . . . had, in early years at least, no political moderation; the young Welshman takes fire and expresses his hot indignation in the reckless language of a partisan. A similar passionate tone will appear in later secular poems and will even disturb the remote air of *Silex Scintillans* and his religious meditations in prose." And see his comments, pp. 121–26, on the way "allusions to contemporary events. . . . mar some of Vaughan's best poems." In the prose, for the most part, Vaughan's anti-Puritan satire is pure invective, pure denunciation. This abusive rhetoric was characteristic of religious polemics in the sixteenth and seventeenth centuries—cf. the material surveyed by William P. Holden, *Anti-Puritan Satire, 1572-1642* (New Haven, 1954), and, on the other side, Milton's anti-prelatical tracts. This is the "railing" or "malcontent" satire studied by Alvin Kernan, *The Cankered Muse: Satire of the English Renaissance* (New Haven, 1959), and, in relation to the lore of melancholy, by Lawrence Babb, *The Elizabethan Malady: A Study of Melancholia in English Literature from 1580 to 1642* (East Lansing, Mich., 1951). Northrop Frye, *Anatomy of Criticism* (New York, 1966 [1957]), pp. 223–24, describes "sheer invective or name-calling"—*flyting*, or "attack without humor"—as "one of the boundaries of satire," and R. C. Elliott, *The Power of Satire: Magic, Ritual, Art* (Princeton, 1960), traces the origin of the satirist as "hard attacker" to primitive forms of magical and ritual cursing. In his verse satire, on the other hand, Vaughan more frequently achieves that distancing of the satiric spokesman and the satiric point of view from the writer which Elliott considers crucial in the transition from primitive to literary satire.

4. Vaughan's point of view associates his anti-Puritan satire with the first phase of Northrop Frye's scheme—see the section on "The Mythos of Winter: Irony and Satire" in the third essay, "Archetypal Criticism: Theory of Myths," *Anatomy of Criticism*, pp. 223–39. In this "satire of the low norm," or "conventional satire on the unconventional," the objects of attack are ridiculed as grotesque dreamers and cranks. But, because most of it is predicated on the victory of the Puritans, Vaughan's anti-Puritan satire is more closely identifiable with Frye's ironic phases, which express "the non-heroic residue of tragedy, centering on a theme of puzzled defeat." As in sixth-phase irony, Vaughan's central theme is "the nightmare of social tyranny"; he "presents human life in terms of largely unrelieved bondage," which "differs from a pure inferno mainly in the fact that in human experience suffering has an end in death," and thus "brings us around again to the point of demonic epiphany, the dark tower and prison of endless pain, the city of dreadful night in the desert." Thus Vaughan's anti-Pur-

itan satire—indeed, his work as a whole—is replete with the "demonic" imagery which presents "the world that desire totally rejects"; see Frye, and my discussion of Vaughan's imagery in chapter 6.

5. Hutchinson, *Henry Vaughan: A Life and Interpretation*, pp. 41-42, recounts the public tumults of 1640-1641, which Vaughan might have seen while in London, associated with the impeachment and execution of Strafford, but declines Imogen Guiney's argument that "the 'tumultuous fate' of Sejanus . . . was in the translator's mind paralleled by Strafford's," remarking: "There was little resemblance between Strafford and Sejanus except that they were subjects who grew 'prodigious high' and that their sudden destruction was the occasion of wild popular rejoicing. Yet, without naming Strafford, the ardent young royalist could give to discerning readers an expression of his hatred of the Parliament and of popular passion."

6. For earlier notice of this poem's political overtones, see E. L. Marilla, ed., *The Secular Poems of Henry Vaughan* (Uppsala, 1958), pp. 172-73, and his article, "The Secular and Religious Poetry of Henry Vaughan," *MLQ*, IX (1948), 394-411. Helen C. White, *The Metaphysical Poets: A Study in Religious Experience* (New York, 1936), p. 303, must have been thinking of "They are all gone into the world of light!" rather than of "The Charnel-house" when she wrote that "it is not death as the leveller of all pride and the dissolution of beauty that he celebrates, but death as the dark gate to the radiance of eternity."

7. On the first three lines of this passage, George Williamson, *The Donne Tradition: A Study in English Poetry from Donne to the Death of Cowley* (Cambridge, Mass., 1930), p. 95, remarks that "this conceit . . . [gives] the emotion of death that peculiar Metaphysical strangeness," adding (p. 133) that it "echoes the mood of Donne, catching the very manner of thought of the *Second Anniversarie*." Vaughan's use of the "Think then" formula may be an echo of Donne, but it is as likely to be due to the fact that, like Donne's poem, "The Charnel-house" reflects—in its structure, tone, and mode of development rather than its theme—the pattern of Ignatian meditation on death expounded by Louis L. Martz, *The Poetry of Meditation: A Study in English Religious Literature of the Seventeenth Century* (New Haven and London, 1954); see also Robert G. Collmer, "The Meditation on Death and Its Appearance in Metaphysical Poetry," *Neophilologus*, XLV (1961), 323-33, and cf. my analysis of "The Book" in chapter 6.

8. Cf. Vaughan's translation from Plutarch, *Of the Diseases of the Mind and the Body* (Martin, p. 111): "But if thou wouldst but search thy self within, where no eys shine but thy own, what variety of distempers shouldst thou find there? giddie distractions, blind conceits, crooked affections, shuffled wils, and phantastick humours." And compare "The Charnel-house" with the still more powerful vision of mortality (translated from Petrarch) in *Man in Darkness* (Martin, pp. 172-73).

9. See Hutchinson, *Henry Vaughan: A Life and Interpretation*, chapter 9, "The Puritan Régime," esp. pp. 109–15.

10. E.g., Lib. 1, Metrum 5 (Martin, p. 78), which is also structurally similar to "The Constellation"; Lib. 2, Metrum 7 (Martin, p. 84)—cf. esp. the conclusions; and Lib. 4, Metrum 6 (Martin, p. 651).

11. Hutchinson, *Henry Vaughan: A Life and Interpretation*, p. 121: "Charles I is the father they kill, and the Church of England is the mother they harry." This is one of those topical allusions which, according to Hutchinson (p. 121), "mar some of Vaughan's best poems." The charge of hypocrisy is intensified by the comparison of the Puritans to the beast in Revelation 13:11, which "had two horns like a lamb, and he spake as a dragon," and which, according to Revelation 13:14, "deceiveth them that dwell on the earth."

12. *Henry Vaughan: A Life and Interpretation*, pp. 125–26.

13. Since it was added to *Silex Scintillans* in 1655, the poem very likely was written at a time when Vaughan thought death was imminent; see Appendix I.

14. *On the Mystical Poetry of Henry Vaughan* (Cambridge, Mass., 1962), pp. 99–111, published earlier as "Vaughan's Pilgrim and the Birds of Night: 'The Proffer,'" *MLQ*, XXI (1960), 45–58.

15. *Henry Vaughan: A Life and Interpretation*, p. 97.

16. From internal evidence, Hutchinson, *Henry Vaughan: A Life and Interpretation*, pp. 220–21, argues convincingly that "Daphnis" was begun as an elegy on the death of William Vaughan in 1648 and adapted to commemorate the death of Thomas Vaughan, the poet's twin, in 1666.

17. Like several expressions in this prayer, "We drink our own waters for money, and our wood is sold unto us" is a quotation from the fifth chapter of Lamentations. Hutchinson, *Henry Vaughan: A Life and Interpretation*, pp. 22–23, thought it might refer to punitive taxes or fines levied against the Vaughans' estate of Newton, but his researches did not uncover any details.

18. Kernan, *The Cankered Muse*, describes the pervasive influence of Juvenal on Renaissance satire as a major source of its violent, savage tone (*saeva indignatio*). Vaughan occasionally displays the milder, more good-humored and lighthearted style characteristic of Horace, but he usually writes satire like a true disciple of Juvenal—and of Ben Jonson.

19. In other words these poems rely primarily, as most of Vaughan's anti-Puritan satire does not, on satiric irony as a structural and stylistic principle. Cf. the excellent discussion of satiric irony by Alvin B. Kernan, *The Plot of Satire* (New Haven and London, 1965), pp. 81–91. However, Vaughan's "classical" satire does resemble his anti-Puritan satire in its heavy reliance on reductivist rhetoric, discussed by Kernan, pp. 30–35, 51–65, as "the diminishing tendency."

20. Most of the poems discussed in this chapter have been mentioned

by Pettet, *Of Paradise and Light*, p. 191, as examples of "objective, observational writing that is usually directed towards everyday and social life, that is explicit in statement, vigorous (and sometimes violent) in tone, colloquial, humorous, and often generally satirical."

21. I see in these poems the sort of "vital and compelling rhythmical impulse" which Pettet, *Of Paradise and Light*, p. 183, identifies in the sacred poems, describing how Vaughan "gives some potentially rigid, even constricting, metrical form suppleness and motion by freely running his sense across line endings, by employing strong mid-line pauses, and by expressing himself in varied cadences and long sweeps of rhythm extending over many lines."

22. This passage is one of two chosen by Pettet, *Of Paradise and Light*, pp. 191–92, "to remind us that there are good things to be found in *Poems* and *Olor Iscanus*." It should be added that writing of this sort is the rule rather than the exception in Vaughan's early work. The reference to "some rough statue of *Fetter-lane*" is puzzling. Martin, p. 708, notes that "Edward Marshall, 1578-1675, master mason, resided as a 'stonecutter' at Fetter Lane." Marilla, *Secular Poems*, pp. 213-14, quotes Grosart's guess that "there must have been 'statues' placed in some of the public buildings," but dismisses it because "neither Stow nor any other writer ... finds statues a distinctive feature of this street." Grosart also observes that "both extremities of the 'lane' were used for more than two centuries as places of public execution." Perhaps Vaughan refers to the body of a criminal hanged in the lane after flogging—he compares his skin to "some rough statue of *Fetter-lane*" because "such *strokes* were drawn."

23. Hutchinson, *Henry Vaughan: A Life and Interpretation*, p. 59, quotes from Whittier's *In War Time*: "So on his Usk banks, in the blood-red dawn / Of England's civil strife, did careless Vaughan / Bemock his times." In reply to this and Courthope's similar charge that "epicurean indifference" made Vaughan "a bad citizen," Hutchinson aptly points out "how passionately concerned he was with the fortunes of Church and State" (pp. 59–60).

24. In 1652, in the note to the reader of *Flores Solitudinis*, Vaughan confirmed that "those black deeds" had indeed brought on a "darksome day": "I write unto thee out of a land of darkenesse, out of that unfortunate region, where the Inhabitants sit in the shadow of death: where destruction passeth for propagation, and a thick black night for the glorious day-spring" (Martin, p. 217).

25. According to Hutchinson, *Henry Vaughan: A Life and Interpretation*, p. 64, this virtual surrender to the Parliamentarians took place before August 1645. But, on the basis of "since *Charles* his raign" (line 48), which he reads literally, Hutchinson dates the composition of the poem early in 1649, after the King's execution (pp. 82-83). Marilla, *Secular Poems*, pp. 189–90, argues convincingly for a date around 1645.

26. Pettet, *Of Paradise and Light*, pp. 15-16, cites the "flippant vein" of lines 37-42 in support of the notion that "there is nothing in his early life or in the poetry he wrote up to 1648 to suggest that he took religion at all seriously." But the passage mocks severe asceticism, not religion; and we must remember that it is part of a speech by a highly developed persona in a dramatic situation, not a direct expression of Vaughan's personal attitude.

27. *The Cultural Revolution of the Seventeenth Century* (London, 1951), p. 132.

28. *Secular Poems*, p. 126.

29. J. B. Leishman, *The Metaphysical Poets: Donne, Herbert, Vaughan, Traherne* (Oxford, 1934), p. 147: "The . . . description of London at night is admirable, and reminiscent of Donne in his realistic vein." Pettet, *Of Paradise and Light*, p. 191, says it "might almost be something out of Dryden." Again it should be stressed that this is a typical example of Vaughan's secular poetry.

30. L. C. Martin, "Henry Vaughan and 'Hermes Trismegistus,'" *RES*, XVIII (1942), 302. Other illuminating parallels with the *Hermetica* are cited, pp. 303-04: Maren-Sofie Røstvig compares these lines and the central portion of "The World" with Casimire's earlier paraphrase of the same Hermetic passage—*The Happy Man: Studies in the Metamorphoses of a Classical Ideal*, vol. I, *1600-1700*, 2nd ed. (New York, 1962 [1954]), pp. 206-11.

31. The phrase "our share" in line 55, together with the opening lines of "Upon the Priorie Grove" (Martin, p. 15), is the foundation for the view that the Amoret poems were addressed to Catherine Wise and that Vaughan was married to her by the date of publication, 1646. See Appendix II.

Chapter VI: The Form of Nature

1. "The Silurist," *The Dial*, LXXXIII (1927), 261.

2. See chapter 1.

3. Sir Thomas Browne, *Religio Medici*, as printed in the Everyman's Library, *"Religio Medici" and Other Writings by Sir Thomas Browne*, introduction by Frank L. Huntley (New York, 1951), p. 17.

4. "The Private Imagery of Henry Vaughan," *RES*, n.s. I (1950), 206.

5. Browne, *Religio Medici*, p. 18.

6. Pioneering studies of the importance of this conception to the literature of the period were E. M. W. Tillyard, *The Elizabethan World Picture* (London, 1948), Theodore Spencer, *Shakespeare and the Nature of Man* (New York, 1942), pp. 1-50, and Arthur O. Lovejoy, *The Great Chain of Being* (Cambridge, Mass., 1936). In articles published in the early 1950s, S. L. Bethell and Joseph A. Mazzeo argued that it was the fundamental source of the Metaphysical style. See Bethell, "The Nature of Metaphysical

Wit," reprinted in *Discussions of John Donne,* ed. Frank Kermode (Boston, 1962), pp. 136-49; Mazzeo, "A Seventeenth-Century Theory of Metaphysical Poetry," and "Metaphysical Poetry and the Poetic of Correspondence," reprinted in his *Renaissance and Seventeenth-Century Studies* (New York, 1964), pp. 29-59. Vaughan's symbolic and emblematic use of Nature is discussed by Rosemary Freeman, *English Emblem Books* (London, 1948), pp. 149-53; Maren-Sofie Røstvig, *The Happy Man: Studies in the Metamorphoses of a Classical Ideal,* vol. I, *1600-1700,* 2nd ed. (New York, 1962 [1954]), pp. 195-212; Arno Esch, *Englische religiöse Lyrik des 17. Jahrhunderts: Studien zu Donne, Herbert, Crashaw, Vaughan* (Tübingen, 1955), pp. 160-82; Ross Garner, *Henry Vaughan: Experience and the Tradition* (Chicago, 1959), esp. pp. 92-127; Frank J. Warnke, *European Metaphysical Poetry* (New Haven and London, 1961), esp. pp. 16-18, 74-75; and Louis L. Martz, ed., *The Anchor Anthology of Seventeenth-Century Verse,* vol. I (New York, 1969), pp. xxiii-xxv.

7. Cf. my discussion of "The Water-fall" in chapter 1.

8. The list is from Pettet's chapter on the subject, *Of Paradise and Light: A Study of Vaughan's "Silex Scintillans"* (Cambridge, 1960), pp. 169-78.

9. This subject is treated in more detail in my "Henry Vaughan and the Great Chain of Being," one of the progenitors of this chapter, in *Studies in English Renaissance Literature,* ed. Waldo F. McNeir (Baton Rouge, La., 1962), pp. 149-67.

10. Garner, *Henry Vaughan: Experience and the Tradition,* esp. pp. 10-45, 92-127, learnedly expounds these philosophical and theological problems in relation to Vaughan's poetry.

11. Cf. Warnke, *European Metaphysical Poetry,* pp. 74-75, who believes that the later Metaphysicals, such as Vaughan and Traherne, "lean heavily on observed nature read as a set of meaningful hieroglyphics" because "the new philosophy has triumphed, and the older view has become merely quaint." Warnke believes that this shift in source of imagery, from the "traditional astronomy, cosmology, logic, and physics" on which Donne and Herbert drew, to the Book of Nature, is "the major historical development within the Metaphysical movement."

12. Merritt Y. Hughes, ed., *John Milton: Complete Poems and Major Prose* (New York, 1957), p. 313. The quotation at the end of the next paragraph also follows Hughes's text (p. 257).

13. The classic study of circle symbolism in this period is Marjorie Hope Nicolson, *The Breaking of the Circle: Studies in the Effect of the "New Science" Upon Seventeenth-Century Poetry,* rev. ed. (New York, 1960).

14. Discussed by R. A. Durr, *On the Mystical Poetry of Henry Vaughan* (Cambridge, Mass., 1962), pp. 60-74, 99-111.

15. Most critics of Vaughan comment on his light imagery; of particular interest is Fredson Bowers, "The Star Symbol in Henry Vaughan's Poetry,"

in *Renaissance Papers 1961*, ed. George Walton Williams (Durham, N. C., 1962), pp. 25-29. Fewer recognize the invariable conjunction with imagery of darkness; but see Pettet's remarks on the cloud-star image, *Of Paradise and Light*, pp. 24-26, 135-36. S. Sandbank, "Henry Vaughan's Apology for Darkness," *SEL*, VII (1967), 141-52, is exceptionally good. Sandbank clearly recognizes that the characteristic form of Vaughan's light imagery is the light-in-darkness oxymoron, and that this is because Vaughan's themes are essentially dialectical.

16. The terms "apocalyptic," "romantic," "demonic," and "ironic" are borrowed from Northrop Frye and used (I hope without distortion) in the sense which he gives them; see *Anatomy of Criticism* (Princeton, 1957), esp. the sections on "Theory of Archetypal Meaning" in the third essay, "Archetypal Criticism: Theory of Myths."

17. The verse is in Latin. I have quoted part of Louis L. Martz's prose translation, *Anchor Anthology*, I, 333-34. Another prose translation, by John Carey, appears in *The Complete Poetry of Henry Vaughan*, ed. French Fogle (New York: Doubleday, 1964; New York University Press, 1965), p. 137.

18. The phrase is from Edward Dawson, *The Practical Methode of Meditation* (1615), as printed by Martz in *Anchor Anthology*, I, 495-514. The principal studies of relationships between the art of meditation and seventeenth-century poetry are Helen Gardner's introduction to *John Donne: The Divine Poems* (Oxford, 1952), and Martz's books, *The Poetry of Meditation: A Study in English Religious Literature of the Seventeenth Century* (New Haven and London, 1954) and *The Paradise Within: Studies in Vaughan, Traherne, and Milton* (New Haven and London, 1964).

19. Dawson, *Practical Methode of Meditation*, in Martz, *Anchor Anthology*, I, 495.

20. Few paid much attention when James Smith, "On Metaphysical Poetry," in *Determinations*, ed. F. R. Leavis (London, 1934), p. 24, claimed that Metaphysical poetry is metaphysical in the proper sense of the word, that it is overwhelmingly concerned with problems deriving from or resembling "the problem of the Many and the One," but his view has been corroborated by Martz's studies of the affinities between Metaphysical poetry and the art of meditation, and, as Martz points out, *Anchor Anthology*, I, xxii-xxvi, by the arguments of Bethell and Mazzeo (see n. 6) that the Metaphysical style depended basically on a view of the cosmos as a system of analogies.

21. A modified version of this analysis of "The Tempest" appeared in my "Henry Vaughan and the Great Chain of Being," in *Studies in English Renaissance Literature*, pp. 153-59.

22. Most critics, commenting on Vaughan's contrasts between the other creatures and man, state or imply that he presents them as naïvely or simply obedient—that is, free of the conflicts and vicissitudes which beset man.

This suggests an idealized picture of Nature as romantically harmonious: the shadow of Wordsworth has fallen across the page again. The theological equivalent of such a picture would be the heresy that Nature was exempt from the Fall and is therefore spiritually superior to man. Garner, *Henry Vaughan: Experience and the Tradition*, pp. 95-105, saves Vaughan from the heresies of Hermeticism by arguing that his poetry reflects the theological distinction between natural obedience, which is instinctive and unconscious, and the superior spiritual obedience of man. But, as Sidney said, the poet asserts nothing, and therefore never lies. Vaughan does personify the creatures, and he does present them as succeeding where man fails, but this is imaginative vision, not heresy. And, if we attend closely to the language and imagery of such poems as "The Tempest" and "The Morning-watch" we can see that here the obedience of the creatures is not the simple, uncomplicated thing it is in "And do they so?" and "Man." And, if we attend to the prominence of the imagery which I have categorized above as "demonic and ironic," which powerfully conveys the corruption of Nature, we can see that Vaughan's picture of Nature is neither Wordsworthian nor naïvely idealized, but ambivalent, dialectical, and baroque.

23. But see A. W. Rudrum, "Henry Vaughan's 'The Book': A Hermetic Poem," *AUMLA*, XVI (1961), 161-66. My reply, "Vaughan's 'The Book': Hermetic or Meditative?" *Neophilologus*, XLVII (1963), 320-27, is a primitive version of the (much briefer) analysis which follows.

24. In its complex time perspectives, the poem exhibits the structural use of time which Lowry Nelson, Jr., *Baroque Lyric Poetry* (New Haven and London, 1961), pp. 21-84, considers distinctive of baroque style (together with "dramaticality"). Nelson's categories are congenial with the meditative structures elucidated by Martz and with the emphasis in much criticism of Donne and Herbert. A great many of Vaughan's poems, both secular and sacred, are susceptible to analysis in these terms, and such a study would provide a welcome counterweight to the prevailing view of his poetry as brilliantly haphazard.

Chapter VII: Archetype and Wit: The Bed-Grave Image

1. See Louis L. Martz, *The Poetry of Meditation: A Study in English Religious Literature of the Seventeenth Century* (New Haven and London, 1954), passim, and Robert G. Collmer, "The Meditation on Death and Its Appearance in Metaphysical Poetry," *Neophilologus*, XLV (1961), 323-33.

2. My basic thinking about Vaughan's imagery in this chapter has been influenced in broad and general ways by Northrop Frye, *Anatomy of Criticism* (Princeton, 1957), especially the third essay, "Archetypal Criticism: Theory of Myths"; by D. C. Allen, *Image and Meaning: Metaphoric Tradi-*

tions in Renaissance Poetry (Baltimore, 1960); and by such studies of Renaissance poetics as Rosemond Tuve, *Elizabethan and Metaphysical Imagery: Renaissance Poetic and Twentieth-Century Critics* (Chicago, 1947), and George Williamson, *The Proper Wit of Poetry* (London, 1961).

3. *The Secular Poems of Henry Vaughan* (Uppsala, 1958), pp. 172-79. See also my discussion of the poem in chapter 5.

4. For an interesting discussion of this figure in Vaughan's poetry, see Fredson Bowers, "The Star Symbol in Henry Vaughan's Poetry," in *Renaissance Papers 1961*, ed. George Walton Williams (Durham, N.C., 1962), pp. 25-29.

5. Actually the situation is somewhat problematic, and has elicited various interpretations. For the most recent attempts to clarify it, see Marilla, *Secular Poems*, pp. 335-37, and my "Henry Vaughan's 'Fellow-Prisoner,'" *English Studies*, XLV (1964), 454-57.

6. I.e., the escape of Charles I, disguised as a gentleman's servant, from Oxford to the Scottish camp on April 27, 1646, the subject also of a poem by John Cleveland, with which Vaughan's may be profitably compared.

Appendix I: Vaughan's Illness

1. The ensuing discussion has been rewritten from my "The Problem of Henry Vaughan's Illness," *Anglia*, LXXVIII (1960), 353-56.

2. *Sacred Poems and Private Ejaculations by Henry Vaughan*, ed. H. F. Lyte (London, 1847), p. xxxi.

3. *Of Paradise and Light: A Study of Vaughan's "Silex Scintillans"* (Cambridge, 1960), pp. 11-12.

4. "The Religious Conversion of Henry Vaughan," *RES*, XXI (1945), 20.

5. *Henry Vaughan: A Life and Interpretation* (Oxford, 1947), pp. 106-07.

6. Ibid.

7. *Hermetical Physick* (1655), Martin, pp. 547-92.

Appendix II: Amoret, Etesia, and Catherine Wise

1. *The Poems of Henry Vaughan, Silurist*, ed. E. K. Chambers, introduction by H. C. Beeching (London, 1896), II, 330.

2. *The Secular Poems of Henry Vaughan* (Uppsala, 1958), p. 100.

3. Ibid., pp. 325-26.

4. *Henry Vaughan: A Life and Interpretation* (Oxford, 1947), p. 52; see also pp. 50-54.

5. Marilla illustrates the discussion, *Secular Poems*, pp. 147-48.

6. *Henry Vaughan: A Life and Interpretation*, pp. 52-53.

7. *Secular Poems*, p. 333.

8. The details are set forth in my "Henry Vaughan's Amoret and Etesia," *PQ*, XLII (1963), 137-42, of which the present discussion is a modified version.

Appendix III: Immorality and Profane Literature

1. The discussion which follows is a modified and expanded version of my "The Identity of Henry Vaughan's Suppressed Poems," *MLQ*, XXII (1961), 390-98, and attempts to provide the "new interpretation of the entire preface" which I promised the reader at that time (p. 390*n*), though perhaps not as "soon" as suggested.

2. In "The Date of Henry Vaughan's *Silex Scintillans*," *N & Q*, n.s. VII (1960), 64-65, on the basis of the flimsy data available, I have speculated that composition of the first *Silex* occupied Vaughan from about March 1648 to July 1649. Harold R. Walley, "The Strange Case of *Olor Iscanus*," *RES*, XVIII (1942), 27-37, and E. L. Marilla, "The Religious Conversion of Henry Vaughan," *RES*, XXI (1945), 15-22, stress the fact that Vaughan's composition of secular poems continued into the 1650s, after publication of his first volume of sacred verse, but many commentators remain unaware of it.

3. *Olor Iscanus* is described on the title page as "Published by a Friend," and the prefatory "The Publisher to the Reader" (Martin, p. 36) claims that the author had long ago condemned these poems to obscurity and that they are now published without his "Approbation." Taken at face value, these remarks, together with the dating of the dedication four years earlier, encourage the belief that Vaughan repudiated secular verse about 1648. For example, see William Riley Parker, "Henry Vaughan and His Publishers," *The Library*, XX (1940), 401-11; Walley, "The Strange Case of *Olor Iscanus*"; and F. E. Hutchinson, *Henry Vaughan: A Life and Interpretation* (Oxford, 1947), pp. 73-77. Contradictorily, all of these scholars recognize that Vaughan wrote some secular pieces after 1648 and that a number of them are included in *Olor Iscanus*. Hutchinson and Walley follow Parker in arguing that the "friend" who "published" the book was Thomas Powell, who was indeed Vaughan's very close friend, and all acknowledge that Powell was unlikely to have violated his wishes and that, in any case, he could gain access to Vaughan's manuscripts only with the poet's permission. Thus we have an argument which begins by assuming Vaughan's repudiation of his secular verse, proceeds by acknowledging that he continued to write it, and ends by inferring that he cooperated in its publication. As E. L. Marilla points out, "Henry Vaughan's Conversion: A Recent View," *MLN*, LXIII (1948), 394-97, this yields a picture of Vaughan as an accomplished hypocrite. Marilla, " 'The Publisher to the Reader' of *Olor Iscanus*,"

RES, XXIV (1948), 36-41, argues more convincingly that, in view of the political implications of a number of the poems, Powell deliberately obscured Vaughan's responsibility for the publication in order to shield him from political reprisals.

4. For the dating, see Walley, "The Strange Case of *Olor Iscanus*," 30.

5. Edward W. Tayler, ed., *Literary Criticism of Seventeenth-Century England*, vol. IV of *The Borzoi Anthology* (New York, 1967), p. 79.

6. Parker, Walley, and Hutchinson all identify the love poems in *Thalia Rediviva* as those suppressed in 1648, but only one critic, to my knowledge, suggests that they deserved such a fate. S. L. Bethell, *The Cultural Revolution of the Seventeenth Century* (London, 1951), p. 128, says "We can see why a seventeenth-century penitent would suppress them," but does not elaborate. Hutchinson, *Henry Vaughan: A Life and Interpretation*, p. 88, remarks that "*Fida*: Or the Country-beauty" (Martin, p. 638) "is the only one of his printed poems that could be thought to consort ill with *Silex Scintillans*."

7. Thus the most likely explanation of the strange case of *Olor Iscanus* is that it was the deletion of these poems from the volume planned in 1647 that caused the delay in the book's appearance.

8. This aspect of Vaughan's purpose in the preface is discussed in chapter 2.

BIBLIOGRAPHY

Editions

Chambers, E. K., ed. *The Poems of Henry Vaughan, Silurist.* Introduction by H. C. Beeching. 2 vols. London and New York, 1896.
Fogle, French, ed. *The Complete Poetry of Henry Vaughan.* New York: Doubleday, 1964; New York University Press, 1965.
Grosart, A. B. *The Works in Verse and Prose Complete of Henry Vaughan, Silurist.* St. George's, Blackburn, Lancashire, 1871.
Lyte, H. F., ed. *Sacred Poems and Private Ejaculations by Henry Vaughan.* London, 1847.
Marilla, E. L., ed. *The Secular Poems of Henry Vaughan.* Uppsala, 1958.
Martin, L. C., ed. *The Works of Henry Vaughan.* 2nd ed. Oxford, 1957.
———. *Henry Vaughan: Poetry and Selected Prose.* London, 1963.

Bibliographies

Berry, Lloyd E. *A Bibliography of Studies in Metaphysical Poetry, 1939–1960.* Madison, Wis., 1964.
Marilla, E. L. *A Comprehensive Bibliography of Henry Vaughan.* Tuscaloosa, Ala., 1948.
Marilla, E. L., and Simmonds, James D. *Henry Vaughan: A Bibliographical Supplement, 1946–1960.* Tuscaloosa, Ala., 1963.
Spencer, Theodore, and Van Doren, Mark. *Studies in Metaphysical Poetry, 1912–1938.* New York, 1939.

References

Allen, D. C. "Vaughan's 'Cock-Crowing' and the Tradition." *ELH*, XXI (1954), 94–106.

———. *Image and Meaning: Metaphoric Traditions in Renaissance Poetry.* Baltimore, 1960.

Babb, Lawrence. *The Elizabethan Malady: A Study of Melancholia in English Literature from 1580 to 1642.* East Lansing, Mich., 1951.

Bennett, Joan. *Four Metaphysical Poets: Donne, Herbert, Vaughan, Crashaw.* Cambridge, 1934. Reprinted, with an additional essay on Marvell, as *Five Metaphysical Poets.* Cambridge, 1964.

Bethell, S. L. *The Cultural Revolution of the Seventeenth Century.* London, 1951.

———. "The Nature of Metaphysical Wit." In *Discussions of John Donne,* ed. Frank Kermode. Boston, 1962.

Blunden, Edmund. *On the Poems of Henry Vaughan: Characteristics and Intimations.* London, 1927; rpt. New York, 1969.

Bowers, Fredson. "The Star Symbol in Henry Vaughan's Poetry." In *Renaissance Papers 1961,* ed. George Walton Williams. Durham, N.C., 1962.

Bush, Douglas. *English Literature in the Earlier Seventeenth Century, 1600-1660.* Oxford, 1945.

———. *Science and English Poetry: A Historical Sketch, 1590-1950.* New York, 1950.

Chambers, Leland H. "Vaughan's 'The World': The Limits of Extrinsic Criticism." *SEL,* VIII (1968), 137-50.

Christopher, Georgia B. "A Study of the Jonsonian, Pastoral, and Apocalyptic Strains in *Silex Scintillans.*" Diss. Yale, 1967.

Clough, Wilson O. "Henry Vaughan and the Hermetic Philosophy." *PMLA,* XLVIII (1933), 1108-30.

Collmer, Robert G. "The Meditation on Death and Its Appearance in Metaphysical Poetry." *Neophilologus,* XLV (1961), 323-33.

Curtius, Ernst Robert. *European Literature and the Latin Middle Ages.* Trans. Willard R. Trask. New York, 1953.

Datow, Wulf. "*The Water-fall* von Henry Vaughan (1621-1695)." *Die Neueren Sprachen,* XV (1966), 410-20.

Denonain, Jean-Jacques. *Thèmes et Formes de la Poésie "Métaphysique": Étude d'un Aspect de la Littérature Anglaise au Dix-Septième Siècle.* Paris, 1956.

Dick, Oliver Lawson, ed. *Aubrey's Brief Lives.* London, 1949.

Duncan, Joseph E. *The Revival of Metaphysical Poetry: The History of a Style, 1800 to the Present.* Minneapolis, 1959.

Durr, R. A. *On the Mystical Poetry of Henry Vaughan.* Cambridge, Mass., 1962.

Eliot, T. S. "The Silurist." *The Dial,* LXXXIII (1927), 259-63.

———. "The Metaphysical Poets." In *Selected Essays,* pp. 281-91. London, 1932.

Elliott, R. C. *The Power of Satire: Magic, Ritual, Art*. Princeton, 1960.
Ellrodt, Robert. *L'Inspiration Personelle et L'Esprit du Temps chez Les Poètes Métaphysiques Anglais*. 3 vols. Paris, 1960.
Empson, William. "An Early Romantic." *The Cambridge Review*, 31 May 1929, pp. 495-96.
Enright, D. J. "George Herbert and the Devotional Poets." In *From Donne to Marvell*, pp. 142-59. Vol. III of *A Guide to English Literature*, ed. Boris Ford. Baltimore, 1956.
Esch, Arno. *Englische religiöse Lyrik des 17. Jahrhunderts: Studien zu Donne, Herbert, Crashaw, Vaughan*. Tübingen, 1955.
Farnham, Fern. "The Imagery of Henry Vaughan's 'The Night'." *PQ*, XXXVIII (1959), 425-35.
Freeman, Rosemary. *English Emblem Books*. London, 1948.
Frye, Northrop. *Anatomy of Criticism*. Princeton, 1957; rpt. New York, 1966.
Gardner, Helen, ed. *John Donne: The Divine Poems*. Oxford, 1952.
―――, ed. *The Metaphysical Poets*. Baltimore, 1957.
Garner, Ross. *Henry Vaughan: Experience and the Tradition*. Chicago, 1959.
Grierson, H. J. C., ed. *The Poems of John Donne*. 2 vols. Oxford, 1912.
―――, ed. *Metaphysical Lyrics and Poems of the Seventeenth Century: Donne to Butler*. Oxford, 1921.
―――. *Cross Currents in English Literature of the XVIIth Century*. London, 1929.
Holden, William P. *Anti-Puritan Satire, 1572-1642*. New Haven, 1954.
Holmes, Elizabeth. *Henry Vaughan and the Hermetic Philosophy*. Oxford, 1932.
Hughes, Merritt Y. "The Theme of Pre-existence and Infancy in *The Retreate*." *PQ*, XX (1941), 484-500.
Hutchinson, F. E. *Henry Vaughan: A Life and Interpretation*. Oxford, 1947.
Itrat-Husain. *The Mystical Element in the Metaphysical Poets of the Seventeenth Century*. Edinburgh and London, 1948.
Judson, A. C. "Cornelius Agrippa and Henry Vaughan." *MLN*, XLI (1926), 178-81.
―――. "Henry Vaughan as a Nature Poet." *PMLA*, XLII (1927), 146-56.
―――. "The Source of Henry Vaughan's Ideas Concerning God in Nature." *SP*, XXIV (1927), 592-606.
Kermode, Frank. "The Private Imagery of Henry Vaughan." *RES*, n.s. I (1950), 206-25.
Kernan, Alvin B. *The Cankered Muse: Satire of the English Renaissance*. New Haven, 1959.
―――. *The Plot of Satire*. New Haven and London, 1965.
King, James Roy. *Studies in Six Seventeenth-Century Writers*. Athens, Ohio, 1966.

Leardi, Margherita. *La Poesia di Henry Vaughan*. Firenze, 1967.
Lehmann, Ruth Preston. "Characteristic Imagery in the Poetry of Henry Vaughan." Diss. Wisconsin, 1942.
Leishman, J. B. *The Metaphysical Poets: Donne, Herbert, Vaughan, Traherne*. Oxford, 1934.
―――. *The Monarch of Wit: An Analytical and Comparative Study of the Poetry of John Donne*. London, 1951.
Lewis, C. S. *The Allegory of Love: A Study in Medieval Tradition*. London, 1936.
Lovejoy, Arthur O. *The Great Chain of Being*. Cambridge, Mass., 1936.
McMaster, Helen. "Vaughan and Wordsworth." *RES*, XI (1935), 313-25.
Mahood, M. M. *Poetry and Humanism*. New Haven, 1950.
Manley, Frank, ed. *John Donne: The Anniversaries*. Baltimore, 1963.
Marilla, E. L. "Henry Vaughan and the Civil War." *JEGP*, XLI (1942), 514-26.
―――. "Henry and Thomas Vaughan." *MLR*, XXXIX (1944), 180-83.
―――. "The Significance of Henry Vaughan's Literary Reputation." *MLQ*, V (1944), 155-62.
―――. "The Religious Conversion of Henry Vaughan." *RES*, XXI (1945), 15-22.
―――. "Henry Vaughan's Conversion: A Recent View." *MLN*, LXIII (1948), 394-97.
―――. " 'The Publisher to the Reader' of *Olor Oscanus*." *RES*, XXIV (1948), 36-41.
―――. "The Secular and Religious Poetry of Henry Vaughan." *MLQ*, IX (1948), 394-411.
―――, ed. *The Secular Poems of Henry Vaughan*. Uppsala, 1958.
Martin, L. C. "Henry Vaughan and the Theme of Infancy." In *Seventeenth-Century Studies Presented to Sir Herbert Grierson*, ed. John Purves, pp. 243-55. Oxford, 1938.
―――. "Henry Vaughan and 'Hermes Trismegistus'." *RES*, XVIII (1942), 301-07.
Martz, Louis L. *The Poetry of Meditation: A Study in English Religious Literature of the Seventeenth Century*. New Haven and London, 1954.
―――. "Henry Vaughan: The Man Within." *PMLA*, LXXVIII (1963), 40-49.
―――. *The Paradise Within: Studies in Vaughan, Traherne, and Milton*. New Haven and London, 1964.
―――, ed. *The Meditative Poem*. New York, 1963.
―――, ed. *The Anchor Anthology of Seventeenth-Century Verse*. Vol. I. New York, 1969. Revised edition of *The Meditative Poem*.
Mazzeo, Joseph A. *Renaissance and Seventeenth-Century Studies*. New York, 1964.

Merrill, L. R. "Vaughan's Influence Upon Wordsworth's Poetry." *MLN*, XXXVII (1922), 91-96.

Miner, Earl. *The Metaphysical Mode from Donne to Cowley*. Princeton, 1969.

Morris, Muriel. "A Note on Wordsworth and Vaughan." *MLN*, XXXIX (1924), 187-88.

Nelson, Lowry, Jr. *Baroque Lyric Poetry*. New Haven and London, 1961.

Nicolson, Marjorie Hope. *The Breaking of the Circle: Studies in the Effect of the "New Science" Upon Seventeenth-Century Poetry*. Evanston, Ill., 1950. Rev. ed. New York, 1960.

Oliver, H. J. "The Mysticism of Henry Vaughan: A Reply." *JEGP*, LIII (1954), 352-60.

Olson, Paul A. "Vaughan's *The World*: The Pattern of Meaning and the Tradition." *Comparative Literature*, XIII (1961), 26-32.

Parker, William Riley. "Henry Vaughan and His Publishers." *The Library*, XX (1940), 401-11.

Pettet, E. C. *Of Paradise and Light: A Study of Vaughan's "Silex Scintillans."* Cambridge, 1960.

Richmond, H. M. *The School of Love: The Evolution of the Stuart Love Lyric*. Princeton, 1964.

Rickey, Mary Ellen. "Vaughan, *The Temple*, and Poetic Form." *SP*, LIX (1962), 162-70.

Ross, Malcolm M. *Poetry and Dogma: The Transfiguration of Eucharistic Symbols in Seventeenth-Century English Poetry*. New Brunswick, N.J., 1954.

Røstvig, Maren-Sofie. *The Happy Man: Studies in the Metamorphoses of a Classical Ideal*. Vol. I, *1600-1700*. 2nd ed. New York, 1962 [1954].

Rudrum, A. W. "Henry Vaughan's 'The Book': A Hermetic Poem." *AUMLA*, XVI (1961), 161-66.

―――. "Henry Vaughan and the Theme of Transfiguration." *Southern Review* (Australia), I (1963), 54-68.

―――. "Vaughan's 'The Night': Some Hermetic Notes," *MLR*, LXIV (1969), 11-19.

―――. "The Influence of Alchemy in the Poems of Henry Vaughan," *PQ*, XLIX (1970), 469-80.

Sandbank, S. "Henry Vaughan's Apology for Darkness." *SEL*, VII (1967), 141-52.

Sencourt, Robert [pseud.]. *Outflying Philosophy: A Literary Study of the Religious Element in . . . John Donne . . . Sir Thomas Browne and . . . Henry Vaughan the Silurist . . . With also some Notes on Witchcraft*. London, 1925.

Simmonds, James D. "The Date of Henry Vaughan's *Silex Scintillans*." *N & Q*, n.s. VII (1960), 64-65.
———. "The Problem of Henry Vaughan's Illness." *Anglia*, LXXVIII (1960), 353-56.
———. "The Identity of Henry Vaughan's Suppressed Poems." *MLQ*, XXII (1961), 390-98.
———. "The Publication of *Olor Iscanus*." *MLN*, LXXVI (1961), 404-08.
———. "Henry Vaughan and the Great Chain of Being." In *Studies in English Renaissance Literature*, ed. Waldo F. McNeir, pp. 149-67. Baton Rouge, La., 1962.
———. "Some Traditional Oxymora in Vaughan's Secular Verse." *Die Neueren Sprachen*, XII (1962), 569-73.
———. "Vaughan's Masterpiece and Its Critics: 'The World' Revaluated." *SEL*, II (1962), 77-93.
———. "Henry Vaughan's Amoret and Etesia." *PQ*, XLII (1963), 137-42.
———. "Vaughan's 'The Book': Hermetic or Meditative?" *Neophilologus*, XLVII (1963), 320-27.
———. "Henry Vaughan's 'Fellow-Prisoner'." *English Studies*, XLV (1964), 454-57.
———. "Vaughan's Love Poetry." In *Essays in Honor of Esmond Linworth Marilla*, ed. Thomas Austin Kirby and William John Olive, pp. 27-42. Baton Rouge, La., 1970.
Smith, Arthur J. M. "Some Relations Between Henry Vaughan and Thomas Vaughan." *Papers of the Michigan Academy*, XVIII (1933), 551-61.
Smith, James. "On Metaphysical Poetry." In *Determinations*, ed. F. R. Leavis. London, 1934.
Spencer, Theodore. *Shakespeare and the Nature of Man*. New York, 1942.
Spurgeon, Caroline F. E. *Mysticism in English Literature*. Cambridge and New York, 1913.
Starkman, Miriam K., ed. *Seventeenth-Century English Poetry*. Vols. I and II of *The Borzoi Anthology of 17th-Century English Literature*, ed. Joseph A. Mazzeo. New York, 1967.
Stewart, Bain Tate. "Hermetic Symbolism in Henry Vaughan's 'The Night'." *PQ*, XXIX (1950), 417-22.
Sylvester, Richard S., ed. *The Anchor Anthology of Seventeenth-Century Verse*. Vol. II. New York, 1969.
Tayler, Edward W., ed. *Literary Criticism of Seventeenth-Century England*. Vol. IV of *The Borzoi Anthology of 17th-Century English Literature*, ed. Joseph A. Mazzeo. New York, 1967.
Tillyard, E. M. W. *The Elizabethan World Picture*. London, 1948.
Tuve, Rosemond. *Elizabethan and Metaphysical Imagery: Renaissance Poetic and Twentieth-Century Critics*. Chicago, 1947.
———. *A Reading of George Herbert*. Chicago, 1952.

Walley, Harold R. "The Strange Case of *Olor Iscanus*." *RES*, XVIII (1942), 27-37.

Walters, R. H. "Henry Vaughan and the Alchemists." *RES*, XXIII (1947), 107-22.

Wardle, Ralph M. "Thomas Vaughan's Influence Upon the Poetry of Henry Vaughan." *PMLA*, LI (1936), 936-52.

Warnke, Frank J. *European Metaphysical Poetry*. New Haven and London, 1961.

Watkin, E. I. *Poets and Mystics*. London and New York, 1953.

White, Helen C. *The Metaphysical Poets: A Study in Religious Experience*. New York, 1936.

Willey, Basil. *The Seventeenth-Century Background*. London, 1934.

Williamson, George. *The Donne Tradition: A Study in English Poetry from Donne to the Death of Cowley*. Cambridge, Mass., 1930.

———. *The Proper Wit of Poetry*. London, 1961.

———. *Six Metaphysical Poets: A Reader's Guide*. New York, 1967.

Wright, Herbert G. "The Theme of Solitude and Retirement in Seventeenth-Century Literature." *Études Anglaises*, VII (1954), 22-35.

INDEX

Abels blood, 108
Activa vita, 40
Affliction, 152–53
Agreement, The, 93
Agrippa, Cornelius, 19. *See also* Hermeticism
Allegory, 18, 26, 143
Amoret poems, 6, 65–84 passim, 204–07. *See also* Love poetry; Secular verse
—*Song to Amoret, A*, 52–53, 81–82, 82–84
—*To Amoret gone from him*, 3–4, 78, 81–82, 206
—*To Amoret, of the difference 'twixt him, and other Lovers, and what true Love is*, 63–64, 81–82
—*To Amoret, Walking in a Starry Evening*, 81–82
—*To Amoret Weeping*, 81–82, 83, 96, 132, 134–36
Amyntas goe, thou art undone, 81
Analogy (correspondence), universal system of. *See* Imagery; Metaphysical style; Nature
And do they so?, 49–50
Anglican Church, 13–14, 37–41 passim, 85–116 passim, 144, 146–49, 154–55, 209, 216–17. *See also* Church; Puritanism
Anselm, Archbishop of Canterbury, 104
Antichrist, 86, 97, 105, 182. *See also* Puritanism
Aquinas, St. Thomas, 166
Archetype. *See* Imagery
Aristotle, 101, 131, 166
Ascension-Hymn, 60–61, 63
Asceticism, 29, 125–26, 209, 133n26. *See also* Conversion; Mysticism
Ass, The, 49–50
Astrology, 73–82 passim, 88, 145, 147. *See also* Imagery; Nature
Aubrey, John, 85, 86, 147

Bacon, Sir Francis, 26, 27, 34, 147
Baroque. *See* Metaphysical style
Beaumont, Sir Francis, 210, 211, 215
Beeching, H. C., 205
Begging, 58
Bennett, Joan, 6
Berkeley, Bishop George, 184
Bethell, S. L., 66, 75, 78, 125
Bible: Exodus, 101; Ezekiel, 61; Genesis, 141, 146; Gospels, 101, 112; Job, 189; Psalms, 25–26, 36,

[249]

138, 146; St. Paul, 139, 146; Song of Solomon, 69, 100; Revelation, 112, 141
Biographical criticism, 4–21 passim, 38, 197–99, 202–03, 204–07. See also Conversion; Inspiration
Blunden, Edmund, 7, 16
Boehm, Jacob, 19. See also Hermeticism
Boethius, 88, 101–02, 123
Book, The, 49–50, 161–64
Book of Common Prayer. See Anglican Church
Book of the Creatures. See Nature
Brecknockshire, 144
Brecon, 124–26, 232n25
Brecon Priory, 205
Brittish Church, The, 20, 61–62, 63
Browne, Sir Thomas, 138–39
Burial Of an Infant, The, 58

Caesar, Julius, 128
Caligula (Emperor Gaius Caesar), 96, 128
Calvinism. See Puritanism
Carew, Thomas, 3, 72, 84
Carpe diem, 173
Catholic Church. See Church
Catullus, 119
Cavaliers, 72, 125–26
Chambers, E. K., 204, 205, 207
Charles I, 13, 39, 103, 108, 110, 179–83, 237n6
Charnel-house, The, 93–95, 170–74, 175, 176, 182, 189
Chaucer, Geoffrey, 216
Christs Nativity, 49–50, 62–63
Christus victor, 113–16, 182
Church 67, 98–101, 144–45. See also Angelican Church; Puritanism
Church Fathers, 146
Civil War, 12–13, 20–21, 39–41, 85–137 passim, 181–83, 198–99. See also Anglican Church; Charles I; Puritanism
Cleveland, John, 3, 237n6
Cock-crowing, 60
Come, come, what doe I here?, 183–84
Commonwealth regime. See Puritanism
Conceit, the. See Metaphysical style
Consensus gentium, 30–31, 144. See also Imitation of Nature
Constellation, The, 20, 49–50, 101–03, 114, 147–48, 181
Conversion, 4–16, 20–21, 29, 39–40, 66, 197–99, 209–10, 212, 224–25n13. See also Biographical criticism; Inspiration
Corbett, Richard, 3
Correspondence, universal system of. See Imagery; Metaphysical style; Nature
Corruption, 58, 114–15
Counter-Reformation, 35
Couplets. See Versification
Courtly love. See Love poetry

Dante, 22, 77
Daphnis, 108–09, 231n16
Daughter of Herodias, The, 58
D'Avenant, Sir William, 23, 31
Dawson, Edward, 155
Day of Judgement, The, 49–50, 114
Death. A Dialogue, 58, 185, 189–91
Democritus, 21, 97, 122
Discordia concors, 32, 43–44, 59–60, 145, 155–56. See also Metaphysical style; Nature
Dispositio, 22–24. See also Metaphysical style
Dissociation of sensibility, 9. See also Metaphysical style
Donne, John, 3, 4, 8, 9, 11, 19, 22–23,

26, 42, 66, 71, 75, 76, 143–44, 145, 192, 206, 233n29
Dressing, 37
Drummond, William, 23, 26, 30, 32, 44
Dryden, John, 3, 6, 233n29
Dualism. See Manicheanism
Durr, R. A., 8–9, 10, 11, 12, 14–15, 106

Easter-day, 61–62
Easter Hymn, 183, 184–85
Egerton, Sir Charles, 202
Elegie on the death of Mr. R. Hall, An, 108, 175–76, 191
Elegie on the death of Mr. R. W., An, 92, 108, 174–75
Eliot, T. S., 7, 9, 16, 19, 138
Elizabethan Settlement, 89
Elliott, R. C., 229n3
Empson, William, 16
Erasmus, Desiderius, 35, 86
Esch, Arno, 6–7
Etesia poems, 65–84 passim, 204–07, 214, 215, 239n6. See also Love poetry; Secular verse
—Character, to Etesia, The, 75–77, 81, 206
—Etesia absent, 78–81, 206
—In Etesiam lachrymantem, 78
—To Etesia (for Timander,) the first Sight, 73
—To Etesia going beyond Sea, 78
—To Etesia looking from her Casement at the full Moon, 73
—To Etesia parted from him, and looking back, 77–78
Eucherius, Bishop of Lyons, 102

Felix culpa, 59
Fida: Or the Country-beauty: to Lysimachus, 72–73

Flores Solitudinis (1654), 103, 201–02. See also Prose works
Fogle, French R., 7, 220n14
Frye, Northrop, 225n14, 229–30, 235n16

Galen, 87
Gardner, Helen, 6, 66
Garner, Ross, 12, 19–20, 222n46
Gilbert, William, 177, 178
Globe Tavern, 126–27
Great Chain of Being. See Nature
Grierson, Sir H. J. C., 66
Grosart, A. B., 205

Habington, William, 3, 204, 205
Hannibal, 89–90
Harvey, William, 87
Herbert, George, 6, 8, 11, 34, 36, 39, 41, 133–34, 149, 208, 209
Hermes Trismegistus, 19. See also Hermeticism
Hermetical Physick (1655), 87–88, 104–05
Hermeticism, 19–20, 38, 131–32, 143, 222n46
Herrick, Robert, 3
Hieroglyphics. See Imagery
Hobbes, Thomas, 23, 31
Holmes, Elizabeth, 8
Homer, 22, 26
Housman, A. E. 198
H. Scriptures, 58
Hutchinson, F. E., 6, 7, 17, 105, 106, 108, 199–200, 202–03, 204–06

Idle Verse, 58, 210–11, 214–15
Imagery, 7, 8, 10, 12, 14–15
—archetypal imagery, 18, 106–07, 113–16, 144–45, 151, 154, 157, 160, 165–93 passim, 235n16
—childhood motif, 16, 20, 46–48, 98, 225–26n2

—circle (cycle), 47–48, 59–60, 149–50, 157, 159–60
—darkness and light, 19, 21, 42, 47–48, 50–51, 54–57, 61, 62, 63, 67, 75, 98, 101–03, 104, 108–09, 126–28, 129, 142, 144, 150–64 passim, 169, 171, 175–76, 180–81, 184–85, 189–93, 234–35n15
—emblematic (hieroglyphic) imagery, 8, 17–18, 59, 94–95, 118, 153, 156–58, 159, 161–64, 185–87
—"everyday" imagery, 6, 145
—motion, 42, 47–49, 50, 51–52, 58–59, 60–61, 62–63, 127–28, 149–64 passim, 192–93
—quest (pilgrimage) motif, 18, 47–49, 58–60, 74–75, 79–81, 129–32, 149–52, 187–93 passim
Imago Dei, 76
Imitatio, 155, 166. See also Metaphysical style
Imitatio Christi, 35
Imitation of Nature, 22–41 passim, 43–44. See also *Consensus gentium*
Importunate Fortune, written to Doctor Powel of Cantre, The, 74, 130–32, 134, 136
In Amicum foeneratorem, 71, 132, 136–37
Incarnation, and Passion, The, 58, 179
Inspiration, 6, 8–9, 10–11, 12–14, 14–16, 23–41 passim, 97–98, 125–26, 128, 198–99, 203. See also Biographical criticism; Conversion
Inventio, 22–41, 143–44, 166, 168, 169. See also Metaphysical style
Itrat-Husain, 10, 11
I walkt the other day (to spend my hour,), 61–62, 176, 185–89, 192

Jacobs Pillow, and Pillar, 49–50

Jesus weeping (II), 49–50
Johnson, Dr. Samuel, 184
Jonson, Ben, 3, 6, 22–41 passim, 44, 49, 50, 210, 211, 212–13, 215, 223n2
Joy of my life!, 61–62, 63, 191–93
Judson, A. C., 19
Juvenal, 85, 86, 87, 89–91, 93, 97, 116–17, 205

Keats, John, 198
Kermode, Frank, 4, 11, 139
Kernan, Alvin, 229n3, 231n18, 231n19
King Disguis'd, The, 39, 176, 177, 179–83
Knot, The, 58

Lampe, The, 49–50
Leardi, Margherita, 8, 9, 15
L'Envoy, 86, 114, 202
Les Amours, 169–70, 175, 177
Lewis, C. S., 65
Life of Paulinus, 90, 93, 100–01, 104, 201
Locus amoenus, 17
London, 120, 127–28, 128–29
Lovelace, Richard, 3, 84
Love poetry, 3, 7, 40, 52–53, 65–84, 125–26. See also Amoret poems; Etesia poems; Secular verse
Love-sick, 50–52, 58
Loyola, St. Ignatius. See Meditation
Lyte, H. F., 197–98

McMaster, Helen, 16
Man, 61–62
Manicheanism, 146–47, 209
Man in Darkness, Or, A Discourse of Death, 98, 115–16, 139–40, 168–69, 200
Man in Glory, 104
Marilla, E. L., 4, 5, 78, 126, 172, 199, 200, 204–06

Martin, L. C., 131, 197–98
Martz, Louis L., 225n14, 230n7, 235n18
Maximus Tyrius, 91–92
Meditation, 8–9, 18, 35, 54–57, 93–95, 101–03, 155–56, 156–64 passim, 165, 165–93 passim, 180, 200–01, 225n14, 235n18
Men of War, The, 92–93, 107–08, 112, 113
Metaphor. See Imagery
Metaphysical style, 7, 9, 18, 19, 20–21, 22–41 passim, 139–40, 143–44, 145, 166–93
Milton, John, 32–33, 47, 69, 149, 150, 166, 177
Mimesis. See Imitation of Nature
Misery, 49–50, 111
Monsieur Gombauld, 50
More, Sir Thomas, 86
Morning-watch, The, 44, 63
Mount of Olives, 61–62
Mount of Olives: Or, Solitary Devotions, The (1652), 13–14, 91, 97–98, 100, 107, 108, 109, 111, 115, 169, 200–01. See also Prose works
Mysticism, 7, 9, 10–14, 15, 16, 20–21, 26–27, 29, 35, 145, 224n6. See also Asceticism; Conversion
Myth. See Imagery—archetypal; Typology

Nature, 7, 9, 14, 16–19, 19–20, 33, 43–44, 88–89, 101–03, 126–27, 129, 130–32, 133, 138–64, 180, 188–89, 190, 191–93, 233–34n6, 235–36n22. See also Imagery; Pastoral mode; Wordsworth
Neoplatonism, 18, 19, 26–27, 76, 138, 166
Newman, Cardinal John, 12
Nierembergius, Johannis Eusebius, 89, 103

Night, The, 21, 61–62, 123
Nollius, Henry, 87, 104–05, 203
North, Dudley, 3rd Baron North, 23, 32

Of Life and Death, 103–04
Of Temperance and Patience, 89, 113
Of the Benefit Wee may get by our Enemies, 109–10
Olor Iscanus (1651), 6, 10, 210, 214, 238–39n3, 239n7. See also Secular verse
Orinda. See Philips, Katherine
Orphic mysteries, 26
Otherworldliness. See Mysticism

Palm-tree, The, 58–60
Paracelsus, 87
Parliament, 9, 86, 87, 89, 90, 96, 128, 174. See also Civil War; Puritanism
Pastoral mode, 46–49, 66–84 passim, 99–101, 101–03, 108–09, 114–15, 126–28, 129–30, 137, 138–64 passim, 206. See also Imagery; Nature
Petrarch, 65, 66, 77, 165, 168, 205
Pettet, E. C., 8, 9–10, 11, 14, 16, 17, 198–99, 226–27
Philips, James, 205
Philips, Katherine, 205
Pilgrimage motif. See Imagery—quest motif
Plato, 16, 26, 28, 29, 32, 48, 65, 73, 74, 75, 76, 123, 138, 146
Plotinus, 138
Plutarch, 91, 109–10
Poems, with the Tenth Satyre of Juvenal Englished (1646), 6, 10, 81, 85, 86–87, 204–05, 206, 210, 211. See also Secular verse
Poetic theories, 22–41 passim, 43–44,

139–44. See also Metaphysical style
Pope, Alexander, 119
Powell, Thomas, 91, 177–79, 238–39n3
Prayer. See Anglican Church
Primitive Holiness. See Life of Paulinus
Priory Cardigan, 205
Proffer, The, 20, 61–62, 105–07, 108
Prose works, 13–14, 39–40, 86–116 passim, 123. See also Flores Solitudinis (1654); Mount of Olives, The (1652)
Providence, 38, 39, 40, 146
Ptolemaic cosmology, 145
Puritanism, 7, 12–14, 21, 38, 39–40, 65, 85–116, 116–37 passim, 146–47, 209. See also Antichrist; Church; Civil War; Parliament
Pythagoras, 26

Quatrains. See Versification
Queer, The, 58
Quest motif. See Imagery
Quickness, 58

Randolph, Thomas, 3
Reformation, the, 35
Regeneration, 61–62
Regicide. See Charles I
Religion, 58, 99–101, 114
Repentance, 49-50
Retreate, The, 16, 46–49, 123
Reynolds, Henry, 26–27, 28–29, 139
Rhapsodis, A, 96, 116, 126–28, 204, 233n29
Rhys, Ernest, 205
Romantic agony, 9. See also Metaphysical style
Romantic criticism, 7, 14–17, 138, 139, 144, 145, 197–99, 203, 235–36n22. See also Conversion; Inspiration; Mysticism
Romanticism, 16–20
Rome, 86, 124, 128
Royal Society, 87
Rudrum, A. W., 222n46

Sacred verse, 3–21 passim, 33–41, 45–64 passim, 75, 86–116 passim, 144–46, 150–54. See also Silex Scintillans
St. Mary Magdalen, 98
Satire, 3, 9, 40, 49, 82, 83–84, 85–137, 228–30, 231n18, 231n19
Scholasticism, 146
Secular verse, 3, 3–7, 8, 23, 44–64 passim, 66, 85–137 passim, 145–46, 208–17 passim. See also Olor Iscanus (1651); Poems, with the Tenth Satyre of Juvenal Englished (1646); Thalia Rediviva (1678)
Seed growing secretly, The, 57–58
Sejanus, 89–91
Shakespeare, William, 24, 58, 65, 66, 121, 166–68, 173, 190
Sidney, Sir Philip, 52, 65, 139
Silex Scintillans (1650, 1655), 6, 10, 14, 15, 16, 18, 33–41, 49, 86, 141, 150, 153, 197–98, 202, 203, 208–17. See also Sacred verse
Skelton, John, 86, 119
Socrates, 165
Spenser, Edmund, 26, 65, 66, 67–68, 69, 71, 81, 205
Spiritual biography, 152
Stanley, Thomas, 3
Starkman, Miriam K., 17
Starre, The, 49–50
Stoicism, 111–13, 117, 122–23, 134, 165–68, 173
Storm, The, 61–62
Strafford, Thomas Wentworth, Earl of, 90, 230n5

Strong lines. *See* Metaphysical style
Suckling, Sir John, 3
Sulla, Lucius Cornelius, 128
Symbolism. *See* Imagery

Tears, 58
Tempest, The, 58, 140, 148, 154–60
Tesauro, Emanuele, 139
Thalia Rediviva (1678), 207. *See also* Secular verse
They are all gone into the world of light!, 21, 54–57, 141–42, 143, 147–48, 176–77, 179–80
Thou that know'st for whom I mourne, 57–58
Timber, The, 57–58
To his friend ———, 132–34, 136
To his Learned Friend and Loyal Fellow-Prisoner, Thomas Powel of Cant., 91, 177–79, 189, 190
To his retired friend, an Invitation to Brecknock, 91, 116, 122–26, 134
To I. Morgan of White-Hall Esq; upon his sudden journey and succeeding Marriage, 66–68
To Lysimachus, the Author being with him in London, 128–30
To Mr. M. L. upon his reduction of the Psalms into Method, 25–26
To my Ingenuous Friend, R. W., 22, 70–71, 204
To my worthy friend Master T. Lewes, 88, 123
To Sir William D'avenant, upon his Gondibert, 210, 211, 212, 215
To the best, and most accomplish'd Couple ———, 68
To the Editor of the matchless Orinda, 28
To the Holy Bible, 49–50, 202
To the most Excellently accomplished, Mrs. K. Philips, 30, 34, 204, 210, 211, 215
To the pious memorie of C. W. Esquire, 92
To the River Isca, 17, 64, 68–69, 70
Townsend, Aurelian, 3
Trench, R. C., 16
Typology, 70, 106–07, 166, 182. *See also* Imagery

Unconscious, the, 8. *See also* Conversion; Inspiration; Mysticism
Upon a Cloke lent him by Mr. J. Ridsley, 118–22, 199
Upon Mr. Fletchers Playes, 22, 95–97, 210, 211, 215
Upon the Poems and Playes of the ever memorable Mr. William Cartwright, 27–28, 30, 34, 210, 211–12
Upon the Priorie Grove, His usuall Retyrement, 17, 69–70, 205
Usk River, 17, 18, 68–69

Vanity of Spirit, 63, 142–43
Vaughan (née Wise), Catherine, 204–07
Vaughan, Thomas, 19, 143, 231n16
Vaughan, William, 108, 231n16
Versification, 6, 44–64 passim

Waller, Edmund, 3
Warnke, Frank J., 20
Water-fall, The, 17–19, 49–50, 141
White, Helen, 11
White Sunday, 57–58, 98
Whittier, John Greenleaf, 122, 232n23
Wise, Catherine, 204–07
Wit. *See* Metaphysical style
Wits, the, 34–35
Wordsworth, William, 16–19
World, The, 6, 15–16, 21, 148
World Contemned, The, 102, 201

DATE DUE